Subjectivity

transitions
General Editor: Julian Wolfreys

Published Titles
TERRY EAGLETON David Alderson
JULIA KRISTEVA AND LITERARY THEORY Megan Becker-Leckrone
BATAILLE Fred Botting and Scott Wilson
NEW HISTORICISM AND CULTURAL MATERIALISM John Brannigan
HÉLÈNE CIXOUS Abigail Bray
GENDER Claire Colebrook
POSTMODERN NARRATIVE THEORY Mark Currie
FORMALIST CRITICISM AND READER-RESPONSE THEORY Kenneth Womack
    and Todd F. Davis
IDEOLOGY James M. Decker
QUEER THEORY Donald E. Hall
MARXIST LITERARY AND CULTURAL THEORIES Moyra Haslett
LOUIS ALTHUSSER Warren Montag
RACE Brian Niro
JACQUES LACAN Jaen-Michel Rabaté
LITERARY FEMINISMS Ruth Robbins
SUBJECTIVITY Ruth Robbins
DECONSTRUCTION • DERRIDA Julian Wolfreys
ORWELL TO THE PRESENT: LITERATURE IN ENGLAND, 1945–2000 John Brannigan
CHAUCER TO SHAKESPEARE, 1337–1580 SunHee Kim Gertz
MODERNISM, 1910–1945 Jane Goldman
POPE TO BURNEY, 1714–1779 Moyra Haslett
PATER TO FORSTER, 1873–1924 Ruth Robbins
BURKE TO BYRON, BARBAULD TO BAILLIE, 1790–1830 Jane Stabler
MILTON TO POPE, 1650–1720 Kay Gilliland Stevenson
SIDNEY TO MILTON, 1580–1660 Marion Wynne Davies

Forthcoming Titles
NATIONAL IDENTITY John Brannigan
HOMI BHABHA Eleanor Byrne
POSTMODERNISM • POSTMODERNITY Martin McQuillan
ROLAND BARTHES Martin McQuillan
TRANGRESSION Julian Wolfreys
DICKENS TO TROLLOPE HARDY, 1837–1884 Julian Wolfreys

---

transitions Series
Series Standing Order ISBN 0–333–73634–6
(*outside North America only*)

You can receive future titles in this series as they are published. To place
a standing order please contact your bookseller or, in the case of difficulty,
write to us at the address below with your name and address, the title of
the series and the ISBN quoted above.

Customer Services Department, Macmillan Distribution Ltd
Houndmills, Basingstoke, Hampshire RG21 6XS, England

---

transitions

Subjectivity

Ruth Robbins

First published in 2005 by
PALGRAVE MACMILLAN
Houndmills, Basingstoke, Hampshire RG21 6XS and
175 Fifth Avenue, New York, N.Y. 10010
Companies and representatives throughout the world.

PALGRAVE MACMILLAN is the global academic imprint of the Palgrave Macmillan division of St. Martin's Press, LLC and of Palgrave Macmillan Ltd. Macmillan® is a registered trademark in the United States, United Kingdom and other countries. Palgrave is a registered trademark in the European Union and other countries.

ISBN-13: 978–0–333–75278–4 hardback
ISBN-10: 0–333–75278–3 hardback
ISBN-13: 978–0–333–75279–1 paperback
ISBN-10: 0–333–75279–1 paperback

This book is printed on paper suitable for recycling and made from fully managed and sustained forest sources.

A catalogue record for this book is available from the British Library.

A catalog record for this book is available from the Library of Congress.

10 9 8 7 6 5 4 3 2 1
14 13 12 11 10 09 08 07 06 05

Printed in China.

Contents

General Editor's Preface

Transitions: *transition-em*, n. of action. 1. A passing or passage from one condition, action or (rarely) place, to another. 2. Passage in thought, speech, or writing, from one subject to another. 3. a. The passing from one note to another. b. The passing from one key to another, modulation. 4. The passage from an earlier to later stage of development or formation ... change from an earlier style to later; a style of intermediate or mixed character ... the historical passage of language from one well-defined stage to another.

The aim of *Transitions* is to explore passages and movements in critical thought, and in the development of literary and cultural interpretation. This series also seeks to examine the possibilities for reading, analysis, and other critical engagements which the very idea of transition makes possible. The writers in this series unfold the movements and modulations of critical thinking over the last generation, from the first emergences of what is now recognized as literary theory. They examine as well how the transitional nature of theoretical and critical thinking is still very much in operation, guaranteed by the hybridity and heterogeneity of the field of literary studies. The authors in the series share the common understanding that, now more than ever, critical thought is both in a state of transition and can best be defined by developing for the student reader and understanding of this protean quality.

This series desires, then, to enable the reader to transform her/his own reading and writing transactions by comprehending past developments. Each book in the series offers a guide to the poetics and politics of interpretative paradigms, schools, and bodies of thought, while transforming these, if not into tools or methodologies, then into conduits for direction and channelling thought. As well as transforming the critical past by interpreting it from the perspective of the present day, each study enacts transitional readings of a number of well-known literary texts, all of which are themselves conceivable as having been transitional texts at the moments of their first appearance. The readings offered in these books seek, through close critical reading and theoretical engagement, to demonstrate certain possibilities in critical thinking to the student reader.

It is hoped that the student will find this series liberating because rigid methodologies are not being put into place. As all the dictionary definitions of the idea of transition above suggest, what is important is the action, the passage: of thought, of analysis, of critical response. Rather than seeking to help you locate yourself in relation to any particular school or discipline, this series aims to put you into action, as readers and writers, travellers between positions, where the movement between poles comes to be seen as of more importance than the locations themselves.

Julian Wolfreys

Acknowledgements

This book about subjectivity is also a book about the relationships of self and other, and I want here to register my gratitude to those 'others' who have helped me to form my thinking on the subject of subjectivity.

I owe an especial debt of gratitude to my former colleagues at the University of Luton with whom I used to teach a module about Confessional and Autobiographical Writing: Jill Barker, Martin Gray, Moyra Haslett and Claire Jones all made an immense difference to what I have produced here, by getting me to read other books, and by sharing their interests and enthusiasms with me. I learned a very great deal from participating in their classes – and I hope the reflections of what they taught me are fairly represented in what follows. Thank you to all of you.

Those classes, and the ones I have subsequently taught at University College Northampton on the same kinds of subject, also depended on the active and thorough participation of some of the most engaged and engaging students it has been my pleasure to know. To the classes of 1998 and 1999 at Luton, and those of 2000, 2002 and 2003 at Northampton in both the undergraduate and Masters programmes, I want to express real gratitude. Whatever I was supposed to be teaching you, I'm extremely aware that I was also learning from you. Thank you for making teaching a pleasure.

The chapter on the Sense of an Ending was presented, in embryonic form at the Life After Theory Conference in April 2002. The audience at that conference asked pointed questions that made me sharpen my thoughts – I am grateful for their intervention. Similarly, parts of Chapter 5 were presented as a seminar to the Midlands Interdisciplinary Victorian Studies Seminar series in 2003. The small and very select audience also had their part to play – my thanks to them as well. The slightly larger audience at the Victorian Gothic Colloquium at Trinity and All Saints College Leeds in April 2003 heard a rather different version of parts of Chapter 3. My thanks to Karen Sayer and Rosemary

Mitchell for inviting me; my thanks to the audience and fellow speakers for a stimulating exchange of views.

To Julian Wolfreys, as always, there is yet another debt. It was he who suggested this book, and he who chivvied me along: still the best of friends, as Joe Gargery might say, and still the best of editors.

This book is dedicated to my husband, Richard Andrews, without whom ... nothing.

Introduction: Who Do You Think You Are?

What would it mean, this
I?
(D. H. Lawrence, 'Humiliation', 1972, 214)

Near the beginning of Virginia Woolf's 1927 novel *To The Lighthouse*, the painter Lily Briscoe asks Andrew Ramsay about the nature of his father's philosophical work:

> She asked him what his father's books were about. 'Subject and object and the nature of reality', Andrew had said. And when she said, Heavens, she had no notion what that meant, 'Think of a kitchen table', he told her, 'when you're not there'. (Woolf 1992, 28)

There is much that could be said about this tiny exchange. Andrew's succinct response to the question implies a certain mockery of his father's project, a mockery that is largely upheld by the novel. Mr Ramsay conceives of his philosophical work as an alphabetical sequence, with each problem neatly laid out in turn, ready to be solved – except that he gets stuck at the letter Q, and never progresses beyond it, undermining his position as a sage who possesses the *alpha* and the *omega* of knowledge. It might also tell us something about gender relations in the period when the book is set. Lily is shown presenting herself as incapable of understanding the abstract nature of the questions Mr Ramsay pursues, and might as well simper as she says, effectively, 'silly me'; and Andrew may also be mocking her in his homely analogy of the unobserved kitchen table, an image chosen in part for its suitability to feminine preoccupations with the domestic sphere. (Of course, it's not quite so simple as that: the image of the deserted table also prefigures the desertion of the house near the lighthouse during the war years, a prolepsis which is testament to Woolf's highly patterned fiction.)

I

I begin here, however, because the answer Andrew Ramsay offers is also in part what this book is about. We might never quite get to the 'nature of reality', and there is certainly a risk of getting stuck at Q. But in that brief moment, Andrew suggests both a close link between the subject (the perceiving consciousness) and the object (the matter that is perceived), whilst also stating their apparent opposition. In thinking about what subjectivity might mean, the complexities of this simple statement in Woolf's novel are writ large. Our common sense (which is seldom to be relied upon in intellectual matters)[1] tells us that subjectivity and objectivity must be a binary opposition; and as such these concepts structure our understanding of the world, differentiating neatly between what is going on in our heads and what is really going on 'out there', in 'reality'. The inverted commas serve as an admonition, of course. As Woolf had commented elsewhere, 'What is reality, and who are the judges of reality?' The question is intended as a rebuke to the unqualified acceptance that reality is an unmediated, total, objective system that 'really' exists 'out there'. For if reality is available to be *judged*, someone must be doing the judging, with the consequence that reality might just as well end up being some other person or group's subjective or ideologically motivated version of it. Reality can be a word used by people with a Humpty-Dumptyish disregard for other people. (Humpty-Dumpty says to Alice that he makes words mean whatever he chooses, 'The question is ... which is to be master?' [Carroll 1970, 269]. And this is indeed a profound statement, for if one has mastery over the language in which the world is described, perhaps one also has mastery over the people in that world.) It might just be the case that subject and object (and their derivatives) are much more slippery customers than the alleged security of their opposition implies.

Depending on the context, the title of this Introduction might mean a number of things. In its colloquial senses, the question 'Who do you think you are?' could 'just' be a question rhetorically asked in everyday life, perhaps as an implied rebuke to an interlocutor with an inflated sense of his or her own self-importance. It is an interrogative sentence which strongly suggests that the 'you' in the question thinks too highly of the self that s/he is. It is a sentence that could be used as a reprimand – by exasperated parents and teachers to articulate their irritation with those younger and less powerful than themselves; and it is also a sentence which might just be a prelude to an extremely unpleasant passage of social life – it can be uttered as a threat, as the ritualized beginning of acts of violence and humiliation (fights in bars, dismissals from employment). It is potentially, that is, a threatening question, even when asked, as it were, 'innocently' – that is free from any explicit philosophical positioning.

But the question also makes oblique reference to what is perhaps the best-known sentence in Western philosophy: René Descartes' *cogito, ergo sum* (I think, therefore I am), first stated by him in his *Discourse on Method* (1637). Its familiarity to even non-philosophers is signalled by its ubiquity in parodic renditions, from Monty Python's representation of the western philosophic tradition as a history of alcoholic excess (beginning with Aristotle being a 'bugger for the bottle', and culminating in the *reductio ad absurdam* of the *cogito* to 'I *drink*, therefore I am'), to one of my own favourite childhood jokes – 'I'm pink, therefore I'm spam' – which even at the age of 10 I understood as a satisfyingly subversive reference to something much more serious.[2] In asking this question here, at the head of a book entitled *Subjectivity*, I want to signal the importance of the connection Descartes makes between thinking and human existence in the making of selfhood. This is a book about the kind of self that can think. The *making* of the self, the *construction* of an identity, I will argue, takes place in language, and there is therefore a close relationship between thinking and being, which the titular interrogative reflects.

The story of how René Descartes got to the proposition that thinking and being are essentially linked has been often repeated. Descartes wanted to begin from first principles to uncover how we know our world and our own place in it. He began by adopting a sceptical position in relation to his knowledge of the world; in other words, he worked on the basis that there must be severe doubts about our ability to 'know' anything at all particularly in relation to the common-sense version of the world deriving from sense perceptions. He narrates himself in the imagined situation of man locked up in a room alone, where he asks questions about what he could 'know' in this limited position. The things that we think we know – from our sense impressions of the world around us, for instance – were rejected as a basis for knowledge. Sense impressions might be mere figments of our imagination, or have been planted there to deceive us by a cunning demonic presence. If such a demonic presence existed and exercised its demonic will upon us, it would, of course, prove our own existence, since we would have to exist in order to be acted upon. Proof of existence, however, is a very limited notion of 'being'. From the position that we can know nothing

with certainty simply from the bodies that we inhabit, Descartes
decided that the only certainty we have is our consciousness of
ourselves as thinking beings. The consciousness of the process of
thought is the nearest thing we have to any certainty about our existence, and for this reason, it might actually be better to translate the
famous *cogito* as 'I am conscious of thinking, therefore I am conscious
as being' rather than the simplified version of 'I think, therefore I am'.
The mind that Descartes posits from this statement is one capable of
autonomy in that it is not reliant on external stimulus for its operation;
and it is a mind founded on reason, on the rationality which supposedly differentiates human beings from animals. Rationality – the ability
to reason from cause to effect, and to follow up lines of inquiry in a
systematic way – is dependent on language; this mind must be able to
narrate to itself the consciousness of which it is allegedly conscious.
The kind of thought in which consciousness of being takes place, in
Descartes' formulation is a rationalistic and necessarily linguistic
process.[3]

   In fact, Descartes was in part referring to a much older philosophical
tradition in positing articulate consciousness as the best basis for
defining being. As Charles Taylor has noted, the idea goes back at least
as far as Aristotle who defined man as the rational animal in the Greek
phrase *zôon logon echon* – meaning 'animal possessing *logos*', where
logos means 'speech'. Taylor's discussion, however, demonstrates the
ways in which *logos* itself is a fairly slippery word, whose meaning
'straddles speech and thought because it means, inter alia, "word",
"thought", "reasoning", "reasoned account", as well as being used for
the words deployed in such an account' (Taylor 1985, 217). In Plato's
philosophy, it's true, one had to be able to 'give an account' of one's
knowledge to another person as guarantee that one possessed it as
knowledge rather than as mere opinion (Taylor 1985, 222), thus creating a necessary relationship between subjectivity and the Other. And
this is one of the aspects of Cartesian thought that is distinctive from
the tradition he at once belonged to and departed from: for Descartes
argued that knowledge (of the self) came from within and did not
demand to be communicated to be possessed. Warren Montag makes
the case that this was a revolutionary moment in philosophy:

> a tradition dating from Aristotle, … which includes Christian, Jewish and
> Islamic philosophy, regarded rationality or truth as necessarily *collective*
> in nature, residing in the totality of an ever present archive of authoritative

works. An individual, in order to escape the particularity of individualized existence, had to accede to and participate in this archive to formulate universally valid propositions. Descartes shocked his contemporaries ... Instead of referring to a tradition of inquiries and findings, he would begin his reasoning from a point of absolute certainty, not simply the position agreed upon by a majority as valid or true. (Montag 2002, 4, my emphasis)

In breaking from a collective (and possibly conservative) tradition of the communality of knowledge, with its insistence on communication of that knowledge as the guarantee of its possession, Descartes proposed a paradigm shift in the understanding of both what knowledge itself might consist of, and in the location of that knowledge in the individual as opposed to in the community.

The Cartesian answer to the question 'who do you think you are', then, is an answer based on the *mental* attributes of the subject. Descartes' writings describe a man deliberately isolating himself from the outside world in order to reach his conclusion of human selfhood as being defined through thinking as being. In other words, he describes relying on his subjective view of the world and his place in it as the opening gambit of his discussion. Since the sense impressions of the body cannot be trusted, only the knowledge that one is capable of thinking, of doubting or believing, of willing actions or refusing them, is appropriate evidence of one's existence. The human subject in Descartes' view is a thinking subject, *homo cogitans* in Latin, a mind rather than a body. One might, of course, comment in a spirit of a slightly different kind of scepticism, that the separation of mind and body is problematic: one could certainly doubt the continued existence of a mind whose housing body had died, for instance. The binary opposition of mind and body – often referred to as Cartesian dualism because it sees selfhood as split between these two parts of existence – privileges the mental world at the expense of the physical world. But other kinds of thought, for instance, theories deriving from materialist and Marxist accounts of the world, might well argue, on the contrary, that the kinds of thought one is able to think are determined not by one's will, but by the material circumstances in which the individual finds him/herself. Such a critique might argue that, far from securely possessing our own intellects, and using our intellectual faculties rationally, we are made in the image of the material world we inhabit. A human being might also be *homo laborans* (a working being who exists primarily in his or her body and in the necessity to labour – to produce and reproduce – to fulfil the demands of that body). Having the time and the leisure to *think* might just be a function of a level of material privilege, rather than a defining human characteristic.[4] As Terry Eagleton puts it:

> Only on the back of an economic surplus can you float a full-time intelligentsia; before that point, the thinkers have to pitch in with the hunters. 'I think, therefore somebody has been doing the donkeywork' might be the anti-Cartesian motto of this vein of inquiry. (Eagleton 2001, 57–8)

And this is not the only possible objection to the Cartesian *cogito*. Descartes' position is ultimately theistic in which the ultimate guarantor of consciousness is man's creation by a beneficent deity. Since the existence of God is notoriously difficult to 'prove', the problem of our knowledge of our epistemological and ontological status cannot be demonstrated by recourse to theology. Moreover, the very logic of Descartes' discussion is open to question. As Peter Burke has observed, 'the "I" of "I think" assumes exactly what the writer is trying to prove', rendering the Cartesian *cogito* a circular argument (Burke 1997, 17); it is a statement, that is, which always already presupposes the existence of the conscious 'I'. More importantly, perhaps, it also implies a radical instability at the heart of the selfhood it appears to inscribe; for if (consciousness of) being is dependent on (consciousness of) thought, there must be times when being is unsettled by lapses in the rational mind – simple activities like sleeping or daydreaming imply a certain loss of selfhood.

Nonetheless, despite the many problems that the *cogito* throws up, that statement connecting thinking and being is extremely significant in the founding of a kind of modern consciousness. In its emphasis on the apparently immaterial mind over the grossly material body, it inscribes a model of selfhood founded on interiority: on the inner life, not the corporeal one. In valuing mental and intellectual faculties, it produces a version of selfhood strongly aligned to the subjective – a word which is, of course, one of the root words for subjectivity. And in its insistence on thought as the defining proof of existence, it focuses attention on language. What this book seeks to investigate, then, through the analysis of a number of textual selves from different points in modern history, is the question of the relationships between the interior selves we inhabit (our existence as thinking beings) and the forces outside ourselves which, despite the solipsism of the *cogito*, also have their effects on us. Thus, although the *cogito* is a foundational concept, the subjectivity it describes is a limited conception of what a human self might be. There are reasons for broadening the investigation beyond the closed room and the mind communing with itself to think out the processes by which we have become the selves we are and the selves that we are in the process of becoming.

Definitions

Look up the word 'subjectivity' in the *Oxford English Dictionary*, and one of the striking things about the supporting quotations the dictionary provides is their relative modernity. The word is used repeatedly, on the dictionary's evidence, by the poet Samuel Taylor Coleridge; first, in 1821 to mean 'consciousness of one's perceived states'. One who possesses subjectivity is therefore supplementarily 'a conscious being' – and again the evidence for the word's usage comes from Coleridge, this time from a text published in 1838. The third offering of the *OED* extends the definition a little further: 'The quality or condition of viewing things exclusively through the medium of one's own mind or individuality; the condition of being dominated by or absorbed in one's personal feelings, thoughts, concerns, etc.; hence individuality, personality.' This meaning appears to date from 1812, and the evidence for its existence in this form is from another Romantic poet, and an associate of Coleridge, Robert Southey. This definition focuses on subjectivity as a purely subjective (internal or mental) process. And, importantly, it also states a relationship between what is going on inside the head and our self-perception as individuals – as unique beings. The fourth definition focuses on the world of artistic production. Subjectivity is 'That quality of literary or graphic art which depends on the expression of personality or individuality of the artist; the individuality of [the] artist as expressed in his art'. Coleridge is again the provider of the first supporting quotation. In this definition, the internal mental processes are externalized through artistic practice, made concrete in an artistic or literary artefact, turning the abstraction of the mind into a material object in the world. The kind of object one produces, it suggests, is a function of the kind of subjectivity one inhabits. Subjectivity and objectivity, as I note above, are usually understood as a binary opposition, but it may just be that the object is determined by the subject, and that inside and outside are not so neatly divided. This leads to the final definition in which subjectivity is defined in opposition to 'objectivity'; 'The quality or condition of resting upon subjective facts or mental representation; the character of existing in the mind only.' Here alone is the supporting evidence from a discipline other than literature–philosophy; but again, the word's usage is modern, dating from 1864. And this apparently simple opposition is far from secure.

One of the interesting things about this trawl through the dictionary is the way in which the emphasis in all the definitions is firmly placed on the mind as opposed to the body, with the dictionary itself formalizing an intriguing example of Cartesian dualism. Subjectivity covers a multiplicity of possibilities, but at its heart is the idea that human beings living in normal circumstances – though, as the dictionary suggests, they may also have to be quite *modern* human beings – possess subjectivity: the consciousness of their own being, their own personality, their own individuality. This consciousness implies that we might well be preoccupied with our own selves, and, if the dictionary is correct, it is foundational in the construction of our personalities. This consciousness might be expressed artistically – if we are lucky. But it is also a risky business, since in our self-absorption, we may well find ourselves behaving in a dangerously solipsistic manner, taking the consciousness of our minds as the sole evidence on which to base our behaviour. 'Resting on subjective facts … existing in the mind only', is presumably a dangerous proposition to live by (and even the apparently objective dictionary cannot quite disguise its distaste for this view), though it represents fascinating possibilities for making our world in our own image. Perhaps the trickiness of the issue is best expressed in the ambiguity of a phrase such as 'self-consciousness'. To be conscious of oneself is part of what subjectivity appears to mean; and from that self-knowledge all other personal traits proceed – self-consciousness can mean self-possession, poise, confidence. At the same time, however, self-consciousness also means awkwardness and embarrassment, clumsiness and discomfort, which may also rob us of our self-possession, suggesting in fact that self-possession is a fragile property. (All the potential puns here are intended.) And we lose our self-possession and become self-conscious at precisely those moments when we are forced to remember that we are not only subjective selves (selves with beautiful interiors, as it were), but also objective selves – selves with a material presence in the world, selves with bodies that may in fact be *subject to* actions and forces that we cannot control, which are in fact the *objects* of the actions and desires, whether hostile or friendly, of others, of 'laws' of the physical world, and of our own unwilled and unconscious actions.

Thus, the sense that subjectivity contrasts with objectivity, and that its possession emphasizes the workings of the mind as opposed to those of the body, may be merely illusory, a linguistic structure of binary opposition rather than an accurate description of the 'real'. The binaries – as is so often the case – are really not simply opposed. The original distinction between subjective and objective, Raymond Williams argues, was in fact the absolute reverse of their definitions today. Subjective originally meant 'things as they are in themselves (from the sense of subject as substance)'; and objective thus stood for the internal workings of the mind, 'as things are presented to consciousness ("thrown before" the mind)'. Williams identifies the philosophical tradition inaugurated by René Descartes in the seventeenth century as an inaugural moment for the process of reversing the terms to their current position, where *subjective* relates to the individual self and *objective* to the empirically observable world; Descartes' view 'proposed the thinking self as the first substantial area of knowledge – the subject – from the operations of which the independent existence of all other things must be deduced – as *objects* thrown before this consciousness' (Williams 1988, 309). He ends his discussion of the term 'subjective' with a serious warning:

> It is easy enough to say [that the range of possible meanings for the words subjective and objective] is both a subject and an object of concern. But the real problem lies in the historical layering within each word and in the surpassing confidence of the very different surviving traditions which now shape the alternative senses. What must be seen, in the end, as deeply controversial uses of what are nevertheless, at least in subject and object, inevitable words, are commonly presented with a certainty at times a glibness that simply spread confusion. Subjective and objective, we might say, need to be thought through – in the language ... – every time we wish to use them seriously. (Williams 1988, 312)

With that warning in mind, we need to remember that the word *subjectivity* is a modern coinage drawing on the meaning of the word *subject*. The *OED* has nearly four pages of definitions and supporting quotation of this apparently simple word in its many forms as noun, adjective and verb, with its noun form alone producing

eighteen different major headings and a multiplicity of sub-headings
as testament to its almost infinite variety. The word *subject* has come to
be very important in contemporary literary theory because of its adoption by strands of psychoanalysis deriving from the works of Jacques
Lacan. The social scientist Anthony Elliott has recently observed that
there are a lot of words to describe selfhood bandied around in contemporary sociological, psychological and cultural theory. He distinguishes between models of selfhood that 'deny the agency of human
subjects and argue in favour of the person's determination by social
structures on the one hand, and those that celebrate the authenticity
and creativity of the self on the other'. Depending on the view one
takes, he suggests, there is a wide vocabulary of selfhood:

> the language used by social theorists and social scientists to analyse
> selfhood varies considerably: sometimes theorists refer to 'identity',
> sometimes to 'the subject' or 'subjectivity', and sometimes simply to 'the
> self' ... such terminological differences are worth close attention, if only
> because these differences reflect deep historical and political transitions.
> For example, it can plausibly be argued that the concepts of 'the self' and
> 'identity', though similar, are not coextensive, since there are forms
> of identity which are not based on the self, namely, forms of collective
> identity, such as nationalist identities. ... the self is also shaped and
> defined against the backdrop of ... political and public forces; yet the
> fabrication of the self, psychologically and emotionally, is rightly under-
> stood to involve something more subjective, particularly in the ways in
> which desire, emotion and feeling influence the conscious and uncon-
> scious experience of sexuality, gender, race and ethnicity. (Elliott 2001, 9)

The choice of subjectivity over other conceptual words describing
selfhood implies a particular emphasis, in this case, drawing on the
psychoanalytic tradition inaugurated by Lacan in his rereadings of
Freud, and adapted by Julia Kristeva in her rewritings of Lacan. At the
same time, however, subjectivity may well include reference to political and public forces, modes of identity related to sexuality, gender,
race and ethnicity, as well as the psychological and emotional frames
of the individual psyche. Although I want in part to pursue a psychoanalytic approach here, the discussions in this book are also involved
in a critique of the potential limitations of the psychoanalytic systems
it describes.

What, then, is the subject from which Lacanian subjectivity is
derived? In his account of the psyche, post-Freudian psychoanalyst

Jacques Lacan (1901–81) returns to the Freudian model of the making of the self, but offers a radical critique and rewriting of that account. Whatever selfhood is, Freud argues that it begins with the body, a turn of the wheel away from Descartes. The newborn child – helpless and absolutely dependent – experiences his (the Freudian account concentrates on boy-children) world initially as a state of oceanic bliss. The child can perceive no differentiation between himself and the world he inhabits or the people (notably his mother) who minister to his needs. In this state of bliss, he learns that certain activities such as suckling, masturbation and the satisfactory filling of his nappy are pleasurable, and that other states of being are unpleasurable – not being fed on demand or being left in the filled nappy, for instance. The pleasure and displeasure he experiences are his sole sense of being, though he does discover that he can find surrogate activities to replace their satisfactions: for instance sucking on a dummy or a thumb is almost as good as actually being fed. For Freud, these are libidinal activities, in some sense sexually motivated as any quest for pleasure that is not driven purely by biological necessity must be.

The illusionary state of belief in his oneness with the universe, however, cannot last. As the child grows, he is necessarily inserted into a pre-existing culture which forces him to recognize that he is in fact different from his mother, that he does not control his universe at all and that powerful forces are insisting on rules that they have made before the child came into the world. In his passage through the Oedipus Complex, the child discovers that one of the major sources of his own pleasure, his penis, might be at risk – that it could be lost. He makes this discovery in relation to the female body, for women, of course, have no penises, and he posits to himself that the woman or girl child he has seen without her clothes has been punished by castration for some infraction of barely understood social rules. To avoid such a consequence being played out on his own body, he has to regulate his desires, and become obedient to the powerful social order represented by his father. But desire cannot just be turned off at will; the child represses his desires for the nurturing body of the mother, for instance, or for the pleasures he has discovered in his own body, and they take up residence in his unconscious mind, pushed away from consciousness because of the terror of the consequence of castration. The unconscious, however, is permeable: in dreams, reveries, physical tics and sensations, and, eventually (when the child begins to speak) in slips of the tongue and verbal errors and *impolitesses*, it mounts escape bids. The stage is set for a lifelong battle between the conscious mind or ego, which is rational and rule governed, obedient and pliable, and the anarchic space of the unconscious (sometimes also called the id) which is chaotic and intractable. 'The id wants its wishes satisfied, whether or not they are compatible with external demands. The ego finds itself threatened by the pressure of unacceptable wishes', writes Elizabeth Wright (Wright 1998, 11). The threatened ego bars the unacceptable thought from consciousness and hopes for the best, which never quite happens.

Lacan's rewriting of this story contains many of the same elements, but has a very different emphasis signalled in part by his replacement of the Freudian ego with his own 'subject' and by his focus on the newborn (still male) child as an infant (a word significant because its etymology signals 'without speech' from the Latin *infans* meaning 'speechless'). The newborn infant, like Freud's child, is helpless and dependent, but does not know this. He also experiences his world as an undifferentiated realm of oceanic bliss – the little man (whom Lacan calls punningly *l'homelette*) is like an omelette (*l'omelette*), an eggy chaos (Lacan 1977, 197). He has no sense of himself as a complete body, because in his state of infantile uncoordination, he can actually see his body only as momentary fragments as his foot or hand moves fleetingly into view, unwilled by him in this underdeveloped phase of motor-control. This state of bliss, however, is an illusion that cannot last. In his essay 'The Mirror Stage as Formative of the Function of the *I* as Revealed in Psychoanalytic Experience', Lacan posits that at some point between the ages of six and eighteen months, the infant either literally or metaphorically catches sight of himself in a mirror, and becomes fascinated by the image he sees there. He plays with the image, glorying in the facts that it replicates his every movement, and that it reflects his familiar environment. At this moment he begins the process of experiencing himself as different from the world, and as a complete and integrated being (as opposed to being made up of just the bits of his body he can see without the mirror's aid). Lacan, however, is anxious to emphasize that the child is in error in identifying the image with himself. He compares and contrasts the human infant's fascination with his image with the almost immediate recognition made by a similarly aged chimpanzee that the reflection can be 'mastered and found empty' (Lacan 1988, 2).[5] In other words, the infant passes from one state of illusion (the oceanic bliss of the *l'homelette*) to another (the imagined totality and wholeness of the mirror's reflection). For what the child sees in the mirror and identifies as himself is not himself, but only a signifier for the self, which he merely *imagines* to be real. It is this illusory image that the child will eventually name 'I'.

In focusing on the idea that the mirror image is a signifier, Lacan draws extensively on the theories of structuralist linguistics, inaugurated by Ferdinand de Saussure, and popularized in France by the anthropologist Claude Lévi-Strauss. Saussure's thought revolutionized the study of language in its insistence that the relationships between words and things are purely arbitrary, conventional, relational and dependent on difference. Beginning from the view that there is no necessary relationship between a thing and the word used to describe it – that simple nouns like *chair* or *dog* have nothing about them that signals their meaning intrinsically – he proposed that the way in which meaning occurs is in relation to the conventions of a given language community: English-speaking people recognize *chair* and *dog* because they belong to a group of people who have learned and agreed that this is what these sounds or marks on the page must mean: this is what the system of the English language (or *langue*, as Saussure called it) decrees. For people who speak English, the signifiers chair and dog – the sound or its graphic equivalent – produce mental images of chairs and dogs. Saussure called these mental images *the signified*, but stressed that there was no real relationship between the signified and the thing itself, real dogs and chairs in the world outside language (he called the real object *the referent*). If verbal signs made up of signifiers and signifieds have no real relationship with the objects they ostensibly describe, meaning must be derived from some other structure than the words themselves. He proposed that relationality and difference were the mechanisms by which meaning comes about. The placing of a word in a particular place in the syntactical unit of a sentence – its relation to other words in a time sequence – is one way in which meaning occurs; and the individual word's difference from other similar-sounding or semantically similar words is another. The speaker of any given language learns the grammar (rules of combination) of that language, and learns the conventions of vocabulary. From the speaker's individual utterances (*parole*) the linguist can uncover the entire system of the *langue*.[6]

This version of the workings of language systems is essential to an understanding of Lacan's views of the human subject. His most famous statement is 'The unconscious is structured like a language', and the

version of language he means is one derived from a rewriting of
Saussure's model. As the speechless infant develops from *l'hommelette*
into a speaking being – a subject – he experiences feelings of both loss
and power. Loss because, Lacan argues, the infant begins to speak in
reaction against unfulfilled desires: not being fed, changed, or cuddled
whenever he wishes. He must relinquish speechlessness to voice his
needs because those needs are not being (immediately) met. In beginning to speak, he experiences power because in asserting himself in
speech he discovers that words can sometimes have a transitive effect
on the world: the child speaks and something happens in response to
his speech. Like the image in the mirror, however, the sense of power of
the speaking subject is also an illusion.

There is not space here to reproduce the whole of the *OED*'s pro-
nouncements in defining the subject, but any good modern standard
dictionary will offer something like the following (from *The Chambers
Dictionary*):

> **subject** ... *adj* (often with *to*) under rule, government, jurisdiction, or
> control; owing allegiance; under obligation; subordinate; subservient;
> dependent; liable; exposed; prone; disposed ... dependent upon condi-
> tion or contingency ... *n*. a person who is subject; a person who is under,
> or who owes allegiance to, a sovereign, a state, a feudal superior, etc ...
> a thing over which a legal right is exercised; a piece of property
> (*Scot*) ... the mind regarded as the thinking power (as opposed to the
> *object* about which it thinks) ... that part of a sentence or clause denoting
> the person or thing about which something is said ... a topic; a matter of
> discourse, thought or study ... a person or thing upon which an opera-
> tion is performed ... sufferer from disease, a patient; a dead body suit-
> able for dissection; a person peculiarly sensitive to hypnotic influence;
> the person or thing an artist or photographer seeks to represent or
> express ...

The vast majority of these definitions focus on the extent to which the
subject is powerfully *subjected to* forces outside itself and the ghosts of
all those other meanings to do with subordination and lack of power or
control are central to the Lacanian concept of the subject, and thence
to the making of subjectivity. The institution of language in the individual is necessary for normal function, and is exhilarating (ask any new
parent) and exciting, despite its origin in loss and lack. The child who
learns to say 'I want' gains a powerful sense of autonomy through
the articulatory gestures of its first speech. The feelings of power come

from a combination of sources: from grammar (the subject of the sentence is that which *does the verb*, producing the feeling that the subject is an actant on the world); and from the appearance that language is transitive – that it acts on the world (the 'I want' demand is [sometimes] met when it is spoken). But all of these feelings of power are, according to Lacan, following his readings in Saussurean linguistics, illusory – misrecognitions of the facts of the matter. Simply using the word 'I' is, after all, to substitute the referent for a linguistic sign, the real being for a word. Moreover, it is a shared word. The 'I' appears to be unique because it refers to 'myself' (my self); but you also all use that word to designate yourselves (and your selves), implying that I have no ownership of the very word that allows me to say who 'I' am, and possibly therefore no ownership over the being that I am referring to. Similarly, the grammatical object of the 'I want' demand, once turned into language, is a similar substitution of a word for a thing. Moreover, in speech, if the aim is communication, the subject who does the verb is hemmed in by rules and prohibitions – rules of language, such as grammar, appropriate vocabulary for age, situation and context, register, tone, phatic tags, gender and so on. As the dictionary definition shows, the subject is always *subject to* a pre-existing social, linguistic, and economic order over which he has very little control. Thus, although conscious selfhood and language are codependent, and come into existence at the same moment, and although there is much pleasure to be derived from speech, its acquisition is also always a process in which there is a near-total surrender of perceived autonomy. If Descartes hoped to stabilize his universe in the conflation of thinking and being, Lacan's views of the issue suggest that this will not happen. And as Malcolm Bowie shows, Lacan in fact made great play with the *cogito*'s essential instability:

> [In Lacan's writing] the *cogito* is not flatly repudiated; its terms and its prepositional structure are refashioned in a sequence of parodic alternatives:
>
> I think where I am not, therefore I am where I do not think.
> I am not wherever I am the plaything of my thought.
> I think of what I am where I do not think I'm thinking. (Bowie 1991, 77)[7]

What is attractive to the literary critic (one of the things that *I* think I am) about the Lacanian account of subjectivity is its emphasis on

language twinned with its openness to the sense that an entire social
system might just be at work in the process of learning to speak. The
prohibitions that hedge language round are not merely linguistic in
Lacan's thought, but are laws that derive from family relationships and
from the family's participation in a larger social structure. In his acquisition of language, Lacan suggests, the infant leaves behind the
Imaginary realm of illusory non-differentiation and enters the
Symbolic order. The Symbolic is defined by the language of rationality,
which is necessarily a language which has submitted to laws outside
the speaking subject's control, to those laws of conventionality and
differentiation. It also depends on the repression of desire. Writing in
patriarchal Western Europe, Lacan posited that the impetus to repress
comes from the figure of the father, both the child's literal 'daddy', and
also – metaphorically or *symbolically* – all those other patriarchal
structures which legislate appropriate behaviour in a given culture: the
Church, the state, the law, the education system, for example. All of
these are forbidding figures and organizations: they operate, quite as
much literally as figuratively, by saying 'no: thou shalt not' to the child.
Lacan punned in French that these structures, from Daddy to God, are
all part of *le non du père*. Literally this phrase means 'the no of the
father', but in French it is indistinguishable from the phrase *le nom du
père* – the name of the father. In Western Europe the legitimate child's
identity is generally signalled by his being given his father's surname
(which is also a word which designates a part of the speaking subject's
identity), so that on one level, simply by being named, the child begins
the unavoidable process of entering the social world ruled by his
father. But because *le nom du père* is indistinguishable to the French
ear from *le non du père*, acceptance into the social world depends on
the child's submission to the father's laws and rules, and to his submission also to the rules the father represents (and is also subject to) in the
world beyond the immediate family context. Family and nation state,
amongst other structures, hold the child in a nay-saying embrace. It is
the recognition of the possibilities of coercion into an acceptable
subjectivity via the complex interactions of particular parents and
particular social organizations that makes Lacanian thought more
than a merely psychic (interior) explanation of the subject's development. Yet because of its origins in Freudian thought, Lacan's explanatory framework also undoes Cartesian dualism: the mind and the body
as well as the social world all potentially come into his purview.

Well, perhaps. There are many problems with Lacanian thought, just as there are with the Cartesian *cogito*. It is certainly possible to object to the sexism of Lacan's account of child development, just as feminists have also objected to the Freudian account.[8] Marxist critiques also note that any psychoanalytic account is unlikely to take sufficient notice of the materialist basis of any society, and Lacan's account is certainly also Eurocentric, inhabiting an Occidentalism which takes Western values as a universalist norm. And most devastating to any account of selfhood that depends on language is the implication that those without language, those human animals who do not possess the *logos*, because they have no subjectivity that can be *subjected to* the rationalist analysis of psychoanalysis or to the social laws that psychoanalysis attempts to describe, are outside the definition of the human and have no place in human society. As Michael Newton has recently observed, there is an ongoing fascination in Western cultures and beyond with the figure of the so-called feral child in both fiction and scientific documents (Newton 2002, 1–15). These are children who, for a variety of reasons, have been deprived of human contact and normal socialization. In some cases, the children have clearly been deliberately abandoned or mistreated by their birth families; in other cases, children have been lost in the wilderness and apparently 'adopted' by wild animals. Whatever the cause, however, the documented cases demonstrate a continuity of features: when the children are rescued, they are rarely able to learn to speak, seemingly rendered incapable of hearing the significance of human speech because of the developmental failures consequent on being deprived of human contact. They can possess neither the *logos* nor even a minimal capacity for the exchange of signs. Such children raise extremely uncomfortable questions about the nature of selfhood and the extent of the differences between people and animals. In the case of Victor, the Wild Boy of Aveyron, who was 'rescued' or 'captured' in France in 1800, Newton's account shows the presumption of an absence of humanity beyond his human shape by those who first examined the child. 'Incapable of attention, he was therefore necessarily "destitute of memory, of judgement, even of a disposition to imitation" ' opined one French physician: 'His life had annihilated his humanity' (Newton 2002, 102–3). The symptoms of this lack or loss of humanity were first, the lack of language – the lack even of an ability to recognize that the sounds made by others might have anything to do with communication; and second, the inability to empathize with the pains or pleasures of others. Victor was consigned to the care of a doctor named Jean Itard, who had begun his career working in an institution for the deaf. It was Itard who named him, thereby attempting to bring him into an exchange of signs with others and into contact with the Symbolic order; and it was Itard who attempted to refute the argument that the child was merely savage and inhuman by the process of educating him. He sought to show that the concept of the Noble Savage, the notion that man in a state of nature is an ideal, popularized in the previous century by Jean-Jacques Rousseau, was nonsense. The child, who was about twelve years old when he came into Itard's care, and demonstrated in his person that Rousseau's view of the state of nature was absurd. Immediately after his capture, Itard describes Victor thus:

> [He was] a disgusting, slovenly boy, affected with spasmodic, and fre-
> quently with convulsive motions, continually balancing himself like
> some of the animals in the menagerie, biting and scratching those who
> contradicted him, expressing no kind of affection for those who attended
> upon him; and, in short, indifferent to every body, and paying no regard
> to any thing. (Malson and Itard 1972, 96)

Fascinatingly, in Itard's account there is a moment which reads very much like a (failed) version of Lacan's mirror stage (Newton even calls it a 'failed mirror' [Newton 2002, 116]). Itard describes how Victor would spend as much time as possible outside in the gardens attached to his nurse's home. Even in the worst weather, he would 'seat himself on the edge of a bowl of water'; in this position, he would sit for hours, and his spasmodic gestures would be suspended: 'his face, insignifi-cant or distorted as it might be, took the well-defined character of sor-row, or melancholy reverie, in proportion as his eyes were steadily fixed on the surface of the water, and when he threw into it, from time to time, some remains of withered leaves' (Malson and Itard 1972, 104). As Newton observes of this passage, however, Victor was not looking at his own reflection when he sat silently in the garden. The sadness of his situation is that, like the chimp in Lacan's example, the image in the water is empty, if not mastered, in Victor's enclosed world. This implies strongly that the Lacanian account depends – though he does not say so – on the reinforcement of the child's sense of self in the mirror image by others: clapping and cooing parents who ensure that the child rec-ognizes himself. Without that socialization, as Itard argues, man is 'one of the most feeble and least intelligent animals' (Malson and Itard 1972, 91). Without language, moreover, he lives continually in the present. His memory is entirely made up of fleeting and disarticulated images; his desires (or wishes for the future) are attenuated to almost nothing, beyond his immediate physical needs. In Lacan's thought, as Malcolm Bowie argues, desire is scandalously divorced from simple need; and part of his definition of the subject's desire is precisely that it is insatiable (Bowie 1991, 135–6). Victor, however, was easily satisfied – too easily for comfort. Without the consciousness of either past or future (both of which require language with its multiple tenses), Victor's selfhood was reduced to almost nothing.

None of which is to say that he did not deserve to be treated humanely, nor that his selfhood was worthless. Victor's story does, however, point up the limitations of any version of selfhood which presumes a norm of development. There are other kinds of example which are equally disturbing: aphasia (or loss of speech) attendant on strokes and head injuries has produced an entire literature of its own, from the varied points of view of medical practitioners and patients. The acuteness with which the sense of loss of self is felt by such subjects and their families (the dictionary definition includes 'patients' amongst its many possibilities for the meaning of 'subject') is painful to behold. One of the problems of psychoanalysis might just be, however, that in describing a norm, it risks prescribing a norm; and those who stand outside the limits of that normality find no place in the narratives of culture, or find only a pathologized place. And returning for a moment to the idea that man is the animal who possesses *logos*, we should remember that the Greeks themselves described all the peoples who did not speak their language as 'barbarians', from the apparent gibberish (*bar-bar* or 'rhubarb-rhubarb') that they muttered into their beards (*barba* is the Latin for beard). What is problematic here is that psychoanalysis is necessarily a culturally specific explanation for the development of personality. Those who do not share its script because they do not come from that culture or because they do not have fair access to that culture, are disadvantaged by its descriptions. Moreover, linguistic prowess has often been the preserve of a cultural elite within a given culture. The language of psychoanalysis is also the language of privilege. Amongst the limitations of these concepts, then, is the blindness they exhibit to the cultural specificity they inhabit. Other groups, other nations and ethnicities, other classes and – perhaps most importantly since the numbers are greatest, the other gender – need always to be mindful of the story's lacunae, and may have to rewrite the script from their own points of view.

In his Introduction to *Rewriting the Self*, Roy Porter produces a slightly tongue-in-cheek version of the usual history of self and self-representation. 'There is', he writes:

> a standard way of telling the story of the self, one that embodies and bolsters core Western values. Its climax is the fulfilment of the cherished ideal of 'being yourself' (or, as Polonius puts it in *Hamlet* ... 'above all to thine own self, be true'). In other words the secret of selfhood is commonly seen to lie in authenticity and individuality, and its history is presented as a biography of progress towards that goal, overcoming great obstacles in the process. (Porter 1997, 1)

He traces this 'history' of progress, from primitive societies to the present, suggesting that the way we describe the past presumes that at the beginning of human time, there was not much consciousness or subjectivity about. Primitive societies are presented as inhabiting collective consciousness, communal views in which the individual self is subjugated to the needs of the community. In Ancient Greek society there were the first stirrings of modern individuality, in which man was pitted against an inexorable fate. The Greeks were followed rapidly by the Christians and their paradoxical beliefs – that everyone has a soul and that the soul is uniquely important, but that the highest human ideal is self-denial or even self-annihilation in the spectacular martyr-doms that re-enacted the example of the Crucifixion. During the Renaissance, 'mankind' (implicitly literate, gifted, elite males) began to liberate itself from the chains of custom. And the movement towards the liberation and autonomy of the individual is a narrative towards the post-Romantic ideals to which we adhere today.

Given that (I think) I am a literary critic, the emphasis in this book is on modes of subjectivity that are written down. This necessarily produces a set of biases. The kinds of text to which we have easy access are those kinds of writing which a given culture privileges as valuable, and that value is measured aesthetically, morally, ideologically and – crucially – economically. I in no way wish to suggest that the subjectivities that are, and were, the lived experiences of cultures without writing are less valuable than literate subjectivities. But, as Walter Ong has shown in *Orality and Literacy*, people who can read and write think very differently from those who cannot, and especially those from 'primary oral cultures' where reading and writing has not even been imagined:

> functionally literate human beings are ... beings whose thought processes do not grow out of simply natural powers but out of these powers as structured, directly or indirectly, by the technology of writing. Without writing, the literate mind would not and could not think as it does, not only when engaged in writing but normally even when it is composing its thoughts in oral form. More than any other single invention, writing has transformed human consciousness. (Ong 1980, 78)

As someone *writing* in the literate west, I necessarily inhabit that transformation of consciousness in fundamental ways. I cannot and perhaps I should not speak or write for those others who inhabit very different structures of emotion, belief and practical engagement with the world. Part of my argument is that the kinds of subjectivity we have developed and lived within are intimately connected to the societies we live in: we draw our models of selfhood from the models that our culture makes available to us. In literate cultures, some of those structures come from books and the transformation of human consciousness that Ong identifies is traceable to texts. There is a very real sense that, in the West (broadly conceived), we are what we read (and, indeed, write). Those cultures where writing does not exist have their own modes of transmission and self-articulation which may, indeed, function in quite similar ways to textual transmission – the audience to an oral performance, for instance, seeking to emulate the heroism described in the poem is not so very dissimilar from a reader's engagement and empathy with characters in a solitarily consumed fiction. But there are differences – differences between communality and solitariness, between a necessary conservatism in a subsistence culture and the high value placed on individual uniqueness and originality in a culture of relative luxury. If I focus on the latter, it is not because I think the former is either inferior or unsusceptible to analysis. It is rather that the interiority that subjectivity describes is more easily available to an interpreter from my place and time.

Porter's ironic presentation of this history of selfhood is a warning against the presumption that the procession of history necessarily implies evolutionary progress. Having said that, however, this book is organized in a broadly chronological fashion, but not because the subjectivities it describes are progressive. It is important to place these textual subjectivities in their material and historical moments because that is part of the argument I am seeking to make. But I do not wish to suggest that there is an easy relationship between time passing and a point of imminent arrival at the apotheosis of human selfhood. The following chapters discuss, amongst other things, the textual formation of subjectivity in relation to the subjectivities of other textual formations. The relationship between self and reading is an important on-going thematic concern. They also focus on the varieties of selfhood that are possible in different material circumstances, and argue that subjectivity produces a necessary illusion of autonomy that is always at odds with the problems of subjection. I have tried to wear my theoretical leanings lightly, so that the chapters are readable. Interested readers can pursue the implications of what I say – and its theoretical roots – through close attention to the notes and to the bibliography.

Notes

1. The critics of the 1980s had much to say against the presumption that just using our common sense is an appropriate way to approach the literary. Terry Eagleton, for example, writes: 'Common sense generally holds that things have only one meaning and this meaning is usually obvious, inscribed on the faces of the objects we encounter. The world is pretty much as we perceive it, and our way of perceiving it is the natural, self-evident one. We know the sun goes round the earth because we can see that it does. At different times common sense has dictated burning witches, hanging sheep stealers, and avoiding Jews for fear of fatal infection' (Eagleton 1996, 94). And Catherine Belsey warns us against any intellectual activity that approaches its subject 'not as a self-conscious or deliberate practice … but as the "obvious" mode of reading, the "natural" way of approaching' the issues (Belsey 1980, 2).
2. For readers not brought up in Britain, or who are rather younger than me, before 'spam' came to mean junk email, it was a kind of tinned meat made from spiced ham.
3. For a highly lucid account of Descartes' position for the non-philosopher, see Sedgwick 2001, 3–11.
4. See Haslett 2000 for an account of the materialist basis of Marxist theories.
5. Of course, there is another way of 'reading' this foundational moment. It is in fact one of the major distinctions between human beings and animals that they do not find the mirror image 'empty'. One can, as Lacan does,

suggest that this is problematic; or, alternatively, one might argue – as I am certainly tempted to do – that the human child who recognizes itself in the mirror is participating in a significant moment in their development: as well as being animals who posses *logos*, human beings might just also be animals who possess an ability to use and exchange signs. (Mis-)recognizing the sign of the mirror image is a cause for celebration at least as much as for mockery.

6. For further eludication of Saussure's theories, see Hawkes 1988, Eagleton 1996. For the absolute beginner, Barry 1995 is a very gentle introduction. To see these ideas in action in the reading of a literary text, see Cowley 1996.

7. I have drawn on a number of sources for this brief description of Lacanian thought. Brave readers can tackle Lacan's own writings (Lacan 1977 and 1988). Those who have not yet had much experience of theoretical writing, especially of the dense kinds can turn to Barry 1995 as a starting place; Moi 1985 and Morris 1993 both give lucid accounts of Lacanian thought in the framework of feminist literary theory. Wright 1998 is an excellent general introduction to psychoanalytic thought more generally. Bowie 1991 is also essential reading. And Payne 1993 is a more detailed and critical discussion, invaluable for the reader seeking to work out ways to *use* Lacanian theories. For a discussion of Lacan's usefulness for approaching literature, see Rabaté 2001.

8. See Gallop 1982 for one such critique.

1   *Pamela*, Rousseau and Equiano: Trousseaux, Confessions and Tall Tales

Subjectivity, as the Introduction suggests, is a very insecure possession. In this chapter, the three texts discussed are produced by writers who, in the words of Julia Kristeva, are *sujets-en-procès* (subjects in process/on trial). Kristeva argues, in fact, that all subjectivities are *sujets-en-procès*, that subjectivity is never complete, but is always in the process of being made and remade by the competing forces of the Symbolic order (the *non du père*) and the semiotic, a space made up of the demands of the body and of the non-signifying parts of language, such as speech rhythms, sounds, intonations and other non-semantic gestures. Additionally, she argues that it is a kind of trial – a trial for one's life, one might say – in which laws made before one's birth compete with the apparently autonomous self's attempts to assert its individuality.[1] In bringing these three very different texts together, I want to suggest a number of possible ideas about subjectivity, and I begin with Kristeva's concept because the paired ideas of trial and process are more acutely felt in some of these texts than in other places. In part, subjectivity depends on pre-existing scripts – you are what you have the ability to say, and, by extension, you are what you have read. This is particularly the case for the two relatively underprivileged subjectivities discussed here, the fictional character Pamela Andrews brought to life in Samuel Richardson's novel *Pamela*, and the real-life historical personage, Ouladah Equiano. Their attempts to make themselves – to achieve self-possession, one might say – depend very heavily on the privileged models of self hood that they find in already-existing texts. On the other hand, whilst Jean-Jacques Rousseau is at pains to argue in his *Confessions* that he is also underprivileged, his subject position is self-consciously produced as a series of acts of resistance against the conventional models available to him. He reacts to those models in part precisely because he is already possessed of and by them, and can take them for granted. For Pamela and Equiano, the situation is much more unstable, and this points out the fact that the subjectivity one is able to inhabit is at least as much a function of the economic and cultural circumstances in which one lives as it is a question of individual choices and will.

'Who *does* she think she is?' The case of *Pamela*

> 'O my good girl', replied [Mr B.] tauntingly, 'you are well read, I see; and we shall make out between us, before we have done, a pretty story for a romance'. (Richardson 1980, 63)

The question in this subtitle is a refinement of the ones I posed earlier. It comes from an essay on the novel *Pamela* (1740) by Carolyn Steedman (Steedman 1992, 8). And amongst all the many things that Samuel Richardson's novel might be, it is, as Steedman argues, a very potent rewriting of a historically and culturally specific script. *Pamela* documents the making of a particular subjectivity against the confines of class and gender; and the important word here is *documents*.

The case of *Pamela* in fact offers serious challenges to readers in my place and time, for we are at some considerable distance from the implications the text offered to its own place and time: modern student readers often struggle to understand what all the considerable fuss was about when the novel was first published.[2] The historian Hayden White comments that 'The reality that lends itself to narrative representation is the conflict between desire and the law' (White 1987, 12). In the West, we live in an era when that conflict is less acutely experienced, though we may well be mistaken in our assumption that our desires are easily met. For Pamela Andrews, however, duty appears a stronger motivation for actions than desire, and many of the problems she confronts are founded on duties that are in conflict with each other – the duty to her 'master', Mr B, duties to her parents (she usually signs herself 'Your dutiful Daughter' [Richardson 1980, 72]), and the duty she owes to her God. The burden of duty is centred on a female protagonist who is established as being especially vulnerable to assaults on her dignity, virtue and self-respect. Duty is not a merely abstract conception.

Pamela produces ideas about emotion and sentiment (the possessions of an interior world) in a world that is very strongly materially realized with specificity of time, place and action. The novel is placed geographically, domestically and socially, implying that the emotions it produces are directly related to the wider cultural values of the mid-eighteenth century in which it is set.

The single most significant thing about Pamela Andrews, however, is that she can read and write. The whole of her existence in the novel, and indeed, the novel's existence, is predicated on the fact that she is 'always scribbling' (Richardson 1980, 54). Her character is constructed entirely out of the words in which she narrates her own story and whenever she is silent, she ceases, for that moment, to exist. The fact that she is able to read and write is a social anomaly caused by the favouritism of her dead mistress: 'my lady's goodness had put me to write and cast accompts, and made me a little expert at my needle, and *otherwise qualified me above my degree*' (43, my emphasis). These skills have rendered her *déclassée*; they have placed her outside the normal skill-set of her social station. She can read, write, count and embroider, and is thus overqualified for many of the servant-type jobs that would otherwise have been open to her. And it is highly likely that it is these attributes – the attributes of a lady in a young girl otherwise socially disadvantaged – that first excite Mr B's unwelcome attentions.

Because Pamela's written language *is* her character, she engages the reader in a series of questions about the nature of the relationship between words and the reality they supposedly describe. Richardson clearly presumed that we would read his novel in good faith: he expected us to believe that Pamela was always telling the truth, and that her motives were as she states them. He went to considerable lengths to reproduce the effects of reality – to create verisimilitude in his fiction so that readers would forget that Pamela is in fact merely an empty sign with no existence beyond the pages in which she appears. He therefore presents Pamela *in medias res*, writing her life story without the benefit of hindsight, and without the knowledge of how it will all turn out. In the excitement of her 'writing to the moment' readers are constructed to respond as if to a series of real, immediate crises. This impression is, of course, false. Even if we accede to a suspension of disbelief and accept Pamela's 'reality', it is obviously the case that whilst ever Pamela is writing the crisis must have receded: no one writes down her thoughts whilst in the very midst of being raped, and there is always a gap between the actions that are narrated and the act of narrating those actions. Her continued narrative signals that she has survived to fight another day. In two senses, then, writing is literally the heroine's whole existence: there is no Pamela (or *Pamela*) without her words; and there is a guarantee of her safety if she is writing 'now'.

At the same time, though, Pamela's writing of her story always risks drawing attention to the fact of her writing, and hence to the fact that her story might be read as fiction or as artifice. Her letters and diaries are not merely the container for the plot (the way in which the story gets told); they are also a major part of the plot. A lot of Pamela's time and ingenuity is taken up with the practicalities of writing. For Pamela, paper, pens and ink are expensive and rare commodities. She must, therefore, 'plot' or scheme to ensure that she has sufficient materials for writing at her disposal, and she must write about these plots. She must find ways to circumvent the watchful eyes of Mrs Jewkes who wishes to see everything her prisoner has written. She must find the privacy in which to write – and in privacy, of course, she is at risk, because once away from the social spaces of the Lincolnshire house, she becomes vulnerable to the predations of her master. Finally, as my students always ruefully notice, even the first two volumes of *Pamela* do not represent a short book. There is an awful lot of paper to be kept away from prying eyes. Ironically, then, Pamela must keep on writing, thereby increasing the bulk of what she has written, about how she is going to keep that bulk hidden. The more she writes, the more she has to write. She is ingenious in her hiding places, hiding her letters in the garden under a sunflower, and eventually sewing them into her petticoats. This last hiding place has the effect of rendering the letters – at least for Mr B – erotically charged because they are close to the body that he wishes to possess. In a novel that is filled with more or less titillatory scenes, the most titillatory is the moment when Mr B threatens to undress Pamela to possess – not her body, this time – but her letters. He describes them as a romance or novel and wants to read them because he wishes to take over the authorship and direct the story's ending: 'there's such a pretty air of romance as you tell your story, in *your* plots, and *my* plots, that I shall be better directed how to wind up the catastrophe of the pretty novel' (Richardson 1980, 268, original emphasis). His desire to read the words she has written eventually becomes a virtual substitute for the sexual conquest he has so far failed to make:

> 'Now', said he, 'it is my opinion that [your writings] are about you; and I have never undressed a girl in my life; but I will now begin to strip my

pretty Pamela, and hope I shall not go far before I find them'. And he began to unpin my handkerchief. (Richardson 1980, 272)

Like pornography, Pamela's writing has seductive effects, acting in a transitive way on Mr B's world. The body of the text and the body of its 'author' are strangely mixed up in the novel, a highly suggestive conflation that tells us something about the possibilities of reading and writing as the sites of erotic encounter. He reads her as the heroine of one kind of fiction, and she resists his interpretation, constructing herself as a heroine in quite another genre.

The answer to the question 'who does Pamela think she is' is largely a matter of her reading. By the standards of eighteenth-century elite culture, although Pamela has been educated above her station, she is nonetheless woefully under-educated and under-read. The education of polite society in this period was one based on the Classics – on the dead languages and literature of Greek and Latin civilization. She may be able to read and write, but what she is able to read and write lays her open to charges of 'vulgarity', the vulgar tongue in this case meaning the vernacular language of English as opposed to the languages of the ancient texts. But it also means another kind of 'vulgarity' – her 'under-reading' is understood as a symptom of her under-breeding, her lack of high-class status. As Moyra Haslett notes, there was a certain discomfort with Pamela's 'homely diction', a lexis which, as it were, named a spade a spade rather than a horticultural implement (Haslett 2003, 213). This discomfort derives from the fact that the eighteenth-century world of polite letters focused strongly on the concept of manners appropriate to an elite class, to an elegant periphrasis that avoided naming things exactly as they are. Nonetheless, Pamela exhibits an attitude to the written word which is testament to its potency, for her reading teaches her moral lessons which her own writing then seeks to replicate for the benefit of her own readers, both those within her text (Mr B and his society friends) and those outside it. There is a focus on the transitivity of the written word.

As a good Protestant, the most obvious text to which Pamela makes reference is her Bible. Her knowledge of this foundational text can be found in structural effects in the novel, such as the fact that her exile at Brandon Hall lasts for forty days and forty nights, the Biblical shorthand for 'a very long time' which covers everything from the duration of the Flood to the wanderings of Christ in the Wilderness. It can also be found in the frankly hilarious version she writes of Psalm 137 ('By the waters of

Babylon, there we sat down, yea, we wept, when we remembered Zion'). This Psalm, which records the emotions of exile experienced by the Israelites in their displacements from the Promised Land, argues that one cannot be oneself, because one cannot be 'at home', in a strange land – exile has serious consequences for selfhood. When Pamela adapts this Psalm, depending on how you look at it, she either elevates her own situation by an appeal to Biblical authority, or she unwittingly ridicules Biblical authority in the bathetic juxtaposition of her own individual situation with that of an entire exiled people. The poem she writes about her imprisonment – 'When sad I sat in Brandon Hall' (349) – strikes modern readers as comic. But the audience inside the book is moved by its pathos and praises Pamela's sensibility, even unto weeping themselves, a move which itself constructs the emotion that Richardson also wished to reproduce in his own readers outside the text through the emotional affect of 'sensibility'. Although Ian Watt's account of the rise of the modern individual as evidenced by the representations of such psychologized characters as Pamela in the era of the rise of the novel has been much criticized, the effect of the Protestant emphasis on the individual quest for salvation via Bible study clearly does mark Pamela's thinking about who she is, and thus also marks her writing of herself and our reading of her.[3]

Pamela, however, has not only read her Bible. In Letter 29 we discover that she has also read both Aesop's *Fables* and the stories of the Protestant martyrs.[4] She uses these texts as very direct examples to apply to her own experience. As she wonders what she will do for a living if she is forced to return to her parents and keep herself by harder kinds of labour than those she is used to, she explicitly compares herself with 'the grasshopper in the fable, which I have read of in my lady's books', and draws the moral lesson that she would have been better off training to do work more fitted to her social position: 'I had better, as things stand, have learned to wash and scour, and brew and bake, and such like' (109). A little later, she compares her own experience to the story of a Protestant bishop who was to be burned at the stake and tested his own fortitude for the coming trial by putting his fingers into a lighted candle:

> so I t'other day tried … if I could not scour a pewter plate … I see I could do it by degrees; it only blistered my hand in two places.
>   All the matter is, if I could get plain-work enough, I need not spoil my fingers. But if I can't, I will make my hands as red as a blood pudding, and

as hard as a beechen trencher, but I will accommodate them to my
condition. (109)

As Margaret Doody has observed of this passage, Pamela founds
her subjectivity on a range of rather incongruously juxtaposed pre-
existing scripts, from real life experience (beechen trenchers and blood
pudding are part of the incontrovertible evidence of the 'vulgarity' or
'lowness' of that experience), to martyrologies (the martyred bishop),
to the concerns of beauty manuals (blistered hands caused by hard
labour) to the language of social duty (to which Pamela will 'accommodate' herself if so required) (Doody 1980, 12). There is both energy and
comedy in this description of what she will do. And Nancy Armstrong
also shows how the genre of the conduct manual – texts explicitly
aimed at reproducing socially exemplary behaviour – are an essential
feature of Pamela's narrative and Richardson's conception of his task as
a writer (Armstrong 1987, esp. 66–7). But the passage also points out
how Pamela habitually makes use of her reading: she always relates
what she reads to her current situation behaving exactly towards the
text as the moralistic fictions and conduct books of her age required
her to do. There are multiple examples of this tendency in the novel.
Fearing she will be raped, Pamela contemplates suicide, but she also
fears becoming 'the subject' of her neighbours' 'ballads and ... elegies'
(Richardson 1980, 212), fears, in other words, that she will be reduced
to a moral fable; yet fables are part of her own process of making
herself and she compares herself to 'the poor sheep in the fable'
(224). Elsewhere, she considers faking her own death, taking her example from a tale she has read 'of a great sea captain' who thwarted his
enemies by pretending to drown (208). And this tendency affects
Mr B as well. His plans to entrap her into a sham marriage – his
'horrid romancing' (219) – are a plot element common in Restoration
comedy.

   The process of reading one's own life into fictional models was one of
the contemporary objections to novel reading, for the Protestant tradition makes great play of the concept of devotional reading which is
designed to produce real effects in readers' lives. If impressionable
young women, in particular, read novels, mostly made up of improbable love stories, they were likely to be led astray into thinking forbidden
thoughts and harbouring untenable aspirations. In this novel, there is
a highly developed sense that reading as well as writing is a material
practice that has material effects on the reader. After all, Mr B is finally

seduced into marriage by reading Pamela's story in her own words; he changes his ways and becomes an interpreter of moral lessons from the written word, just as Pamela herself is, and just as we are supposed to be in the world outside the text.

In becoming an author, Pamela stakes a claim to *authority* (the root word for both author and authority is the same). It is a claim that, in many ways, she has no right to make at all. Apart from her relatively feeble educational status, within the English class system that is the social backbone of the text, Pamela's place is extremely insecure. And one reason why the text goes on at such length is to do with the psychological effects of that position on Pamela's hopes and dreams. The rigidity of the social hierarchy is such that Pamela cannot imagine marrying Mr B like a latterday Cinderella. He is too far above her for this even to cross her mind at the outset. As Doody puts it:

> She belongs to the bottom of the social pyramid; Mr B. and others refer to
> her father as 'Goodman Andrews', as he is not of the class entitled to be
> referred to as 'Mister'. He is master of nothing. Mr B. orders ... the
> servants ... refer to Pamela as 'Madam', 'Mistress Pamela', 'Mrs Pamela',
> as if she were entitled by rank to the dignity of a title. But she knows that
> this is making a 'May-game' of her. By birth, she is mistress of nothing,
> and they are trying to maker her 'Madam' and a 'Mistress' in the sense of
> 'whore'. (Doody 1996, 101–2)

The fact of class not only prevents Pamela from dreaming of a marriage to Mr B, at least at the outset; it also prevents Mr B from dreaming of marrying her. Pamela's worthlessness on the social scale is cruelly exposed in the reactions of the local gentry to her plight during her Lincolnshire imprisonment. As Parson Williams reports:

> I applied to Lady Darnford, and told her, in the most pathetic terms I
> could think of, your sad story, and shewed her your more pathetic letter.
> I found her well-disposed; but she would advise with Sir Simon, she
> said ... She did, in my presence; and he said, 'Why, what is all this, my
> dear, but that our neighbour has a mind to his mother's waiting-maid!
> And if he takes care she wants for nothing, I don't see any great injury will
> be done her. He hurts no *family* by this.' (Richardson 1980, 172, original
> emphasis)

The lady reader in this exchange is touched by sensibility; pathetic stories and pathetic letters move her to action. But the man of the family thinks only in terms of class rather than in terms of individuals; Pamela's fate is unimportant so long as the privileges of his class remain untouched. At the end of the first two volumes, however, those privileges do not remain untouched. *Pamela* was a revolutionary novel in its claim – reiterated in different terms by Pamela on several occasions – that her social status is not the primary marker of her worth. Her soul, she tells Mr B, is the equal of his.

Pamela's literacy, no matter how marginal it is, makes Richardson's novel what it is. It shapes the kind of thoughts that Pamela can think. It even gives her access to the arguments that will protect her; for instance when Mr B proposes a 'mistress contract' to her, its appearance in written form enables her to refute each of its terms in turn. Similarly, she negotiates the meaning of her projected marriage in the conditions of a written contract. She thinks through writing in dialectical structures through which she attains access both to the arguments that threaten her and the means to undermine them. *Who she thinks she is* is absolutely contained in a world of reading and writing.

Pamela is, writes Carolyn Steedman, a story of 'class and gender' which provokes her to think about 'the way some stories simply come and take you, occupy you, make you work out again and again what its they mean, and the meaning of your own obsession with them' (Steedman 1992, 2). Steedman's conclusions about what *Pamela* means are tentatively expressed, but extremely important. She argues that the key difference between *Pamela* and Richardson's later novel, *Clarissa* (which has a very similar plot in many ways) is a difference predicated on class: *Pamela* is comedy and *Clarissa* is tragedy because Clarissa Harlowe is a lady, and Pamela Andrews is a labouring-class woman. We cannot laugh at Clarissa's predicament as we do at Pamela's:

> though our laughter at one is perhaps more terrible in implication than our tragic response to the other, for *Pamela* ... tells us plain that [the] grand issues (bodily integrity, habeas corpus, land tenure, ownership, occupancy and exploitation) affect the poorer sort in every aspect of their existence, but that their story of resistance simply cannot be told as tragedy. (Steedman 1992, 3)

The structures of the class system and the structures of narrative disempower the labouring-class narrative twice over; they do not permit us quite to accept that Pamela's claim of spiritual equality with Mr B is true. At the same time, Steedman sees in *Pamela* not only a plot which describes a particular historically specific subjectivity, but also the process by which that subjectivity comes into being. She considers the ways in which writing – like the Lacanian infant's speech – 'continually spell[s] out both restraint and permission ... draw[s] our attention to the literary forms available to people in different historical epochs, forms that sometimes restrain the writing of the self, sometimes permit it' (14). When she describes her own writing process in the Preface to this book, she emphasizes that she works 'by producing endless drafts': it is only in the process of writing (which she describes, fascinatingly, as a bodily process – 'dragging [it] out of the viscera'), she argues, that you can find out 'what it is, *what it is you mean*' (x). Articulating thought in writing is how she knows she is having a thought at all. In comparison to Descartes' solitary self-communion with thinking, writing is a neatly ambiguous activity. One might write for oneself at least as much as for an audience – Pamela does both, using writing to order her thoughts in the manner of therapy or self-help, as well as to communicate her distress to others.

The voice that speaks to us from this fiction is relatively under-privileged, insecure, threatened in an unstable universe; but this voice nonetheless stakes a claim on the interest of readers, asking us to consider her far from unique situation through the lens of her unique subject position. The kind of self Pamela inhabits and becomes through the process of her relating her story presents us with a powerful mythology of the secure possession of self; of subjectivity as autonomous and resistant as well as powerfully *subjected*. It suggests that the transmission of models of selfhood takes place in a variety of places: in relation to class and socio-economic status as well as to the sense of an interior life of language and thought. It points out that the body cannot be ignored in the making of subjectivity – it is the fact Pamela 'lives' in a female body which is the pre-requisite for her story. It shows that the interior life is very much a product of the exterior life. And it insists that literacy has profound effects on the kind of thought that can take place inside the mind as well as on paper. From the point of view of the literary critic that I think I am, it also demonstrates the power of the written word on subsequent performances of selfhood. There is a transformative effect in a text like *Pamela*; in the wake of its publication it altered what it was possible to imagine being.

Jean-Jacques Rousseau's *Confessions*: refusing to play the game

In Virginia Woolf's 1942 novel *Between the Acts,* Bartholomew, an audience member at a village pageant that represents British history from the Norman Conquest to the present, asks: ' "What's the object," said Bartholomew, "of this entertainment?" ' (Woolf 1992b, 105). No explicit answer is forthcoming to Bartholomew's question, but implicitly the answer is that the pageant dramatizes both communal values – particularly important in the context in which the pageant is enacted, in the foreboding-filled summer of 1939 – and fissures in that community, its breakings-down caused by the forces of both social and political history. It is also, however, a question that can be asked about the performance of subjectivity enacted by autobiographical writings. The potential answers to the question of the purpose of autobiography are similar. On the one hand, readers read 'typical' experience with which they might identify: the writer's experience and the subjectivity that experience has created is similar to their own. And therefore autobiography functions to produce and reproduce communal values despite the evidence of differences between people that it also enacts. On the other, the autobiographical writer also engages in an act which asserts his or her uniqueness and utter difference from those readers: and as a reader, one's interest is piqued by that alterity of subjectivity that autobiography both uncovers and performs.

It is his uniqueness that Jean-Jacques Rousseau seeks to emphasize. When in the opening passages of his *Confessions*, he asserts:

> I have resolved on an enterprise which has no precedent, and which, once complete, will have no imitator. My purpose here is to display to my kind a portrait in every way true to nature, and the man I shall portray will be myself.
>
> Simply myself. I know my own heart and understand my fellow man. But I am made unlike any one I have ever met; I will even venture to say that I am like no one in the whole world. I may be no better, but at least I am different. Whether Nature did well or ill in breaking the mould in which she formed me, is a question which can only be resolved in the reading of my book. (Rousseau 1953, 17)

The tensions inherent in the exercise of the written performance of subjectivity are writ large in this short statement. On the one hand, Rousseau promises truthfulness; on the other, he is always already involved in the conventions of representation – here figured in the metaphor of a portrait. He is unique; but he is also a member of a 'kind', presumably humankind, and he seeks his own validation in the process of this representation. He offers us no explanatory purpose in his confessions: what we will read is 'simply myself'. He already 'know[s] his own heart', so the purpose of the narrative is not a journey of self-discovery, undertaken for his own purposes. He also knows his 'kind', his 'fellow man', so the narrative offers him no purpose in understanding others either. He invites us to judge him – is his uniqueness a good thing or a bad one is the question he poses; but in the narrative that follows, he will be unable to offer any judgement, or any answer to his original question. There is a sense, indeed, in which the personality Rousseau presents is – more than metaphorically – 'unreadable'.

The Confessions have been continuously read and re-read since their publication in 1781, and are often regarded as one of the inaugural texts of modern subjectivity as well as of modern autobiography.[5] Rousseau was, nonetheless, correct in his presumption that he would have no precise imitators for his method. *The Confessions* are a broadly chronological (though also occasionally inaccurate) record of the events of Rousseau's life. But this is not a progressive narrative of a developmental self, and it is not an explanation of the self that Rousseau has become. Finally, it is not even, despite its titular appeal to the sacramental notion of confession adhered to by Roman Catholics, an *apologia*, an expression of regret or distaste for past actions. Moreover, the Catholic confession demands that the confessant seek the origins of his/her actions, pursue them narratively to their source, for by explaining how a particular sin came to be committed, the sinner is thereby able to avoid the same mistake again. Instead, Rousseau presents – interminably – the things that have *happened to him*; he is the object of other people's actions at least as much as the actor of his own destiny – and he presents himself as though the simple act of story-telling in itself is the whole point of the enterprise. He can draw no conclusions; and, indeed, he cannot even very clearly tell the story. A large part of the latter stages of *The Confessions* is taken up with the description of the various plots Rousseau felt himself to be the victim of. But the nature of the plots against him is impossible to disentangle from the knot of events he narrates. His verbatim reproduction of letters to and from the principle plotters is a signal attempt to produce documentary evidence that such a plot existed, but the letters, often couched in the periphrastic language of polite writing, do not disclose the main points at issue. And he repeatedly makes the same kinds of error in his relations with others, misinterpreting them and finding himself misinterpreted. The Russian formalist critics of the 1920s distinguished between the two elements of narrative that they identified as *fabula* (roughly, story, event, unfolding of action in chronological sequence) and *syuzhet* (meaning, subject, purpose, or plot).[6] *The Confessions* has the tendency to remain at the level of *fabula*, presenting 'one dam' thing after another' rather than – as is usual in narrative – providing causes and effects, and reflections thereupon. Moreover, narrative generally operates in relation to climax and dénouement, so that, as Linda Anderson puts it, Rousseau's rambling narrative creates a 'plotless' self (Anderson 2001, 44).

As a representation of subjectivity, then, Rousseau's text is confusing because, whilst he claims that he knows his own heart, he does not disclose it to us, or perhaps cannot expose it to us. This is not to say that he does not tell us anything. In fact, the *Confessions* are a very frank chronicle of the peculiarities and failings of Rousseau's character. He has no hesitation in telling us of activities usually disguised or absent from narrative because of considerations of shame and decency. He, on the other hand, narrates obsessively the erotic pleasure that he derived from beatings at the hands of his tutor's sister, Mme Lambercier; he admits to the pleasures he took in masturbation; he describes a pleasure in self-display which culminates in an act of 'flashing' in a public street; he admits to the fetishization of the female body and its clothing; he steals from his employer and gets an innocent servant girl sacked for his crime; later, he receives his first full sexual experience from Madame de Warens, his adoptive mother, whom he calls 'Mamma' throughout the text; and he abandons all five of the children he fathers on Thérèse La Vasseur to the Paris foundling hospital without so much as an expression of regret. Indeed, in this last instance, he absolutely refuses an explanation for his actions: denying that his abandonment of the children amounts to callousness, he writes:

> If I were to state my reasons, I should say too much. For since they were strong enough to seduce me, they would seduce many others; and I do not wish to expose any young people who may read me to the risk of being misled by the same error. (Rousseau 1953, 333)

The list goes on and on and the word 'chronicle' is the right one for this obsessive listing of experience. As Hayden White has observed (in *Metahistory*), the chronicle form is a narrative genre that focuses on continuity, and he distinguishes between two modes of historical writing, diachronic (or dynamic narrative) structures and synchronic (or static) ones: 'In the former, the sense of structural transformation is uppermost as the principal guiding representation. In the latter, the sense of structural continuity ... or stasis ... predominates. This distinction points ... to a difference of emphasis in treating the relationship between continuity and change in a given representation of the historical process as a whole' (White 1975, 10–11). In this model, Rousseau privileges continuity in the self he inhabits. He has, he repeats, 'always' been like this or that, so that the narrative itself does not furnish explanation for his subjectivity; and he is often mystified about the motives for his own actions, unable to explain anything from why a piece of music moves him (23), to why he is socially inept on pretty much every occasion, to why he steals the old pink ribbon and accuses a servant girl of having done so.

This book does not keep to the rules. Rousseau's subjectivity is not in control, either of external circumstances (he is incapable of acting on the world) or, even minimally, of the language in which it is expressed. Rather than being the doer of the verb, he is its object; and he is the subject of the narrative only inasmuch as he provides its content or *subject matter*. The possession of language generally, and of written language in particular, is usually supposed to confer on the 'possessor' an ability to make sense of events. If life is presumed to be random and contingent, language at least has its rules and imposes a minimal ordering on events. Rousseau knows these rules, and makes use of them, but often does so in such a way as to subvert their ordering force. In a striking passage, Rousseau describes his compositional process as one which begins in disorder and chaos, and then, by long reflection, and without the imposition of his will (this subject does not *do* verbs), the disparate events begin to form themselves into a state of order. The ideas in his head begin by going 'round in dull circles and ferment, agitating me until my heart palpitates'; at this point he 'can see nothing clearly, and cannot write a word'. It is just like, he argues, a trip to the opera in Italy:

> During changes of scenery, wild and prolonged disorder reigns in their great theatres. The furniture is higgledy-piggledy; on all sides things are being shifted and everything seems upside-down; it is as if they were bent on universal destruction; but little by little everything falls into

place, nothing is missing, and, to one's surprise, all the long tumult is
succeeded by a delightful spectacle. That is almost exactly the process
that takes place in my brain when I want to write. If I had known
in the past how to wait and then put down all their beauty the scenes
that painted themselves in my imagination, few authors would have
surpassed me. (Rousseau 1953, 113)

This is, obviously, just like the 'portrait' with which he began, a self-
consciously artistic (even artificial) simile for writing. Writing is a
drama of self-performance, an act of representation rather than an
unmediated presentation of essence. Additionally, though, he is not an
actor in this scene; he has not *made* the order happen, it has merely
happened, with no agency on his part (or indeed, anyone else's); this is
subjectivity *subject to* outside forces, not subjectivity in charge, even if
that autonomy is always a species of illusion. His consciousness does
not guide the outcome of the compositional process. At the same time,
what the simile both disguises and speaks is artistic control. The trip to
Italy he undertakes in his mind's eye is anecdotal and digressive – but it
does have a point (a description of compositional process), to which
Rousseau is able, at length, to return.

This control is not always evident, however. J. M. Cohen notes, in the
Introduction to his translation, that the later parts of *The Confessions*
are carelessly written (Rousseau 1953, 12), and he is quite right.
Rousseau himself admits that his mastery over his own discourse is
lacking. He describes compositional processes on numerous occasions, and as the book goes on, the processes become more chaotic.
Describing the writing of a philosophical essay, he tells us that he
spent his insomniac night hours composing and polishing sentences,
committing them to memory until morning. But when morning came,
'the break caused by my getting up and dressing made me lose everything, and when I had sat down before the paper hardly a sentence
came to me of all those I had composed' (Rousseau 1953, 328). He
therefore dictated his thoughts to his mistress's mother from his bed.
The fact that a short interval between composition and writing (an
interval that presumably always exists in writing) made him forget his
thought, suggests that the thoughts were never securely possessed.
Later, he notes ruefully: 'The further I go in my story, the less order and
sequence I can put into it. The disturbances of my later life have not left
events time to fall into shape in my head. They have been too numerous, too confused, too unpleasant to be capable of straightforward

narration' (574). Whereas the Romantic, Victorian and Post-Freudian writer all have at least a minimal faith in the ability of narrative to 'tell', explain, and – through the process known as abreaction – to render control back to the subject through the control s/he exercises over narrative, Rousseau figures himself as 'alone and without power to act except as fate determines' (Anderson 2001, 46). He is a subject who attempts to exercise no control over his life, remaining determinedly (and irresponsibly) *subject to* external forces and never imposing his subject position.

This is clearly not quite true. *The Confessions* – more than 600 pages long in the current Penguin edition – are really quite an imposition on the subjectivities of their readers. This lengthy demand for his reader's attention is hardly the work of a shrinking violet; and more than that, it is clear from the final paragraphs of the text that he envisages himself reading the whole narrative aloud to a captive audience of his friends and confidants, an even lengthier imposition, one must assume, than reading them silently for oneself. Anderson suggests that the point for Rousseau is to compel readers' attention and to demand their admiration for his wise, evolved, and transparent inner self (50). I, for one, though, am a somewhat resisting reader in this regard. In pursuit of one of his wayside amours, Rousseau describes taking on the pseudonym of a fictional English Jacobite, a M. Dudding (Rousseau 1953, 237), despite the fact that he elsewhere evinces contempt for the English and cannot speak the language. Quite unconsciously, one must presume, he has given himself a name that, in English, implies that this act of forgery is not just an imposition on his fellow travellers, but a really bad forgery, for a dud is an easily spotted fabrication. In this disguise, he is seduced by Mme de Larnage (never suppose for a moment that he is active enough to do the seducing himself), and at the moment when her design on him becomes clear, he writes: 'For once I was myself. Never have my eyes and my senses, my heart and my mouth, spoken so eloquently; never have I so completely atoned for my errors' (239). This transparency is only produced, however, when Rousseau's 'real' self, that man of straw, is well and truly hidden.

This call for the reader to admire the spectacle of self he produces is highly problematic, for it is not reciprocated by the good faith that Philippe Lejeune suggests is an essential part of the 'autobiographical pact' – where the reader agrees to believe, and the writer agrees to be truthful. This is an unequal relationship – and an unethical one. Rousseau describes the absurdity of his work for the Venetian embassy in a way that seems a very apt analogy for his procedure with us. His boss, the Ambassador, an idle and stupid man in Rousseau's description of him, decides that the only way to keep up with external correspondence conducted in complex cipher is to write the replies to despatches before the despatches themselves actually arrive: 'Despite everything I could say about the impracticability and the absurdity of his idea, he thought it so ingenious that I had to give in' (Rousseau 1953, 282). Rousseau, however, presumes on our response to his text in much the same way, refusing to be responsible for, or in, his own text. The problem he presents us with is the problem of interpretation, and he is quite deliberately going to refuse to give us any help in the process, writing elsewhere that although he is trying to make his soul 'transparent to the reader's eye', by presenting all his emotions and all the events without commentary, he is not 'responsible' for the resulting judgements that readers make: 'by relating to him in simple detail all that has happened to me, all that I have done, all that I have felt, I cannot lead [the reader] into error ... [The reader's] task is to assemble these elements and to assess the being who is made up of them. The summing-up must be his, and if he comes to wrong conclusions, the fault will be of his own making' (Rousseau 1953, 169). As is perhaps clear from the tone of my commentary, I make my own judgement, and Rousseau would probably be upset at the result.

The question is, then, whether this chaotic, interminable and repetitive text has any point at all: or does it merely represent life as it is lived, with all the randomness that that implies? One answer, according to Laura Marcus, is that Rousseau's text continues to hold our attention because of its resistance to the characterological types and stereotypes that we are more used to in relation to the conventions of (self-) representation. Marcus quotes from the seldom-reprinted Neuchâtel Preface to the *Confessions* to demonstrate that Rousseau was self-consciously in revolt against the prevailing standards of his day in the narrative relation of personal identities. In the Neuchâtel Preface, he contemptuously dismisses 'Histories, lives, portraits, characters! What do they amount to? Ingenious fictions built on a few spoken words relating to them, on subtle conjectures in which the Author is seeking much more to shine than to discover the truth' (quoted in Marcus 1994, 23). As she comments, Rousseau attacks 'the reduction of a unique and complex identity to a set of characteristics and traits shared with others'. In this resistance, Rousseau asks us to look again at the attributes we passively accept as truthful. Thus, the inaugural text of modern autobiography begins by attacking pre-existing forerunners of the self-representing text.

It is probably for this reason – that the *Confessions* at once announce a genre and announce the grounds of its impossibility – that the text has produced ingenious readings of its own ingenious fictions from post-structuralist critics such as Jacques Derrida and Paul de Man. For Derrida, the point of Rousseau's text is a philosophical one which goes to the heart of the process of signification. Rousseau presents himself 'better' in his written text than he manages to do in social situations, where his shyness and social awkwardness make it impossible for him to cut a dashing figure. Writing therefore acts as a supplement (an addition, a substitution and an attempt at completion) for his 'real' self. Writing 'masks' the real self, but also makes it what it is – for after all, Rousseau is a writer in his self-figuration. The 'dangerous supplement' of writing exposes the failings of the self to live up to its alleged natural plenitude (it is a necessary supplement to self-hood, for without it, we would never know Jean-Jacques's 'true worth'), as well as exposing the failings of the self in its subject matter, altering our perception of his 'true worth' (Derrida 1976, 142). For Paul de Man, on the other hand, in a virtuoso textual exegesis of the ribbon-stealing episode, *The Confessions* is a text that implicitly sets out to generate the very guilt it explicitly seeks to excuse. He distinguishes between two modes of subjectivity in autobiography, both of which are actually purely linguistic in the final analysis. Autobiography can be 'cognitive', in the sense that it narrates the spiritual, emotional, interior journey of the self towards self-knowledge. This mode presents itself as 'referential', realistic and progressive. But autobiography can also be (perhaps is usually) 'performative', in the sense of the speech-act theories of J. L. Austin. A speech act is a moment of speech in which the act of speaking performs the act it describes, as when the parson proclaims: 'I now proclaim you man and wife' or when the Queen proclaims 'I name this ship … ' It is a speech that makes something so, and enacts what it says. For De Man, Rousseau's professions of guilt and shame at his implication of an innocent serving girl in his own crime are performative in this sense, and are not part of a cognitive autobiographical mode. Rousseau does not go on an emotional journey towards spiritual plenitude in his description of what he has done to the girl, Marion. Instead he goes on a purely verbal journey: 'Rousseau can convey his "inner feeling" to us only if we take, as we say, his *word* for it, whereas the evidence for his theft is, at least in theory, literally available [i.e. the evidence provided by the object, a pink ribbon]' (De Man 1979, 280). He says, in other words, that he feels guilt and shame, and the only evidence we have for the guilt and shame is his saying that he felt them. We are at liberty to disbelieve his staging (the word is deliberately chosen) of his self-abasement. For De Man, therefore, the point of the text is a point to do with readers and their interpretation rather than with the writer and his intention. It is precisely because Rousseau cannot explain his motives that he needs to confess his actions: the text is interesting because it suspends 'the referential function' of writing (the function of writing which 'refers' us to the real world), and refuses to explain everything away 'by the cognitive logic of understanding' (De Man 1979, 298).[7]

Perhaps, in the end this is not a subjectivity at all. The chronicle structure of *The Confessions* – emphasized by the reiteration of the dates of events, strongly signalled typographically in the text – militates against the necessary illusion of coherence and progression that the subject is usually supposed to inhabit. Rousseau's text enables us to say many things about language and its problematic functioning. It allows us to say almost nothing about Rousseau himself, for if the problem is language, he is reduced to a linguistic sign. The silence of his non-responsive audience at the end of *The Confessions* speaks of his unreadability. If this is a subjectivity at all, it is a peculiar one, which refuses its ethical obligations to the others that it both calls into being and then – most impolitely – ignores.

Ouladah Equiano's *Interesting Narrative*

If *The Confessions* represent a narrative strategy without a 'point', the purposes of *The Interesting Narrative of the Life of Ouladah Equiano, or Gustavus Vassa, the African, Written by Himself* first published in 1789, has almost too many points to mention. Its primary purpose, as Equiano describes it in his Preface, which is addressed to both British Houses of Parliament, is 'to excite in your august assemblies a sense of compassion for the miseries which the Slave-Trade has entailed on my unfortunate countrymen' (Equiano 2001, 7). It has a palpable design upon the world – to change it, to render the arguments for Abolition of slavery as strongly as possible, and thereby to persuade its audience that there is no possible excuse for its continuation. If that is its primary purpose, however, it touches many other points along its

narrative way. For in order to make this argument, Equiano is appeal-
ing to his own experience; he – a former slave – was 'torn' away from his
country and family by the 'horrors of that trade'; in his case it has been
a providential uprooting, for by meeting Christian white men, he has
'obtained to the knowledge of the Christian religion', which, if not
exactly a compensation for all that he has suffered, is nonetheless seen
by him as a kind of gain. As a former slave, writing against the very
process that both enslaved him, but also that gave him the tools (literacy) to argue against it, Equiano has to produce himself in relation to
the discourse of human rights; he has to assert that, although his experience has been radically different from that of the whole of his (white)
audience, he is a man, a human being, like they are. In that common
humanity there is the fundamental reason why slavery should not be
tolerated. So, as well as producing himself as a coherent and rational
subjectivity, he also calls his audience into being as similarly coherent
and rational. His argument is that he has a subjectivity that is just the
same as the ones his audiences inhabit.

His subjectivity, however, is precisely what is at issue, and he has to
go to considerable lengths to narrate and produce it in a convincing
way, for as a slave, what has been denied him is precisely his status as a
subject, autonomous and individual. Thus, although he claims to be
'an unlettered African' (a contradiction in terms in this context of his
writing, but also, of course, the performance of the modesty that polite
letters demands of its speaking subjects in the late eighteenth century),
the way he demonstrates his subjectivity is in relation to his mastery of
literary discourses; describing himself as 'unlettered' is part of his strategy of mastery, demonstrating that he can speak/write the language of
his 'masters' – that he has mastered it – as well as they have.

Equiano's first narrative genre is ethnography. His first chapters
provide a detailed description of his African home in the Kingdom of
Benin (present-day Nigeria). This world is, if not completely Edenic, at
least self-governing, autonomous and appropriate to the landscape; life
there is 'natural', but not uncivilized. The life that is lived there makes
sense in terms of the geography and the traditions of the people. He associates his homeland with the tribes of Israel, and points out the connections between Jewish practices and customs and those of his own
forefathers, and in doing so, he connects his world and belief system with
those of his readers. All the same, this world is not untouched by contact
with the outside world. Equiano stresses the morality of his people,
especially in relation to sexual relations, and insists that like the White

Christians he addresses, his countrymen are civilized, not primitive savages. Like the Christians, 'the natives believe that there is one Creator of all things', a disembodied God, who lives in the sun. This God of his ancestors smokes a pipe; and the Eboe people grow Indian corn amongst their crops – both tobacco and corn are importations from the Americas and suggest the extent to which the globalization of the slave trade has material effects on both the material conditions of the Africans and, by extension, on their spiritual beliefs. In establishing the similarities between white and black peoples, he also sets out to answer the common objections to the presumption of equality between them, arguing that one should not judge by appearances, and that it is foolish to presume that dark skin colour implies inferiority. When white people write about black people as savages, he argues, it is usually because they are judging by unfair standards of comparison, the chief of which is slavery itself, which 'depress[es] the mind, and extinguish[es] all its fire and every noble sentiment' (Equiano 2001, 31).

Although, as Geraldine Murphy has suggested, the travel narrative genre is hardly one that can be easily made to sit with abduction into slavery – 'travel connotes a voluntary, temporary change of environment', and implies privileges of class, gender and race (Murphy 2001, 368) – Equiano also makes extensive use of this generic mode in his narrative, and begins the process of assuming precisely the identities that slavery necessarily refuses him: as a man, and as an economic entity, an individual with choices and opportunities. As well as his horrific description of the Middle Passage (which is not travel, but kidnap), he spends many years as a sailor in the British Navy, and sees most of the ports of Europe. After he is tricked out of his freedom by the double-crossing Captain Pascal, and sent to the West Indies as the slave of a Quaker plantation owner, he works for several years on the ships that ply various trades, including transporting slaves, between the islands. When he finally buys his own freedom on the back of his enterprise and business acumen, he continues to travel – this time partly for his own pleasure, working as a barber aboard ships bound for the Mediterranean, and participating in a scientific voyage to the Arctic Ocean. Angelo Costanzo emphasizes his indebtedness to the picaresque tradition of European fiction in which the 'hero or rogue journeys from place to place in search of experience that contributes to his growing awareness of the world and to his sense of maturity' (Costanzo 2001, 348). In making use of that genre, he also inserts himself into the discourse of spiritual autobiography, in which a conversion narrative makes it clear that the literal, geographical journey is always also a metaphorical and spiritual one. To those genres, Murphy adds 'the newly emerging secular success story', in which Equiano's enterprise can be compared with that of the fictional Robinson Crusoe; and the political discourse of the Abolitionist movement. Equiano is not merely a speaking subject; he is also a subject who can speak with authority and experience on many different subjects. His experiences have made him, both literally and figuratively, a man of the world, for he has much wider experience of it than the vast majority of his readership. In describing the meaning of the name his parents gave him, he dramatizes his own chameleon status: 'I was named *Ouladah*, which in our language, signifies vicissitude or fortune also, one favoured, and having a loud voice and well spoken' (Equiano 2001, 27). His very name in this gloss speaks generic instability in its accurate characterization of him as at once the victim of bad luck and the beneficiary of good fortune (or divine providence as he eventually explains it), at once a loudmouth and a softly spoken, polite being who has learned the rules of good speech/writing. (Being a loudmouth – attracting the 'imputation of vanity' [Equiano 2001, 19] – is exactly what he fears; and in fearing it, he disables it.) These binary oppositions structure his sense of self – he is both a subject who has agency and can act on the world around him, and an object, tossed back and forth by slavery and by circumstance. The sudden reversals of fortune he suffers are presented almost as the consequence of this naming. But he also denies that there is anything exceptional in his story; despite his trials he still looks on himself as 'neither a saint, a hero, nor a tyrant', and his only claim to special status is that he is able to regard himself as '*a particular favourite of Heaven*' (19, original emphasis), since, compared to the fates of many of his countrymen, he has been relatively lucky.

This mastery, however – of himself, of the language he writes and speaks, and his management of the different modes of writing and address – has been extremely hard won. The condition of slavery is precisely to render the subject into an object, *subject to* the whims of others, and incapable therefore of acting on one's own behalf. In an important passage, this object status is presented to us in his misapprehension of the various objects that surround one of his many masters. On his first landfall after the Middle Passage, Equiano works for a short while on a plantation, and is one day sent for to work in the house, fanning his master, who is unwell, whilst he sleeps in his bed:

> While he was fast asleep I indulged myself a great deal in looking about the room, which to me appeared very fine and curious. The first object

that engaged my attention was a watch, which hung on the chimney and was going. I was quite surprised at the noise it made, and was afraid it might tell the gentleman any thing I might do amiss; and when I immediately after observed a picture hanging in the room, which appeared constantly to look at me, I was still more affrighted, having never seen such things as these before. At one time I thought it was something relative to magic; and not seeing it move I thought it might be the way the whites had to keep their great men when they died, and offer them libation as we used to do to our friendly spirits. (Equiano 2001, 44)

At this point the child Equiano cannot yet speak English. In his reconstruction of the scene and his sense of wonder at it, though, he identifies a key element in the making of his selfhood in this new environment. The technology of the watch and the portrait is presented as a method of surveillance, as if the word 'watch' is already understood by the boy to be both a noun and a verb. As Henry Louis Gates observes about this passage, 'Equiano endows each of these objects with his master's subjectivity', which is no surprise since 'the slave enjoys a status identical to that of the watch, the portrait, and the book. He is the master's object, to be used and enjoyed, purchased, sold or discarded' (Gates 2001, 364, 365–6). The book to which Gates refers comes from a slightly later passage, when Equiano has already left the plantation and is on board ship with his new master. He describes watching his new-found friend, Dick and his new master, reading, and evinces 'a great curiosity to talk to the books, as I thought they did, and so to learn how all things had a beginning: for that purpose I have often taken up a book, and have talked to it, and then put my ears to it, when alone, in hopes it would answer me; and I have been very much concerned when I found it remained silent' (Equiano 2001, 48). Gates suggests that we should pay close attention to the tense structure of this passage, which begins in a retrospective past tense, but proceeds suddenly into the present in a startling dramatization of the African child's sense of wonder at this new object, the book. For him, it represents Equiano's mastery of a discourse of a dynamic subjectivity in process. Equiano the autobiographer, like many later writers, exhibits a double consciousness: the sense of what he was like 'then' with the sense of what he has 'become' (Gates 2001, 365). This developmental, psychologized and individualized self is presumably what Equiano thought he had 'really' become, and I do not doubt his good faith; but it is also essential to his argument. If he is capable of development, from the innocent who causes the reader endowed with the appropriate eighteenth-century dosage of sensibility to empathize and sympathize, and to smile at his inno-cence, to the rational Enlightenment figure he has later become, his argument for a common humanity with his readers is unanswerable: he appeals to their emotions and to their intellects, neatly covering all the bases of their possible objections.

The phrase 'double consciousness', read positively by Gates as the symptom of Equiano's mastery of discourse, can, however, also be seen in a more negative light. The word individual, as Raymond William points out, hovers uncomfortably between contradictory meanings: that which is undivided against itself, and that which is divided from (different from) other objects/subjects in the world. Felicity Nussbaum finds the phrase 'double consciousness' in the writings of the great Black American thinker and theorist, W. E. B Du Bois. In *The Limits of the Human*, she quotes Du Bois's elaboration of the discomfort of doubleness:

> It is a peculiar sensation, this color-consciousness, this sense of always looking at one's self through the eyes of others, of measuring one's soul by the tape of a world that looks on in amused contempt and pity. One ever feels his twoness ... The history of the American Negro is the his-tory of the strife, – this longing to attain self-conscious manhood, to merge his double self into a better and truer self. (Du Bois, qut. Nussbaum 2003, 196)

Nussbaum goes on to suggest that the situation for Black subjectivities in the context of slavery in the eighteenth century is even more com-plex than Du Bois suggests. The consciousness of the Black man is not merely double, she argues, but multiple, and she proposes the term 'diasporic identity' to describe its motility and instability: 'The dias-poric manner of thinking entails constituting oneself as located not simply on both sides of a border, but "in-between" geographical places and available identities, including a repertory of cross-racial borrow-ings instead of a settled hybridity' (Nussbaum 2003, 197). She argues further that Equiano negotiates against the grain of available stereo-types of the Black man in western cultures of the period. He is neither the noble savage figured in eighteenth-century primitivist writings, nor African prince (of the sort favoured on the Restoration and eighteenth-century stage), nor little-boy house-servant (as depicted on multiple occasions in eighteenth-century portraiture). He is trying to find an acceptable masculinity that does not conform to racial stereotypes authored by subjectivities other than his own. The two he chooses in the end are the identity of the bourgeois economic individual to be found in eighteenth-century fictions, and the identity of a convert, chosen by God (he believes in predestination [Equiano 2001, 88]) as moral and spiritual exemplar to others. This subjectivity involves him in a compromise, since Christianity and Capitalism are not completely compatible systems. That compromise has Equiano himself involved in slave-trading, carrying Jamaican slaves to his Nicaraguan plantation (Equiano 2001, 155). In that compromise, however, he demonstrates the extent to which he has successfully learned the double-consciousness of – not just the Black man in a racist and slave-owning context – but also of the white man, who makes this compromise in all his dealings.

There may be loss as well as gain in attaining subjectivity, as the Introduction suggests. All the same, when a writer strives so hard for it, and not only in his own behalf, it is churlish to carp at its basis. Moreover, in his appeal to his readers, there is clearly a great deal more at stake in this narrative than Equiano's own subjectivity. Unlike Rousseau's narrative, which refuses a proper relationship with its readers – refuses us the very structures of plot, development and climax that narrative gives us every right to expect – Equiano's subjectivity is created out of the ethical obligation to insist on a *face-to-face* relationship with readers.[8] His narrative is interesting, as he himself calls it, precisely because it operates within the established parameters and conventions of the textual conversation. He provides an exciting story, with multiple reversals of fortune and climaxes to keep us hooked at the mere level of plot; but he also provides us with a textual self that engages us on what he himself would identify as a more *human* level. The man who was mastered by slavery masters in turn the discourses that enslaved him, and 'writes back' in a reverse discourse that undoes their presumptions. As textual self-performances go, that is no mean feat.

Notes

1. These ideas are discussed by Kristeva in *Revolution in Poetic Language* (1974, trans. 1984). Kristeva's ideas, however, are dense and difficult to read. Useful introductions to her thought can be found in Moi, 1985 and the Introduction to *The Kristeva Reader*, 1986; in Wright 1998, and Robbins 2000a.

2. A really useful account of the *Pamela* controversy can be found in Haslett 2003, 209–25.

3. Watt's *Rise of the Novel* (1957, 1987) discusses the concept of the individual in some detail, in relation to the canonical texts of the eighteenth century. His discussion has been much criticized for its emphasis on those texts, which tend to privilege a particular (elite male) version of the development of modern self-hood in tandem with modern fiction. Some of the most trenchant discussions are to be found in McKeon 1987, Armstrong 1987 and Richetti 1999 and 1996. The importance of Watt's argument, however, is signalled by the fact that we continue to need to respond to it.

4. That she has read Aesop is no surprise. We know that Richardson had prepared and printed a popular translation of the *Fables* in the period immediately before he began to compose Pamela's narrative.

5. Laura Marcus demonstrates the extent to which Rousseau's text is taken as foundational in her *Auto/Biographical Discourses*. See Marcus 1994, especially Chapter 5.

6. For a good introduction to the Russian Formalist thought, see Jefferson and Robey 1986, 24–45.

7. See also Culler 1983 and Marcus 1994 for further explanations of this issue.

8. This phrase – *face-to-face* – is borrowed from the writings of Emmanuel Levinas, who insisted that the ethical relationship is a *face-to-face* relationship.

2 Two Romantic Egos: Wordsworth's *Prelude* and De Quincey's *Confessions of an English Opium Eater*

Of writing many books there is no end;
And I who have written much in prose and verse
For others' uses, will write now for mine, –
Will write my story for my better self. (Barrett Browning 1981, 38)

Poet of nature, thou hast wept to know
That things depart which never may return. (Shelley in Wu 1994, 823)

Wordsworth went to the lakes, but he was never a lake poet. He found in stones the sermons he had already hidden there. He went moralising about the district, but his good work was produced when he returned, not to Nature but to poetry. Poetry gave him 'Laodamia', and the fine sonnets and the great Ode such as it is. Nature gave him 'Martha Ray' and 'Peter Bell' and the address to Mr Wilkinson's spade. (Wilde 1994, 1078)

The stereotypical version of William Wordsworth is as the poet of Nature, a man who describes with enormous enthusiasm in many different places how wandering through rural landscapes has repeatedly provided him with the balm for his soul and the matter for his poetry. Nature taught him, in this version of the Romantic myth, everything he really needed to know. His subjectivity was created by intercourse with the landscape rather than socially constructed by intercourse with other people. The great political events of the French Revolution and the Napoleonic Wars were the ones, which moved him to enormous enthusiasm at the time – 'Bliss was it in that dawn to be alive, /But to be young was very heaven!' (X, 691–92)[1] – became in retrospect a false dawn rather than the herald of a new world. The return from politics to nature is narrated in Book XI of the thirteen-book *Prelude* (1805), and it is clearly with a sense of reconstructed relief that Wordsworth turns away from both emotional and political turmoil back to the assuaging balm of the natural world.

Nonetheless, as the Wilde quotation above suggests, this is not quite an accurate statement of Wordsworth's procedure. In *The Prelude* and elsewhere, like other Romantic poets, he 'asserted the mind's creativity in perception', and continually suggests that the mind 'constitutes, at least to some extent, what it perceives', though this view is not generally regarded as solipsistic or subjectivist (Day 1996, 56, 57). For as well as focusing on the individual mind, Wordsworth is also a poet of experience – a quasi-Lockean empiricist as well as a Cartesian subjectivist, drawing some of his sense of selfhood and subjectivity from his adaptation of the ideas of John Locke – ideas that came to him in modified form through both the writings of David Hartley, the eighteenth century philosopher, and through his friend Samuel Taylor Coleridge's adaptations of them. John Locke's *Essay Concerning Human Understanding* (1690) argued for an experiential version of human development: put rather crudely, we are what we know, and we know what we have experienced and felt. In contrast to Descartes, Locke argued that first and foremost, people are bodies, and that they come to know their world through their bodies. In striking metaphors, he described the new-born child as either like an empty cabinet (a cupboard), waiting to be filled up with experiences; or as a piece of blank paper, waiting to be covered with *impressions* (a metaphor that refers both to the sense impressions and thereby connects the senses with printing – in which characters – a significantly double word – are stamped or impressed onto the waiting paper). The self in this formulation is the sum total of its experiences, combined with its *reflection* or thought on those experiences: the particular (experience) gives rise to the general (principle). What one becomes, then, is in part a function of the impressions you receive from the world, and in part a function of what you do with those experiences: body and mind are not a mutually exclusive dualism, so much as a mutually necessary symbiosis. Moreover, unlike Descartes, the clear implication of Locke's position is that consciousness is to some extent *determined* by corporeal existence and material circumstance.[2] Through the process of the 'association of ideas' (from sense perceptions and the process of reflecting on them), the rightly constituted human mind is then able to propose ideas of its own, which have a basis in the material world, but which are also created out of the individual consciousness. These ideas were developed by David Hartley in the mid-eighteenth century with the result that a slightly more moralistic and theistic bias was added to them. In Hartley's thought, God has so ordered the world that the external stimulus the mind receives from the natural world produces vibrations in the mind that lead inevitably to knowledge of God himself: as Peter Kitson puts it, 'if we subject ourselves to the right environments we are inevitably led to benevolence and a love of God' (Kitson 1998, 37).

The new-born baby is, then, a *tabula rasa*, the Latin phrase that is often used to designate the blank sheet of paper; it literally means 'blank tablet' – as in the tablet of wax that would have been used for writing before paper was easily available, and it designates a surface that will *take an impression* easily when lightly scratched with a stylus or pen. Rather than being an already 'fallen' creature, as Christian thought most usually designates even children, the *tablula rasa* is virgin territory, empty, untouched. This view has a major effect on the way in which the romantic psychology espoused by Wordsworth and Coleridge operates. For if the child is innocent at birth, and if it is dependent on its environment for its subsequent character, there is an obligation on those who have the care of children to ensure that their experiences are the most appropriate for the development of subsequent good character. In Coleridge's 'conversation' poems, especially 'Frost at Midnight', thinking back to his own childhood, 'reared/In the great city, pent mid cloisters dim' where he 'saw nothing lovely but the sky and stars', he vows that his sleeping baby will have a very different experience of childhood: '*thou*, my babe, shalt wander like a breeze/By lakes and sandy shores, beneath the crags/Of ancient mountain, and beneath the clouds' (Wu 1994, 464, original emphasis). The virtues of the natural landscape will thereby *write themselves* onto the child's soul, and ensure his development as a loving human being. Locke's metaphor of the empty cabinet is part of the early argument of Wordsworth's epic of his mind, though he feels at a loss to 'class the cabinet/Of [his] sensations, and ... / Run through the history and birth of each' (II, 228–30) And this same emphasis on the necessity for appropriate stimulus for the growing child is to be found throughout *The Prelude*. 'Blest the Babe' who 'Doth gather passion from his Mother's eye', who is 'subjected to the discipline of love', and who thereby finds 'his organs and recipient faculties' 'quickened' (II, 239, 244, 251–3). The nature he depicts in the poem, however, is not all sweetness and light. He was 'fostered alike by beauty and by fear' (I, 306), because the natural landscape in which he exists is not mere pastoral fantasy, but a place where there is both beauty and hardship. The famous boat-stealing episode, in which the child Wordsworth is provoked into a retreat from his theft by the sudden appearance of a mountain crag round a headland, like some avenging angel (II 372 ff), as well as an episode narrated much later when he comes across the site of an old gibbet (XI, 258ff.), makes the landscape a threatening as well as a comforting place. Nonetheless, his argument is that, far from finding the sermons he had already placed there in the stones of the Lake District, the land itself provokes the moral response.

Whilst, however, Wilde's commentary on Wordsworth is deliberately provocative in its assessment of his poetic achievement, dismissing the *Intimations Ode*, and standing against his century's assessment of Wordsworth as *the* poet to whom one should turn in troubled times, he is right, I suspect, in thinking that the essential morality that Wordsworth found in the natural world will not bear too much inspection. The metaphor of writing and reading derived from the blank piece of paper and the impressions that it takes from the world around it is a central conceit of *The Prelude*, and its centrality in Wordsworth's presentation of his developing subjectivity implies that, far from pure sense impressions being the foundation of his moral self, that morality comes to him from other sources. In all sorts of ways, of books, reading and writing them, there is no end in this text. Wordsworth's central descriptions of his growing understanding of the world around him are figured in the language of reading and the interpretation thereof. The people he meets in his wayside wanderings are like books: 'The face of every neighbour whom I met/Was as a volume to me' (IV, 58–9); he 'read[s], without design, the opinions, thoughts,/Of those plain living people' who live near his childhood home (IV, 203–4); he 'peruses' the outward aspect of a soldier encountered by chance (IV, 420); innocent children can 'read lectures upon innocence' to their supposedly more experienced elders and betters (V, 313); he reads the 'plain Tale' of a tragedy by drowning evidenced by a man's clothes left on a beach (V, 467); during his journey to France to cross the Alps, he meets with wonderful landscape and kind people, and learns from then just as he would if he were reading a book:

> With such a book
> Before our eyes, we could not chuse but read

> A frequent lesson of sound tenderness,
> The universal reason of mankind,
> The truth of Young and Old. (VI, 473–7)

His terror of London is partially about his inability to 'read' the situations that he sees there, so that he 'familiarly peruse[s] [London life] day by day' (VII, 140), but he cannot interpret (read) what he sees there:

> How often in the overflowing Streets,
> Have I gone forward with the Crowd, and said
> Unto myself, the face of every one
> That passes me is a mystery. (VII, 594–8)

In London, unlike in his own rural landscape, he does not know the people or their histories, a point made vivid in his brief encounter with a blind beggar, who carries a label round his neck that explains his story:

>   it seemed
> To me that in this Label was a type
> Or emblem, of the utmost that we know,
> Both of ourselves and of the universe. (VII, 618–20)

One entire book of *The Prelude* is entitled 'Books' (Book V), and it contains both striking examples of Wordsworth mixing up books and people, and a critical account of how the wrong kinds of books – 'manage[d] books' that have an overt didactic purpose – are both immoral and ineffective (V, 374). Still, his wish for children is: 'May books and nature be their early joy!' (V, 447). And I could go on with many more examples. My point is that Wordsworth's nature is, of course, *culture*. It is utterly dependent on his literacy; those lengthy sentences with their multiple digressions and qualifications and complications of analogy are not only far removed from the language ever really *spoken* by any men (it is literate and literary language), but their content is figured in terms that depend not on an oral culture or subsistence economy, but on the possession of material privilege and mastery over literary discourse. Wordsworth is in part responsible for a major shift in the use of the word nature and its derivatives. When Shakespeare describes a character as 'a natural', he means fool, incompetent or idiot; when we use the same phrase, it means innately gifted or talented (see also Williams 1988, 219–24 for the complex history of the word nature). Nature is a word that depends more than most words on the possession of culture, a fact that *The Prelude* at once dramatizes and disguises.

This is not just a question of a prevailing metaphor, no matter how significant that is. *The Prelude* is a Romantic reader, in the sense that it provides us with a kind of anthology or primer for the major themes of Romanticism – nature, the imagination, childhood, revolution and political commitment, desolation and recovery. It also presents Wordsworth himself as a romantic reader – a reader of romances and of other literary texts, which then find their way into his own self-figuration by allusion and direct quotation. At least as much as being the child of nature, Wordsworth is the child that books built. He often sees the figures in his various landscapes in precisely the terms of the fictions he has read, and it is not for nothing that an early reference is made to Cervantes' novel, *Don Quixote*, a text above all about how reading infects reality, how the books you read make the personality you inhabit (see V, 59ff.). A soldier he encounters during his sojourn in France wanders through the events of the French Revolution 'As through a Book, an old Romance or Tale/Of Fairy' (IX, 307–8). And actually, to some extent, so does Wordsworth himself. For when he describes his preparatory process for writing poems, he suggests that he immerses himself in the traditional stories, and prepares to tell old stories in new ways:

> I settle on some British theme, some old
> Romantic tale, by Milton left unsung;
> More often resting at some gentle place
> Within the groves of Chivalry, I pipe
> Among the Shepherds, with reposing Knights
> Sit by a Fountain-side, and hear their tales. (I, 179–85)

When he turns to himself as the source of inspiration, 'to shape out/Some Tale from my own heart', he often finds that 'the whole beauteous Fabric seems to lack/Foundation, and withal, appears throughout,/Shadowy and insubstantial' (I, 220–1, 227–9). His own self – his real self – has less substance than the dreams he finds in fictions.

In addition, of course, *The Prelude* is the romantic reader of the literary genres and movements of the past. Alongside the allusions and quotations from previous generations – from Shakespeare and especially Milton – there is also Wordsworth's stated debt to his contemporary and friend, Coleridge, to whom the poem is addressed. Most importantly, in its very structure it both refers to and modifies the tradition of the epic, most usually a public proclamation of heroic and warlike values, here turned to account for the genius of the poet. *The Prelude* is not a strict epic, as defined by Byron in his own self-mocking recipe for epic poetry in Canto I of *Don Juan*; it is not

> Divided in twelve books, each book containing,
> With love and war, a heavy gale at sea,
> A list of kings and captains, and kings reigning,
> New characters; the episodes are three:
> A panorama view of hell's in training
> After the style of Virgil and of Homer,
> So that my name of epic's no misnomer. (Wu 1994, 782)

Nonetheless, it is massive in scale, does contain accounts of love and war (though the poet was only an onlooker in the latter), and does focus – at times – on stormy weather. The 'Residence in London' (Book VII) is presumably the nearest thing in the poem to the epic hero's descent into hell. Jonathan Wordsworth notes that Wordsworth's original conception of the poem was a far more self-conscious homage to the epic models provided by Milton's Christian epics, *Paradise Lost* and *Paradise Regained*, and originally had the structure of fall and flight, of loss and reacquisition (of peace of mind, if not quite the kingdom of heaven) (Wordsworth 1998, 187). To Milton's influence, one could certainly add that of Alexander Pope of *The Dunciad*, where the view of literary London as one giant sewer of human intellectual filth is alluded to in Wordsworth's typical metaphors for the crowds he passes through in the city: the crowd 'flows', 'overflows', is a 'thickening hubbub' and a 'swarm' (VII, 702, 596, 227, 699). His response to the crowding scenes speaks of alienation and defamiliarization. In the city, unlike his home, he cannot know 'Even next-door neighbours' who remain therefore strangers without histories and stories, or even names (VII, 119).

Wordsworth's ability to interpret depends on perspective. When he stands at a distance from the scenes he observes, as he is able to from the vantage points he adopts in the countryside, he is able – usually – to interpret them. The reason London is so hellish is that he cannot here achieve the distance necessary to focus properly on the scene before him. His confusion is registered in the way he describes the city, as a series of chaotic lists of sights seen, lists which cannot be rendered as anything other than the hopeless juxtaposition of incongruous people and objects. Even when he self-consciously (and literarily) invokes the aid of the Muse to 'lodge [him], wafted on her wings/Above the press and danger of the Crowd' (VII, 557–8), he still cannot see clearly:

> what a hell
> For eyes and ears! what anarchy and din
> Barbarian and infernal! 'tis a dream,
> Monstrous in colour, motion, shape, sight, sound. (VII, 559–62)

In that invocation of the Muse, and in his explicit reference to the infernal anarchy of the scene before his eyes, with every sense assaulted so he is unable to make anything of the view, he situates his own experience in the literary tradition. In his Preface to *Lyrical Ballads*, he lamented the speed and ferocity of urban life: 'For a multitude of causes, unknown to former times, are now acting with a combined force to blunt the discriminating powers of the mind, and unfitting it for all voluntary exertion to reduce it to a state of almost savage torpor' (Wordsworth 1984, 599). 'The encreasing accumulation of men in cities' was greatly to be lamented, he argued. But although he is talking about his own experience, it is crafted through the lens of poetry (poetry, from the Greek word *poeisis*, literally means 'craft'), and especially through the focus offered by the models of the literary tradition.

This issue of *craft*, which is also the *craftiness* of self-conscious artistry, is one of the fundamental issues that renders *The Prelude* a highly complicated textual performance of selfhood. The poem makes a claim for sincerity and authenticity, but makes it in a mode that is necessarily artificial – the poetic line. Moreover, the attempt to write of the self which creates the subjectivity it describes necessarily imposes particular limitations on completeness. *The Prelude* is – for all its length – only the edited highlights of the poet's life, figured in Wordsworth's metaphor of the 'spot of time', the epiphanic and significant moments of a life, which make the subjectivity what it is.

> There are in our existence spots of time,
> Which with distinct pre-eminence retain
> A renovating Virtue, whence, depressed

> By false opinion and contentious thought ...
>   our minds
> Are nourished and invisibly repaired ... (XI, 258–265)

These epiphanies occur primarily when the 'outward sense/Is but the obedient servant' of the mind (XI, 272–3). Thus the empirical evidence of the sense impressions is mastered by subjective interiority, and recreated in the image of that mind. This subtle alteration of the 'facts' by the perceiving consciousness is the craft of the poet, who similarly alters the language really spoken by men into a written order in which they would not speak. In speaking *to* us of this process, Wordsworth is also speaking *for* us – we, too, can experience these moments, and be nourished by our own (probably less efficacious – for we are not poets) mental processes acting on external stimuli. His selectivity of experience is an important fact to hold in mind. This is not the whole story, and never can be, for without editing there really would be 'no end' of this poem. Narrative, that is, structures selfhood into episodes that have beginnings, middles and ends; lives, however, are lived in random continuity in which episodes flow without organization. The structure of the story of Wordsworth's intellectual growth must therefore be a kind of fabrication, and its truth status modified in the consciousness that he is *making* it out of craft.

In a beautiful extended (almost epic) simile, Wordsworth provides us with a metaphor for reading his own poem. He is describing the 'falling off' of his youthful enthusiasm for the natural world during the first of his summer vacations from Cambridge:

> As one who hangs down-bending from the side
> Of a slow-moving Boat, upon the breast
> Of a still water, solacing himself
> With such discoveries as his eyes can make,
> Beneath him, in the bottom of the deeps,
> Sees many beauteous sights, weeds, fishes, flowers,
> Grots, pebbles, roots of trees, and fancies more,
> Yet often is perplexed, and cannot part
> The shadow from the substance, rocks and sky,
> Mountains and clouds, from that which is indeed
> The region, and the things which there abide
> In their true dwelling; now is crossed by gleam
> Of his own image, by a sunbeam now,
> And motions that are sent he knows not whence,

Impediments that make his task more sweet;
– Such pleasant office have we long pursued
Incumbent o'er the surface of past time
With like success. (IV, 247–64)

This is an interesting example of the failed mirror that is also an image
of the very problem of self-representation and of subjectivity that it
sets out to resolve. The self-image is here an interruption of the matter
in hand – the observation of an alien landscape. The world beneath the
water is 'perplexed', but this is a transferred epithet, for the perplexity is
the experience of the observing consciousness, not of the scene itself
(the water, after all, is 'still'). Wordsworth 'cannot part/The shadow
from the substance', the scene he wishes to observe (the substantial
but unfamiliar underwater world) from the solid world above the
water, which becomes, in its reflection on the water's surface, a
shadow, an image or a mere signifier. The simile is productive because
it organizes into a poetic form the confusions of subjectivity – it is creative; but it is also counterproductive because it speaks of the doubtful
success of separating self from world in such a way that analysis of
what is 'really' there and what is really inside the poet becomes impossible. There may be beauty (the 'task [is] more sweet', the duty 'pleasant') in this confusion, but there is also an inability to master the
image, even as the poetic imagery organizes memory and representation into aesthetic form.

The tension between random contingency and coherent wholeness
is what the Romantic reader of *The Prelude* experiences and reflects
upon. This is a subjectivity in process rather than a finished perfected
article; its oscillations are the precise record of the limitations imposed
by the fact that mind and body co-exist in Hartley's symbiosis, speak to
each other in constant intercourse, but do not resolve into wholeness.
The capacity for resolution 'lies far hidden from the reach of words' (III,
185), and the subject is split between two consciousnesses – one available to linguistic analysis, the other elusive, one part of the symbolic
order, the other partaking of the Kristevan semiotic. Speaking of his
memories of his youthful self, Wordsworth writes:

so wide appears
The vacancy between me and those days,
Which yet have such self-presence in my mind
That, sometimes, when I think of them, I seem

Two consciousnesses, conscious of myself
And of some other Being. (II, 28–33)

This speaking subject is a split subject indeed.

Thomas De Quincey's *Confessions*

The Prelude, as well as being an epic, is also a conversation poem. It is addressed to Samuel Taylor Coleridge – the 'Friend' who is often apostrophized. One of the reasons for its double consciousness is probably precisely that it is performance of Self for the Other, and there is a real sense in which Coleridge's subjectivity is formative of Wordsworth's poetic recreation of his own. (Coleridge, after all, read the multiple drafts of the poem, and commented on them for his friend's benefit.) The conversation is perhaps, as in all conversation poems, a little one-sided. Wordsworth turns himself into an ancient mariner figure, compelled to narrate his story apparently interminably, whilst Coleridge, the hapless wedding guest, has to listen in perpetuity. But although it is a social performance, where selfhood is created in response to the other's demands or request, and although it is an epic poem and therefore a public statement (even if it was not published until after Wordsworth's death) it is also a private performance; friend speaking to friend in a kind of face-to-face encounter.

The contrast between this mode of address and that of Thomas De Quincey in his *Confessions of an English Opium Eater* (1822) is rather hard to overstate. Although, throughout the text, De Quincey makes multiple panegyric references to Wordsworth, the Wordsworthian model of subjectivity is not much in evidence, either in the tone or the philosophical positions that the *Confessions* take up. Where Wordsworth is caught up in the double-bind of double consciousness – the attempt to perform sincerity in good faith – De Quincey has no hesitation in demonstrating the extent to which his subjectivity is all performance, all mask of social manners with little sense of the substance behind it. This is, in part, the result of the forum in which the *Confessions* were first published, in the *London Magazine* in 1821. The notion of a confession – a private and sacramental act rendered public and commercial through publication – was a more or less new literary form in the eighteenth century, perhaps first produced in the form that De Quincey uses by Jean-Jacques Rousseau's *Confessions*. What distinguishes De Quincey's version from earlier examples is his concentration on the self as a social being, whose entire personality depends on the validations of others. Earlier autobiographical, confessional writings, like Rousseau's and Wordsworth's *Prelude* (which De Quincey had read as early as 1812) had tended to justify their existence by reference to some larger framework, beyond the mere self of the writing individual, and beyond the give and take of social life. Rousseau's *Confessions*, as we have seen, made large philosophical claims to justify his personal exhibitionism, and refused the category of mere self-indulgence (though his readers may well disagree). Wordsworth was embarrassed by the *Prelude*'s concentration on 'the growth of the Poet's mind'. But he absolved himself from the charge of self-indulgence by relating his personal history to the larger dimension, the universal experience of 'Man'.

De Quincey, whilst he was producing his writings on opium addiction during the height, of what we now call, the Romantic period was nonetheless writing for an audience which was used to an eighteenth-century notion of literary decorum, and which focused on literary production as social in origin and destination. On their first appearance in the *London Magazine*, a journal whose subscribers were urban, but also urbane, and probably largely (upper) middle class, the *Confessions* were carefully placed in relation to their expected audience. For such a readership, it would be regarded as bad taste to reveal one's physical sores in public. And De Quincey shows his awareness of his audience in the way he sets up his confessions, in the Preface.

> TO THE READER – I here present you, courteous reader, with the record of a remarkable period in my life: according to my application of it, I trust that it will prove, not merely an interesting record, but, in a considerable degree, useful and instructive. In *that* hope it is, that I have drawn it up: and *that* must be my apology for breaking through that delicate and honourable reserve, which, for the most part, restrains us from the public exposure of our own errors and infirmities. Nothing, indeed, is more revolting to English feelings, than the spectacle of a human being obtruding on our notice his moral ulcers or scars, and tearing away that 'decent drapery', which time or indulgence to human frailty may have drawn over them: accordingly, the greater part of *our* confessions ... proceed from demireps,[3] adventurers, or swindlers. (De Quincey 1985, 1, original emphasis)

On the one hand, De Quincey constructs an audience of courteous readers who could not possibly be interested in the moral sores of the confessional subject. He also sets himself up as almost one of them – aware of and making use of the conventions of decorum to which they are accustomed in literature. Thus his confessions are to be 'useful' and 'instructive', or so he hopes, and he offers an apology for 'breaking through that delicate and honourable reserve' that ought to prevent the discussion of moral failings. The metaphor here, though, of 'breaking through' is strangely sexualized, as if decency is like the hymen that protects female virginity; and that sexualization is continued in the metaphor of the 'decent drapery' which clothes 'human frailty', but which also – in a moment of quasi-striptease, flaunts that there is a sexy body of work underneath all the fine phrases. To paraphrase Wordsworth, De Quincey is a gentleman speaking to an audience of gentlemen. But at the same time, there is titillation and excitement in confessional writing – an excitement for the reader, but also an excitement for the writer. So whilst De Quincey invokes the 'decent drapery' which masks that which should not be seen or spoken, at the same time, he is also going to lift the curtain so that we can see beneath; this is writing that is 'flashing': now you see it, now you don't. And while it obviously would not be the 'done' thing to accuse one's audience of prurience in the tradition of polite literature, a work narrating the addictions of the writer to a drug implicates the reader in the addiction of reading about forbidden things. As Laura Marcus has observed, it was precisely the titillatory and the prurient potential of autobiographical writing that caused most anxiety about its existence in the early years of the nineteenth century. She quotes from an anonymous commentator in *Blackwood's Magazine* in 1829, who laments that much recent autobiography is really just 'gossip' masquerading as something more substantial:

> But really, if stock jobbers and contractors are to give us accounts of their profits and losses; if every unfortunate female (the sentimental modern designation of those, whom our more jocular fathers termed ladies of easy virtue) – if every swindler and thief taker is to nauseate the public with the detail of their vulgar vices ... for exciting a prurient curiosity that may command a sale, the very name of autobiography will ... be loathingly rejected in the drawing room, as fit only for the kitchen and the servants' hall. (Mary Margaret Busk [1829], qut. Marcus 1994, 32–3)

De Quincey's 'decent drapery' does not amount to much in this view.

Moreover, for all its formal beginnings, De Quincey's text is indecorous in more than its content. The form it takes belies the conventions of politeness that the Preface invokes. *The Confessions* are more like an interminable self-analysis than a rigorous confession. De Quincey's discourse constantly transgresses its own boundaries and meanders away from its course; it does not have, as it were, an identifiable point, and the fact that the reader continues to pursue De Quincey's tale is a sign of our own addiction to the text. The text tells us of intemperance – De Quincey takes opium, writes interminably, borrows money, and borrows quotations. Indeed, Marilyn Butler implies that De Quincey is not confessing himself, but is demonstrating his skills as a plagiarist: 'His *Confessions* are a clever medley of the facts of his life with fables, inconsistencies and probable lies – like … his obviously self-deluding fantasies about his role as a protector of two female waifs in London. His so-called opium dreams read like an amalgam of the oriental poems of Southey and of Beckford's fantasy *Vathek*' (Butler 1981, 175). Just like Wordsworth, then, though with rather different aims and results, De Quincey's subjectivity is a literary construction, made out of the materials of the various books he has read. His dreams are indeed the stuff of fiction, derived from the sources Butler notes, as well as from the illustrations of imaginary prisons produced by Piranesi and reproduced in a book that – significant fact – Coleridge showed to De Quincey (70–1). Just as Coleridge's 'Kubla Khan' derives its opening lines from a book, *Purchas's Pilgrimage* where the author read the words 'Here the Khan Kubla commanded a palace to be built, and a stately garden thereunto. And thus ten miles of fertile ground were enclosed with a wall' (Wu 1994, 522), even so, in what may be a conscious homage to Coleridge's example, do De Quincey's dreams take their décor from artistic and literary examples.

But the process of telling also dramatizes intemperance in its form. *The Confessions* are, as Grevel Lindop puts it 'Gothic both in their weird emotional intensity and in their digressive complexity of structure' (De Quincey 1985, vii). The Piranesi illustrations, to which De Quincey alludes, though, by his own report he has not seen them and is relying on the description Coleridge offered of them, are for Lindop an emblem of his narrative structure – or of its lack. The illustrations show, says De Quincey, terrifying visions of distorted perspective and impossible images of architecture that could not exist outside of the fantasizing mind. That distorted perspective is the foundation of the textual performance. We are never quite sure what we are looking at, and so are forced to keep looking.

But why does De Quincey confess? He does not present himself as an educator; he does not elaborate on the pleasure of opium in order to persuade us to take it too, or on its pains to dissuade us. Rather, De Quincey became a writer of his own life out of necessity; but as no polite writer can confess that he writes principally for money, there is a motive in the text which it is not permissible to admit. De Quincey's confessional writing was almost entirely commissioned work, produced to satisfy the demand of London magazines for fresh copy, and more pressingly, produced to keep De Quincey's own creditors at bay. *The Confessions* originated in a request from the editor of *Blackwood's Edinburgh Magazine*, and they were published in 1821 in the *London Magazine* at a time when De Quincey was virtually bankrupt, and needed to find funds to support his family. Indeed, he was in the middle of writing the first part of the *Confessions* when he had to flee his London lodgings to escape from his creditors. His unsettled private life has a material effect on the shape of the narrative of self that he produces, as well, presumably as having an effect on the self that he actually inhabited. The compositional and publication history of the *Confessions* is at least as protracted and tortuous as that of Wordsworth's *Prelude*. There was no end to writing this book either, with the result that the self it portrays is always in a state of flux, with De Quincey never quite having the last word on himself. Following its publication in the *London Magazine* in September and October 1821, *The Confessions of an English Opium-Eater* was then published in volume form, with minor revisions in 1822, to which edition De Quincey added an appendix in which he apologized for not writing the advertised 'Third Part' of his Confessions, and in which he gave more details of his varied opium intake.[4] In 1845 he also published a sequel to the *Confessions* consisting of narratives of opium dreams entitled *Suspiria de Profundis* (Dreams from the Depths). He collected a miscellany of *Autobiographic Sketches* in 1853, and in 1856 he produced an expanded edition of the *Confessions* which had by then swelled to twice the length of the originally published text. Even after his death, a posthumous collection of more dreams was published. There are also numerous confessional fragments scattered amongst his other writings (see Davies 1998 and Lindop 1981 for more details). The evidence of the publication history of De Quincey's self suggests two things: that he was always desperate to produce writing for money; and that the self that is expressed out of economic necessity is dispersed and fragmentary, requiring a great deal of research for the reader to 'know' De Quincey's self, and implying that De Quincey's own self-knowledge changed through time, and might not have amounted to all that much because it is so incoherent. There is a sense that all the texts of his life are conditional – there is no complete, finished version. Moreover, factual details differ from edition to edition. For example, in the first edition, his reasons for first taking opium are as an anodyne against rheumatic fever. But in later editions the origin of his addiction is 'a very melancholy event' in 1812 – probably the death of one of Wordsworth's daughters, which he avoids making explicit. And the 1856 edition dates his opium taking from his unhappy schooldays at Manchester Grammar School, where the stuffiness of the classroom and the pollution of the city led to liver complaints and stomach problems.

It may, of course, be that the fragmented nature of the text he writes is part of the product he's trying to sell; its incompleteness and rough edges vouch for its 'authenticity', for this incoherence is the condition of persistent intoxication. It needs to be a little rough to be convincing. This *construction* of authenticity is developed in De Quincey's often contradictory portrayals of his own 'character' within the text. Instead of a composite, coherent personality, the text illustrates a dispersal of the self, in which the self turns out to be selves – infinitely plural, and impossible to complete. Moreover, they are distinctly 'artful' or – even – *crafty* constructions of the self.

In his 'Introduction to the Pains of Opium', this artfulness is displayed – a paradox, since artfulness has usually to do with the concealment of the mechanisms of representation. De Quincey asks his audience to picture him at home in his Lakeland cottage. He even introduces a painter to do the job for him, and instructs him carefully in what is to be represented in his 'self' portrait, and he then describes the result – a fictional painting by a non-existent painter – in an act of fantasy ekphrasis:

> I will introduce a painter; and give him directions for the rest of the picture. ... Paint me, then, a room seventeen feet by twelve, and not more than seven and a half feet high. This, reader, is somewhat ambivalently styled, in my family, the drawing-room: but ... it is also, and more justly, termed the library; for it happens that books are the only article of property in which I am richer than my neighbours ... Therefore, painter, put as many as you can into this room. Make it populous with books: and, furthermore, paint me a good fire, and furniture, plain and modest,

befitting the unpretending cottage of a scholar. And, near the fire, paint me a tea-table; and ... place only two cups and saucers on the tea-tray. ... And as it is very unpleasant to make tea, or to pour it out for oneself, paint me a lively young woman, sitting at the table. Paint her arms like Aurora's, and her smiles like Hebe's. – But no, dear M., not even in jest let me insinuate that thy power to illuminate my cottage rests upon a tenure so perishable as mere personal beauty; or that the witchcraft of angelic smiles lies within the empire of any earthly pencil. (De Quincey 1985, 60)

This passage raises several points of interest for the construction of De Quincey's self through his confessions – points which also relate more generally to questions about the nature of subjectivity itself. For example, like the text as a whole, this passage is filled with digressions, as though narrative form – in particular straight-line structures – cannot contain the self which De Quincey is describing. Indeed, when it comes to describing himself in this fictional portrait –

there I demur. I admit that that, naturally, I ought to occupy the fore-ground of the picture, that being the hero of the piece, or (if you choose) the criminal at the bar, my body should be had in court ... why should I confess on this point, to a painter? or why confess at all? If the public (into whose private ear I am confidentially whispering my confessions, and not into any painter's) should chance to have framed some agreeable picture for itself, of the Opium-eater's exterior, – should have ascribed to him, romantically, an elegant person, or a handsome face, why should I barbarously tear from it so pleasing a delusion – pleasing both to the public and to me. No: paint me, if at all, according to your own fancy: and, as a painter's fancy should teem with beautiful creations, I cannot fail, in that way, to be the gainer. (De Quincey 1985, 61).

He refuses to appear in the very painting that has his representation as its very *raison d'être*, and he refuses – ekphrasis's commitment to explanation through description notwithstanding – to interpret the non-appearing apparition of the opium eater as either hero or villain. The tension between authenticity and literary construction is writ large. The metaphor of the painter theoretically stands as a sign of authenticity because a painted scene should be an accurate representation of the scene; but it also stands as a sign of artifice: *ceci n'est pas* Thomas De Quincey – this is merely a representation of him, artfully constructed, and even that representation figures him as an absence. The gap between representation and reality is emphasized in De Quincey's comment that he has no objection to seeing a representation of opium in the fantasy picture, but that he would rather see the 'real' thing. So the passage draws attention to its own constructed nature, its own fictiveness, whilst simultaneously claiming authenticity. De Quincey also appeals to classical, literary models of feminine beauty in his description of a woman with arms like Aurora's and a smile like Hebe's, but insists also on a return to the real woman, 'dear M.' – whose reality, however, cannot be represented. We can also see him here identifying himself by the name of his addiction. These are not the confessions of Thomas De Quincey, but those of a self-styled 'Opium Eater', whose entire identity is bound up with this label. All of this takes place in sentences that are wilful in their refusal to get to the point, and which thereby stand, like Piranesi's buildings, on shaky logical foundations. And finally, there is the joke at our expense: these confessions of the opium eater are being whispered in our ear, and so are private confidences, but the whispering takes place via the public-address system of publication in a freely available magazine. What price a confidence or a secret that can be bought by anyone who has the money and the inclination? What we are seeing in this passage is reproduced throughout the text in varying degrees. De Quincey's language is always double, and it thus refuses the very generic category signalled in the title – the confession.

This is a fragmented subjectivity, a phrase that would normally signal some element of distress in the self-representation. It is, however, part of De Quincey's 'craft' of representation, part of his contract with his polite audience, that he will not put out distress signals, generally revealing his problematic selfhood with rueful, self-deprecating good humour. Moreover, the fragmentation is not only the impetus for the story, but is also part of the story itself. At his lowest ebb in London, De Quincey tells of his resorting to Jewish moneylenders for relief, and his attempt to borrow money on the security of his future inheritance. The moneylenders, not surprisingly, perhaps, eye him with suspicion, doubting his identity.

> To this Jew, and to other advertising money lenders ... I had introduced myself with an account of my expectations; which account, on examining my father's will at Doctor's Commons, they had ascertained to be correct. The person there mentioned as the second son of – , was found to have all the claims ... that I had stated; but one question still remained ... – was I that person? This doubt had never occurred to me as

> a possible one: I had rather feared ... that I might be too well known to be
> that person – and that some scheme might be passing in their minds for
> entrapping me and selling me to my guardians. It was strange to me to
> find my own self, *materialiter* considered (so I expressed it, for I doated
> on logical accuracy of distinctions), accused, or at least suspected, of
> counterfeiting my own self, *formaliter* considered. (p. 25)

It is, of course, precisely that suspicion – that the 'own self' described – is
counterfeit, fabricated and forged, that really ought to cross readers'
minds as well as those of the moneylenders. What this passage illumi-
nates is the possibility that there is a disjuncture between the form and
the content of self: that the self, indeed, depends for its definition on
the recognition that it is *this* self, rather than another self, *by other
people*. On the one hand, the text claims authenticity; on the other, the
writer is faking it.

This doubleness at the heart of the *Confessions* – essential self versus
performed self, truth versus fiction – takes us to the heart of the issue in
the text. In a book that advertises itself as a confession, the truth of the
deep structures of subjectivity is supposed to come out, but 'telling'
and 'being' a particular self might well be two rather different propositions. As Michel Foucault argues in *The History of Sexuality*, whilst
confession sets itself up as an unmediated disclosure of the self, it is
also a discourse, with its own rules of language practice. The spoken,
written self has to fit certain discursive rules which undermine the
possibility of truthfulness, authenticity and sincerity. And one of
these discursive rules is that a confession is always a confession *to*
someone. The act of confession sets up a relationship between confessor and confessant in which the confessant's 'truth' is only validated by
its entrance into a discourse *with* someone else. Or, as Foucault puts it:

> If one had to confess, this was not merely because the person to whom
> one confessed had the power to forgive, console, and direct, but because
> the work of producing the truth was obliged to pass through this rela-
> tionship if it was to be scientifically validated. The truth did not reside
> solely in the subject who, by confessing, would reveal it wholly formed. It
> was constituted in two stages: present but incomplete, blind to itself, in
> the one who spoke; it could only reach completion in the one who assim-
> ilated and recorded it. ... the revelation of confession had to be coupled
> with the decipherment of what it said. (Foucault 1984, 66)

Foucault is here speaking of the tradition of religious confession in
the Catholic church, in which the ultimate confessor – the ultimate

audience – is God himself. In that tradition, the guarantee of confession's authenticity is that there is no point in the confessant lying, since God is omnipotent and omniscient, and will clearly catch out the false confession. In the romantic tradition in which De Quincey is writing, following on from Rousseau, there is no greater power, no divine power, to validate the self, other than those to whom the self addresses itself – no other guarantor of subjectivity except other people's subjectivities. De Quincey remarks in 'The Pains of Opium', in the context of narrating an anecdote about a girl who nearly drowned, and had her whole life flash in front of her, that 'That dread book of account which the Scriptures speak of, is, in fact, the mind itself of each individual' (De Quincey 1985, 69) – not a judgement book produced by the external authority of God and his angels. Foucault saw traditional modes of confession – both religious and scientific / medical – as intrinsically bound up with ideas about power. De Quincey's text, however, suspends that power relationship: his audience is made up of people like him in some essential way, who are therefore not at liberty to judge him because such a judgement would also be a judgement on themselves. Hence the effort he puts into procuring complicity between himself and his implied audience of like-minded (gentle)men.

The self which is constructed in *The Confessions of an English Opium-Eater* is therefore plural, contradictory and incomplete – it evades the judgement which would complete it. And this incompletion rebounds on its readers, for if De Quincey claims in his mode of address to be like us, what does that say about our own sense of self? We may be dissatisfied with his veracity – not a surprising conclusion since De Quincey's very name, the apparent guarantee of his identity, is itself a fiction. De Quincey was snobbish about the origins of his father's fortunes in mercantile trade – the father was a linen merchant. His death permitted the young Thomas some licence in describing his origins. Around 1799 he decided to add the 'de' to his father's plain name of Quincey. 'De' is a fictive index of De Quincey's nobility – so there is, in fact, a sense in which he was impersonating himself as the moneylenders suspicions implied. But whatever our dissatisfaction, we have 'bought into' his fiction – both literally (we bought the book or the magazine) and figuratively (we read on, even when we doubted the good taste, decency and appropriateness of what we were reading).

The doubleness (two-facedness) or multiplicity of De Quincey's discourse is not only a feature of his chosen genre, the confession. It is also intimately bound up with the subject of addiction to a drug.

In De Quincey's narrative, opium is an example of what Jacques Derrida identifies as the problem of the *pharmakon*, meaning both remedy and poison. In Plato's writings on Socractes in *The Phaedrus*, Plato shows Socrates associating the pharmakon, the drug, with writing. As a form of writing, the *pharmakon* is both a remedy in that it supplements or codifies the memory, and a poison, in that it infects and alters the memory. In his book *Dissemination*, Derrida is interested in the implications of a word which contains its own opposition for two reasons. In the first place it indicates the problem of translation when a noun has two precisely opposite meanings in one language, which might not be replicated in target language. In the second; it is an example of how one can see that words, even nouns, do not embody self-evident truths – there is no relationship between the signifier and a single signified in the word 'drug', which in English also contains the undecideablity Derrida notes in the original Greek:

> The *pharmakon* is 'ambivalent' because it constitutes the element in which opposites are opposed, the movement and play by which each relates back to the other, reverses itself and passes into the other: (soul/body, good/evil, inside/outside, memory/forgetfulness, speech/ writing, etc). It is on the basis of this play or this movement that Plato establishes the oppositions or distinctions. The *pharmakon* is the movement, the locus, and the play (the production) of difference. (Derrida 1981, 127; see also Culler 1983, 42–4)

The ambivalent nature of the drug enables De Quincey to oscillate between its meaning as poison and its meaning as cure, without concluding on some 'essential' nature for opium. He can justify his drug-taking for its therapeutic effects; but it is also the source of his guilt and his financial problems; his financial problems are the source of his confessions, which require the 'guilt' of drug-taking for their popularity and interest; the confessions which depend on drug-taking and guilt are the cure for the financial problems that guilt and drug dependency caused in the first place. In the Preface, we can see how he both announces that he has nothing to confess, but is starting, nonetheless, a process of confession. An oscillation between guilt and self-justification is present from the outset:

> on the one hand, as my self-accusation does not amount to a confession of guilt, so, on the other, it is possible that, if it did, the benefit resulting

to others from the record of an experience purchased at so heavy a price, might compensate, by a vast overbalance, for any violence done to the feelings I have noticed, and justify a breach of the general rule. ... Guilt, therefore, I do not acknowledge: and, if I did, it is possible that I might still resolve on the present act of confession, in consideration of the service which I may thereby render to the whole class of opium-eaters. (De Quincey 1985, 2)

On the one hand, he tells us he is not guilty. On the other, that if he were guilty, there's still a whole set of good excuses for telling his story. It is called having one's cake and eating it too. There is an ongoing oscillation between opposing forces in De Quincey's life, an oscillation that renders analysis impossible (and actually undesirable, for if he analyses, then the obvious answer is to give up the drug).

Finally then, there is an element of collapse in the *Confessions*. The text is double in what it claims on the one hand, and what it dramatizes on the other. The written self, that is, appears to speak one thing, and to enact another. Writing as a romantic who took the self as being of central importance, De Quincey finds himself in a double bind in which the statement that he is speaking the unmediated truth is belied by the textual strategies in which he speaks. For all that he would claim otherwise, confession does imply guilt. Or, as Paul de Man suggests throughout his essay on Rousseau's *Confessions*, excuses effectively generate the very guilt they apparently exonerate, because they verbally signal the possibility of guilt (De Man 1979, 278–301). On the one hand, then, the reader recognizes that we have been presented with a fabricated authenticity. On the other, that this constructedness is so very visible is also a virtual guarantee of authenticity. We also oscillate. We can trust him, his text argues, because he has shown us how the trick is done; but it's still a trick. The undecideability that both the form and content of this text produce and invoke puts the joke on the reader. In the intersubjectivity of the text – the gentleman speaking to an audience of his peers – the audience's subjectivities are rendered as unstable as those of the author.

Notes

1. All references to *The Prelude* are taken from the thirteen book version of 1805, reprinted in Wordsworth, ed. Gill 1984. Roman numerals refer to the

Book number, Arabic numerals to the lines quoted. The composition and publication history of *The Prelude* is extremely complicated. It was begun in 1798, and a two-volume version was completed by 1799. Wordsworth returned to his poem at intervals throughout his life, completing the thirteen-book version by 1805, and then his final version shortly before his death in 1850. The process of composition and the variant texts can be examined by the interested reader in Wordsworth, Abrams and Gill, 1979. The title is not his – it was given to the poem by his wife after his death; and the poem was never published in Wordsworth's lifetime, finally going into print shortly after his death in 1850. We know, however, that the various manuscript editions were circulated amongst his friends and fellow poets, with Coleridge in particular having some influence on the developing shape of the narrative (Coleridge is in fact the 'friend' to whom much of the poem is addressed). I have chosen Gill's edition of the 1805 text because it is a scholarly edition that remains in print and is reasonably priced for student readers. And I have chosen the 1805 edition because it seems likely that this was the edition that De Quincey might have read. For quotations from other romantic poets, I use Duncan Wu's *Romanticism: An Anthology* because of its general availability and massive coverage of the period. The protracted compositional process of *The Prelude* is the reason for the epigraph from *Aurora Leigh*.

2. See Sedgwick 2001, 11–16 for a brief account of Lockean empiricism suitable for the philosophical beginner.

3. Demi-rep means prostitute. The reference is to the popular genre of sensational confessions by ladies of easy virtue, a mode that made money, certainly, and had the added pleasure of embarrassing the upper-class clientele of the high-class courtesan.

4. Rousseau also promised a third part for his *Confessions*, and just like De Quincey's promise, it was never fulfilled. One wonders whether, even in this small detail, De Quincey is self-consciously imitating his master.

3 Victorian Individualisms and Their Limitations

Individualism

The prevailing definition of subjectivity in the mid-Victorian period was involved in the concept of individualism, which John Stuart Mill, writing in 1859 in his treatise *On Liberty*, defined in the following terms:

> the end of man ... is the highest and most harmonious development of his powers to a complete and consistent whole; ... the object 'towards which every human being must ceaselessly direct his efforts, and on which especially those who design to influence their fellow men must ever keep their eyes, is the individuality of power and development'; and ... from union of these arise 'individual vigour and manifold diversity', which combine themselves in 'originality'. (Mill 1993, 125)[1]

The manner in which this ideal of self-development is to be achieved is left slightly vague, but Mill went on to say that man must avoid the 'apelike' faculty of 'imitation', employ all his faculties and 'use his observation to see, reasoning and judgement to foresee, activity to gather materials for decision, discrimination to decide, and when he has decided, firmness and self-control to hold to his deliberate decision' (Mill 1993, 126). As a definition of this central ideological formation in mid-Victorian England, Mill's description of the individual is a brilliant example of both an ideal position and its tensions. For, as Raymond Williams has noted, like so many of the other words we might use to designate selfhood, individualism exists in an uneasy state of contradiction: 'Individual originally meant indivisible', Williams writes. 'That now sounds like a paradox. "Individual" stresses a distinction from others; "indivisible" a necessary connection' (Williams 1988, 161). He goes on to show that the word 'individualism' is a nineteenth-century coinage which creates a man's identity in relation to both his unique person-hood, and his '(indivisible) membership of a group'. On the one hand, then, individualism is bound up with ideas about uniqueness, self-expressiveness, internal coherence (the indivisible self) and originality of a man who stands firm by his own observations and ideas. On the other, participation in this particular recipe for individualism implies group identity; otherwise the formula for its possession could not exist.[2]

The qualities that Mill describes are the qualities of the adult middle-class male of the mid-nineteenth century, and his description is both formative of the concept of individualism and formed by the particular historical moment in which he wrote. The aim of mature masculinity in this class grouping and within this discourse is self-development, towards an ideal state of consistency and coherence, power and origi-nality. These things are to be attained by the man who has freedom: moral and intellectual freedom, certainly, but also – and though this is not stated explicitly, it is an implicit part of his discourse – freedom from material want, as well as freedom conceived as the absence of 'slavery'. Such a man, in order to reach the endpoint of maturity, must expose himself to a variety of experiences: he must travel, for example; and he must also confront a variety of different intellectual problems to test the capacity of his mind for sound and moral judgement. He must be a man of the world, with all that that phrase implies. In auto-biographies, both fictional and real, written by the middle-class men of the period then, the narrative goal is self-possession, a kind of confi-dence in the individual man's own judgement and belief attained experientially. This self-possession is both a group and an individual property, which involves it in certain tensions. As Laura Marcus observes, there is 'a pattern of circular influence' between the unique-ness of the individual and his place as an exemplar of general laws of human 'nature' (Marcus 1994, 24). Additionally, there is a similar circle of influence between the written models of manhood and the lived experience of genteel masculinity.

I keep the word 'man' advisably in this definition of individualism, for one of the limitations of individualism as ideal and goal, as this chapter will show, is that it is highly gender specific. Indeed, it might even have been better to choose the word 'gentleman', because it is also a class-based mode of identity. The individual might be 'unique', but he is unique within the quite strict codes and conventions of what

Victorian society came to recognize as proper masculinity. To step outside the bounds of those conventions deliberately (because of a choice of lifestyle or particular behaviour) or to find oneself outside those bounds on the basis of class, ethnicity or gender (or all three) entailed a denial of status, and involved relative difficulty in achieving (self-)respect and self-possession. In this, as in so much else, the story of the Victorian individual was different for girls, as well as for socially disadvantaged men.

David Copperfield – Writing like a man: telling tales and false accounting

In her influential book *Uneven Developments*, Mary Poovey argues that the cultural discourses of literature inscribe and form the meaning of the individual in ways that had direct and traceable effects on Victorian lived experience. She argues that 'one effect of the "literary" in this period was the textual construction of individualist psychology', which operated to construct not merely fictional characters, but also to construct the reader 'as a particular kind of subject – a psychologized, classed, developmental individual' (Poovey 1989, 89–90). Her suggestion is that the mid-Victorian novel both represents and creates reality; novels (and autobiographies) do not merely passively reflect an already existing reality, but help to form that reality by forming the sensibilities through which readers relate to their world. Fiction has real observable effects on the world beyond its own textuality, and reading and writing are material processes. In a text like *David Copperfield*, which critics agree is Dickens's most nearly autobiographical work, even described by him as 'some portion of himself' in the Preface to the first edition of 1850 (Dickens 1985, 45), there is a deliberate blurring of the author and the character, of the real and the fictional. Critics routinely comment on the resemblances between Dickens's father and the satirically conceived Mr Micawber, and on the fact that Dickens and Copperfield share the same initials, albeit reversed, implying something of the nature of the text as the mirror image of its writer, as his textual signifier, though whether he 'masters' the image and finds it 'empty', is a rather moot point. Psychoanalytically motivated biographers have also noted that the book 'writes out' in a lightly disguised form, Dickens's disappointments with romantic love in the case of Maria Beadnell, and thereafter in his marriage to Catherine Hogarth, from whom he eventually separated.[3] And there is also the issue of the famous 'Autobiographical Sketch', given to John Forster, Dickens's first biographer as an account of what Dickens saw as his shameful passage of his early life, which he spent performing manual labour in a blacking factory whilst his family was living in straitened circumstances as the direct consequence of his father's Micawberish financial incompetence. This autobiographical fragment is transcribed, virtually unaltered, in Chapter 11 of the finished novel, describing David's equal sense of shame in relation to his time at Murdstone and Grimby's bottling factory.[4] Most importantly, perhaps, David himself is a successful novelist by the end of the plot, looking back on his early life and (re)creating it through his own writing. Although he evades talking about the textual process, a notable repression in a novel that describes the career of a successful novelist, in textualizing some of the autobiographical incidents of his own life Dickens's novel enacts a process of subjectivity in the making, and places that process as a function of textuality. One can only presume that his refusal to talk about the act of writing is founded on a desire to disguise the processes – technical and artificial – by which the self he narrates has come into being, for to recognize the process explicitly would be an admission of a self whose consistency and coherence were both open to question.

The Personal History of David Copperfield was published in monthly parts from May 1849 to November 1850. To its first readers, therefore, the novel was observably about a self in the process of coming into being, a *sujet-en-procès*, since they did not have a completed text or a completed character to assess until the publication was complete.[5] This is a relationship to the novel that modern readers do not quite share when we read David's story neatly bound into a single – if somewhat weighty – volume. The processes and trials David undergoes in his life story are the dramatization of his identity formation that takes place essentially in writing and in relation to reading. Like Pamela before him, David is in part the product of the cultural materials – the books – at his disposal. Equally, though, he is also a product of a particular mode of literary production. As John Sutherland has noted, serial publication imposes a certain rhythm on narrated events, since the audience must be kept 'hooked' if they are to continue buying the monthly parts (Sutherland 1995, 86–106). And this was also an observation made by contemporary observers, with one review of Dickens's later autobiographical fiction, *Great Expectations* noting that serial publication was a risky venture; and though it was a mode that had brought Dickens great material success, this was often felt to be at the expense of aesthetic value. This is the tension to be found in E. S. Dallas's anonymous review in *The Times* in 1861:

> monthly publication succeeds, and thousands of a novel are sold in minute doses, where only hundreds would have been disposed of in the lump. ... On the whole, perhaps, the periodical publication of the novel has been of use to [the novel's form], and has forced English writers to develop a plot and work up the incidents. Lingering over the delineation of character and of manners, our novelists began to lose sight of the story and to avoid action. Periodical publication compelled them to a different course. They could not afford, like Scheherezade, to let the devourers of their tales go to sleep at the end of a chapter. As modern stories are intended not to set people to sleep, but to keep them awake, instead of the narrative breaking down into a soporific dulness [sic], it was necessary that it should rise at the close into startling incident. Hence a disposition to wind up every month with a melodramatic surprise that awakens curiosity in the succeeding number. (Dallas in Collins 1971, 432)

Just beneath these urbane observations, however, one can detect a certain distaste for the serial form. If novels published 'in a lump' in three-volume format behave like soporific drugs, the serial imposes a necessity for startling incident and cliff-hanging endings which are here compared to stimulants: reading novels in this way is like being on speed. The lives that are thus narrated are problematic in their shape not only because they are necessarily sensational, and not only because they might stand as rather sensationalist examples to unwary readers; they are also problematic because they are necessarily uneven, inconsistent and do not therefore represent an ideal of human character as coherent and 'whole'. The episodic nature that serialization imposes on character and plot is a shape that actually undermines the final goal of individualism.

The fact that David is to become a writer is, retrospectively, important from the outset of the novel. There is a double consciousness at work in *David Copperfield*, divided as it is between David the character who lives in the real time of the novel and David the narrator who recreates that real time with the benefit of hindsight. David the narrator knows things that David the character cannot know at a given point in the narrative – knows, in fact, how the story will turn out. This knowledge produces an ironizing distance into the text, but also undermines any claim to 'wholeness' in David's character. The narrator looks back at the character with a satirical smile which may be affectionate but which is also mocking. It is the distance of fiction rather than of auto-biography which is commonly supposed (usually quite wrongly) to be a transparent, unmediated narrative that sticks to the facts. The novel famously opens with a slightly disingenuous comment that precisely points out the ways in which David the narrator is fictionalizing David the character, and which places the character in an avowedly fictional world:

> Whether I shall turn out to be the hero of my own life, or whether that sta-tion will be held by anybody else, these pages must show. To begin my life with the beginning of my life, I record that I was born (as I have been informed and believe) on a Friday, at twelve o'clock at night. It was remarked that the clock began to strike, and I began to cry simultane-ously. (Dickens 1985, 49)

A hero belongs in a fiction not a life; there is play here on the two mean-ings of the word: as the signifier for the main character of a fiction, and as a larger-than-life figure in historical reality. From the very outset of his tale, David the narrator is constructing his former self as a fictional character, and not only in terms of his doubtful heroic status. There is, in addition, an intertextual reference here to Laurence Sterne's *Life and Opinions of Tristram Shandy, Gentleman* (1759–67) in which Shandy's narrative of his own existence opens with a reference to a clock inaus-piciously remembered at the moment of his conception. And the noto-rious peregrinations of that narrative are affectionately recalled by Dickens's opening passage in *Copperfield*, when David enters a sub-stantial digression on the history of the caul with which he was born, until he catches himself 'meandering' and recalls himself to the matter in hand: 'I will go back to my birth' (Dickens 1985, 50).

Both David the character and David the narrator, however, necessar-ily lack first-hand information about that birth. Both are reliant on what they have been told, and on an act of faith – they *believe* what they have been told. The self that is narrated cannot therefore be the autonomous possession of the narrator, but is rather a relative self, dependent on the narrations of others, at least in the early part of the story. The *infant* David is inarticulate, and cannot speak/write in his own behalf. The narrator David, who is very articulate indeed, nonetheless does not exactly 'know' what happened, and is anxious from the outset that the child he presents to us should not appear as merely an artificial reconstruction:

> If it should appear from anything I may set down in this narrative that I
> was a child of close observation, or that as a man I have a strong memory
> of my childhood, I undoubtedly lay claim to both these characteristics.
> Looking back, as I was saying, into the blank of my infancy, the first
> objects I can remember as standing out by themselves from a confusion
> of things are my mother and Peggotty. What else do I remember? Let me
> see. (Dickens 1985, 61)

There is a tension here between an infancy that is 'blank' because
speechless, and an infancy that can be recalled and narrated. David's
representation of his experience at this point reads like conversation
where his implied interlocutor appears to have raised doubts about
what the speaker can remember, and where the speaker is digressive and anecdotal. This is, of course, an artful deception designed to
make readers forget that David Copperfield is a sign without a referent.
The writing process differs in key ways from the speaking process, not
least because it can be revised and reordered to suit the writer's purposes. As the above quotation suggests, in the 'objects' of his mother
and Peggotty, between whom David totters as he learns to walk and
talk, we see a neat emblem of the aesthetic and sexual choices (beautiful but impractical women versus plain but practical ones) that David
will wrestle with for the rest of the novel. David's facility with the written word seeks to persuade his audience that he is really talking to us:
but, really, he fabricates the authenticity of conversation.

This is a fabricated conversation 'between men',[6] which is not to say
that women cannot read it, but that they are explicitly excluded from
some of its conclusions. The kind of story that David can tell is dependent on his male sex and on the processes by which he achieves the
gendered identity of an adult gentleman. It would not be possible to
tell this story had David indeed turned out to be the girl child Betsey
Trotwood so confidently predicts at his birth. The variety of experience
that Mill identifies as necessary for the development of the individual
is confined to the middle-class male of the species in mid-Victorian
England. David's story describes his experience of an illusorily dreamy
and Edenic domestic sphere with his mother before her marriage to
Mr Murdstone; it shows his expulsion from this Eden into school, and,
following his mother's death, into the world of manual work. From
Murdstone and Grimby's factory, he takes to the road in quest of his

aunt; and after many hardships and dangers on the road – dangers that
would be qualitatively very different if he were a girl child – he achieves
a new kind of domesticity with Miss Trotwood. From there he goes
again to school, before finding a more suitable employment (with
his head as opposed to his hands) as a junior lawyer's clerk, and thence
as a parliamentary short-hand reporter. He then marries the hopeless
Dora Spenlow, an action which serves to displace his mother's mental
frailities onto his wife, thereby enabling him to pass through his Oedipal
conflict without serious regret, and becomes, through application and
effort (the consistency and determination identified by Mill) a successful writer. Finally he is rewarded with a more appropriate Eden in his
perfect marriage to Agnes Wickfield.

   This broad outline of the plot shows the extent to which David's
experiences owe something to the plots of picaresque novels; this
Victorian fictional individual is drawing on his fictional predecessors.
This is no surprise for it is written into the fabric of the novel that the
books David turns to in order to find comfort for the loss of his mother's
affections are precisely eighteenth-century picaresque fictions, significantly once the property of his father:

> My father had left a small collection of books in a little room upstairs, to
> which I had access ... From that blessed little room, Roderick Random,
> Peregrine Pickle, Humphrey Clinker, Tom Jones, the Vicar of Wakefield,
> Don Quixote, Gil Blas, and Robinson Crusoe came out, a glorious host.
> They kept alive my fancy, and my hope of something beyond that place
> and time ... and they did me no harm ... I have been Tom Jones (a child's
> Tom Jones, a harmless creature) for a week together. I have sustained my
> own idea of Roderick Random for a week at a stretch ... This was my only
> and constant comfort. When I think of it, the picture always rises in my
> mind of a summer evening, the boys at play in the churchyard, and I sitting
> on my bed, reading *as if for life*. (Dickens 1985, 105–6, my emphasis)

The picaresque novel derives its name for the Spanish word *picaro*,
meaning rogue, and its rogues are often figured as outlaw heroes. It
designates a narrative mode popular from the sixteenth to the eighteenth century in which rogues and vagabonds evaded, for a time at
least, the stability of normal life. David is more a 'hero' than a rogue,
hence his hasty but necessary parenthesis that his version of Tom Jones
was quite innocent for *Tom Jones* has a notorious barely avoided incest
plot and a vast quantity of extra-marital sexual activity. But he is also a
strangely feminized hero in the sense that far from wishing to escape

the confines of home for the freedoms of the road, his wanderings will be a sustained quest for a home, the domestic goal more usually apportioned to the heroine of such fictions. The novels he reads substitute for the absent father (to whom they once belonged), giving David some slightly odd masculine role models to live up to – though their oddity is certainly preferable to the out-and-out cruelty of his 'surrogate' father, Mr Murdstone. They also provide him with protective camouflage. When Murdstone humiliates him, if he is being someone else at the time, then he still possesses a capacity for heroism that has not been shamed away by cruel treatment. This is the force of his comment that he read these books 'as if for life'. They provide him with escapist fantasies that have real psychological benefits. This tendency to play out fictional roles is not confined to David's childhood misery. It continues long into his adolescence as is evidenced by Chapter 18, 'A Retrospect' in which David narrates the juvenile excesses of his seventeenth year. His love affair with the unattainable Miss Larkins takes place entirely in the terms of bad romantic fiction. This episode is narrated with irony and mocking distance. Similarly, he makes a doomed attempt to teach his hopeless wife, Dora, the principles of domestic economy by recourse to the models to be found in conduct books. She is incapable of sustained attention, and the experiment fails. Nonetheless, there is a clear message that if one is a man, what one *is* may often be intimately related to what one *reads*. And it is reading that gives David the narrator the interpretative facility to judge what he *was*, making him the critic of his former self even as he narrates that self.

As Poovey observes, it is important that David constructs his eventual career as a writer as a strenuously masculine activity (Poovey 1989, 124–5). She describes the debates in the period about apparent feminization of the novel, regarded in the mid-century as a potentially respectable career path for middle-class women because it was work that could be carried out in the safely domestic sphere of the home. David is at pains to create his work as a writer as 'manly' in opposition to the perception that fiction is a feminine form. It is manly in his case because it is capitalistic: he seeks his fortune with his pen rather than the means of simple self-expression, and is a venture capitalist risking his (intellectual) capital for profit in order that he can perform his patriarchal duty and afford his ineffectual wife. His training for writing comes unwilled, through circumstances – he has to make a living somehow. But it is also represented as a direct consequence of the particularity of David's own special character. He not only reads 'as if for life', but also 'narrates' and eventually writes as if for life from very nearly the outset of the story.

When his aunt loses her money, he sets out to increase his income by working as a shorthand reporter for a Parliamentary magazine. That choice, coupled with the real effort he has to put in to learning shorthand, gives him a wider view of the world than would otherwise be available to him – a view, incidentally, available only to men in a period when women were excluded from both Parliament and professionalized status more generally. His widening experience gives him, we are supposed to believe, wider views of the world, views which enable him to judge that world (which he does with evident satirical relish when he describes the workings of both Parliament and the law, the two areas in which he has tested his capacities). What David emphasizes about his writing work is that it registers his near-completion of the process of becoming a proper individual because it requires serious effort and application to make him a productive economic entity in his society, as we see in Chapter 42, 'Mischief':

> ... it is not for me to record, though this manuscript is intended for no eyes but mine, how hard I worked at that tremendous short-hand, and all improvement appertaining to it, in my sense of responsibility to Dora ... I will only add, to what I have already written of my perseverance at this time of my life, and of a patient and continuous energy which then began to be matured within me, and which I know to be the strong part of my character, if it have any strength at all, that there, on looking back I find the source of my success ... I could never have done what I have done, without habits of punctuality, order and diligence, without the determination to concentrate myself on one object at a time ... whatever I have tried to do in life, I tried with all my heart to do well: that whatever I have devoted myself to, I have devoted myself completely; that in great aims and in small, I have always been thoroughly in earnest. (Dickens 1985, 671–2)

The entire passage from which this quotation is taken is a fascinating example of the tensions of masculine individualism as Dickens set out to negotiate them. As James Eli Adams has perceptively remarked, acceptable individualism, whilst self-assertive, was also crucially bound up in self-abnegation: uniqueness had to function in terms of conformity to group identity to be acceptable. Adams suggests we should look to words such as 'reserve' and 'restraint' as key terms in the discourse of Victorian masculinity (Adams 1995, 86–103, 189) to investigate the contradictions of this discursive formation. These are words that imply that the individual must not draw attention to himself, must not assert himself and demand notice; but at the same, he must always behave as if he were being observed. In the opening of Chapter 42, David struggles to express both his pride in his achievement whilst also avoiding the vanity of boasting. He disclaims the very act that we are in the process of reading, the public proclamation of a self, since his manuscript is 'intended for no eyes but mine'; this is self-examination – the private thoughts of the individual on which we are eavesdropping, or sneaking a shifty look without the writer's permission.

In theory at least, anyone with at least a minimal level of education and a bit of luck could do what David does with his life: anyone could write for a living. But when it comes down to it, in fact, in the novel David is unique in his capacity for turning story-telling to profitable account and for controlling the language in which his stories are told. As he admits, slightly uncomfortably to himself, 'many men have worked harder and not succeeded half so well' (671). It is, however, more than luck. David's talent for story-telling is, apparently, innate. It is first noted by Steerforth at Mr Creakle's school, where David, like a latter-day Scheherezade, recounts the plots of his father's picaresque novels to his schoolmate during the small hours of the night. And even here, this is a kind of capitalistic exchange – David tells stories to Steerforth in return for Steerforth's protection from bullying. On the other hand, whilst this is a masculine exchange – between boys who will become men – Steerforth sees David as a partly feminine figure, christening him Daisy and speculating that if David had a sister, he would have liked to meet her: 'she would have been a pretty, timid, little, bright-eyed sort of girl' (140). David narrates *like* a man; but it is an act of impersonation, and certainly at this stage his possession of gender status is far from secure.

As Poovey argues, 'the representative (literary) man was simultaneously considered unique (a "genius") and like every other man (interchangeable)' (Poovey 1989, 110), a comment which, in the context of Steerforth's view of David has some interesting resonances, implying that all men are also potentially merely performing their gender. More importantly, all the other characters in this novel who write – in whatever form (and none of them is a novelist, a creative voice) – are clearly much less talented than David in controlling and shaping their linguistic resources. The examples of failed writers abound. The most significant, perhaps, is the harmless lunatic, Mr Dick, who finds refuge with

Betsey Trotwood, and who exemplifies the linguistic failure to structure his experience into narrative. His attempts to write his Memorial, or autobiography, a therapy for his condition of insanity, are treated comically, but still make a fairly serious point. Mr Dick, whose real name is Richard Babley (a rather cruel joke at the expense of his written babble) has a very attenuated relationship with his own identity, beginning with his very name, which he 'can't bear', as Betsey tells David (Dickens 1985, 257). How, though, can he write a testament to his identity if he cannot speak or write his own name? The answer is that he cannot, losing his own story in endless digressions about the execution of Charles I (258). For him, the articulacy of written language does not serve its usual purpose of putting things into an order of cause and consequence by which he can make sense of experience. Mr Dick's memorial is a wild-goose chase, imaged in the fact that his chosen mode of publication is the unorthodox one of flying his written sheets of paper as a kite: 'There's plenty of string', he tells David. 'And when it flies high, it takes the facts a long way' (259). He has lost the thread, one might say – and has lost the plot, both literally and figuratively. Mr Dick, feminized by his insanity, is incapable – as women were thought to be – of systematic thought, incapable of a larger manly purpose and of originality. On the other hand, he is able to undertake tasks of copying and imitation (the clerk's work he takes up when Miss Trotwood loses her fortune). This activity, as Mill's views on individualism suggest, is indicative of the passivity of a man who is not quite a proper individual, a man who cannot work independently for purposes of his own directing.

   Other writers we see in the text also point out David's linguistic potency and competence in relation to their patent impotence and absurdity. Miss Julia Mill's diary, through which David keeps in touch with Dora when he has been forbidden to see her (Dora is so linguistically inept that one could not expect her to write for herself), is a staccato factual account of the days spent by Dora and Julia in Putney, interspersed with sentimental and utterly banal interpolations by Julia herself, offered as a most inadequate interpretation of each day's events:

> Monday. My sweet D[ora] still very much depressed. Headache. Called attention to J[ip, Dora's lapdog] as being beautifully sleek. D fondled J. Associations thus awakened, opened the floodgates of sorrow. Rush of grief admitted. (Are tears the dewdrops of the heart? J. M.) (Dickens 1985, 624)

No wonder David is a frustrated lover at this point of the story. But Miss Mills is only a girl and cannot be expected to do better. A more serious instance of written language's failure to express appropriate selfhood is Mr Micawber's flood of purposeless words. The novel is speckled not only with his periphrastic and spendthrift conversation, but also with various examples of his epistolary art in which he appears to live by similarly uneconomic rules in language as he does in every other aspect of his life: his outpourings of twenty words where five would do – result: unnecessary complexity and failed communication:

> My dear Copperfield,
>
> You may possibly not be unprepared to receive the intimation that something has turned up. I may have mentioned to you on a former occasion that I was in expectation of such an event.
>
> I am about to establish myself in one of the provincial towns of our favoured island (where the society may be described as a happy admixture of the agricultural and the clerical), in immediate connexion with one of the learned professions ...
>
> In bidding adieu to the Modern Babylon ... Mrs Micawber and myself cannot disguise from our minds that we part ... with an individual linked by strong associations to the altar of our domestic life. If, on the eve of such a departure, you will accompany a mutual friend ... to our present abode, and there reciprocate our wishes natural to the occasion, you will confer a Boon, etc. (Dickens 1985, 592)

Even in its abbreviated form, this is a very long-winded way of announcing a job as a lawyer's clerk and inviting a friend to tea. Mr Micawber's linguistic excesses mark him out as a man failing in manliness. Economy of expression (and time is money, after all) is a marker of efficiency and productiveness. Micawber has none of these attributes.

There is only one serious rival to David in the text, only one other character who has anything like David's facility with words: Uriah Heep. Commenting on the way in which David disperses his own negative attributes through other characters in the novel, Kate Flint suggests that 'The creepily unctuous Uriah Heep, with his clammy hands – and his own unacceptable designs on Agnes – acts as a viscerally repulsive embodiment of David's own social ambitions and capacity for hard work. ([David] never stops to consider, overtly, that as a boy washing empty bottles, he was for a time considerably more " 'umble" even than Uriah)' (Flint 2001, 44). In this comment, she reiterates a point that has become a standard view of *David Copperfield* – that David has 'doubles' throughout the text who stand for the parts of himself of which he has least reason to be proud. As I suggest above, masculine individualism is caught up in a contradictory movement: how is the individual to embody and express his own achieved individuality whilst at the same time appearing both modest and restrained? Uriah Heep embodies this problem, taking the ideal of modesty beyond its proper limits. His catchphrase – 'I'm very very 'umble' – accompanied by his cringing gesture of wringing his hands is a brilliant dramatization of how revolting the *display of modesty* might be. Yet there is a painful connection between David and Uriah, imaged in the fact that they both, eventually, have designs on Agnes Wickfield as a wife. The distinctions between them come from a number of sources. One issue is that we are not given the evidence to feel physically repulsed by David (who surreptitiously wipes his hand whenever it comes into contact with the damp appendage of Heep). Another is that David wields considerable power in terms of representation because he is in charge of the narrative; in that narrative, David presents himself as honest. His 'honesty' is artfully constructed. His autobiography is also a confession of youthful folly and indiscretions, such as, a single instance of alcoholic intemperance, and a series of youthful infatuations, of which his marriage to Dora is the most serious result. A man who can tell us his little faults, the feeling is, must be alright really. Even his disastrous friendship with Steerforth, which produces dire consequences for Little Em'ly and the Peggotty tribe, is the result of genuine affection; no blame attaches to David for consequences he could not predict. Uriah, on the other hand, is presented from the outset as a conscious hypocrite, a man with two faces who deliberately sets out to deceive: he is neither consistent nor coherent in the terms which, according to Mill make up the model of masculinity. David is shown in the process of achieving wholeness; Uriah is represented as refusing it. And as Lyn Pykett puts it, '[Heep's] false accounting is a negative (indeed criminal) version of David's fiction making' (Pykett 2002, 119): two stories, two endings.

The opposition between David and Uriah which is the cover story of the novel's ending, however, is more apparent than real. For in one very important respect they are uncomfortably alike. They both 'buy into' the discourse of individualism, at least, in Uriah's case, in terms of class positioning, and both set out to raise their class position from inauspicious beginnings. A key distinction apart from Heep's self-evident moral obliquity is the position from which they start. David, after all, is born genteel. The class position he achieves at the end of the novel is, in fact, merely the reassertion of his birthright. Uriah, the charity boy, on the other hand, inhabits a social class that, in the world the novel creates, precludes social mobility. To wish to rise and to desire marriage to Agnes are examples of both social and sexual arrogance. It is as if the model of individualism on which the text is predicated is only available to those who inhabit a degree of privilege already, and preferably by birth.

David's achievement of mature masculinity is imaged in his joint achievement of career and wife. He gets there, however, as will always be the case in competitive systems, by the sacrifice of others along the way. His self-assertion leads to the annihilation or exile of other characters. If, for example, it is possible to see Uriah Heep as one of David's displacing doubles, then it is certainly possible to see Steerforth as another. David's dangerous, though immature, desires for Little Em'ly, a woman who is an unsuitable mate for him on the grounds of class, are displaced onto Steerforth who seduces and 'ruins' her in David's stead. And Kate Flint suggests also that Mr Micawber is another double, representing David's immature incapacity to plan properly for the future. Prison, death by drowning and Australia are the fates of these 'other' Davids. What's at stake in this representation of subjectivity, in the end, is a doubled reading of the text, a reading that maps onto the double consciousness with which it is narrated. On the one hand, it is possible to take it all at face value; on the other, it is just possible that it is not only Uriah Heep who is 'two-faced' in the text. The sensitive reader might just start to see the fissures in the ideology of individualism that David represents to us. The assumptions of this discourse, though it never says so in so many words, are actually based on gender and class within a capitalist system of competition between individuals. Identity is certainly not a God-given attribute since it has to be striven for. But it certainly helps to have been born into a privileged class and a privileged gender to make the strife worthwhile.

At the same time, male relationship to class status is far more secure than the female one. As I turn now to Charlotte Brontë's autobiographical fiction, *Jane Eyre* (1847), what becomes clear is that class is possessed by male characters in their own right, but possessed by female characters far more tenuously, *in relation* to the men in their lives – husbands and fathers. Jane Eyre is rather short of male relatives to provide the protection of class identity, and is therefore thrown onto her own resources to make her way in the world. But the kinds of stories she – and, by implication, women in the nineteenth century – can inhabit are absolutely different from those that Dickens's (1861) 'heroes' live in and through. Even the very humble Pip in *Great Expectations*, despite his discomfort and the instability of his class aspirations, is shown to have far more 'right' to be self-assertive than is Jane. Moreover, since individualism depends on an active life, on originality, on variety of experience and intellectual and physical mettle, its meanings are clearly different for women. In a period when the ideal figure of femininity is what Coventry Patmore termed 'The Angel in the House' – an ideal that *David Copperfield* rather heavy-handedly reiterates in its multiple views of Agnes Wickfield as a domestic angel – the space of individualism is registered as essentially masculine. The experiences that make individualism possible are very differently experienced by girls. At Lowood School, having been exonerated from the charge of being a liar, Jane Eyre begins to learn the French language: 'I learned the first two tenses of the verb *Être*', she tells us (Brontë 1996, 87). In this novel, Brontë dramatizes the ways in which female subjectivity is a strange and foreign concept, far less securely possessed and far more difficult to attain than the individualism at the heart of the masculine fictional autobiographies of Dickens. This can be seen in both the plot of Brontë's novel, and in the responses of contemporary readers to this plots.

Circumstanced like me … *Jane Eyre* and Charlotte Brontë's wandering eye/I

We do not know for certain that Charles Dickens read *Jane Eyre*, but I would be prepared to bet that he did. As Lyn Pykett notes, *David Copperfield* is 'Dickens's *Jane Eyre*: David's five-day confinement in his room by Murdstone and his being made to wear, at Salem House, a placard announcing "Take care of him, he bites", echo the early experiences of discipline and punishment in the Red Room and at Lowood School, which Charlotte Brontë had invented for the heroine of her first novel published just two years earlier' (Pykett 2002, 110). David's biting of Murdstone's hand, though it pricks David's conscience, is presented as a justifiable reaction to unjust treatment; and certainly, when I first read *Jane Eyre*, I understood her assault on John Reed as similarly justifiable. 'Be grateful, boy, to them which brought you up by hand', intones Mr Pumblechook complacently over Christmas dinner in *Great Expectations* (Dickens 1965, 57). I can see no evidence that Pip actually is grateful, and have little sense of what he has to be grateful for. The contemporary reviews of Dickens' novels, however, do not pounce on his ingratitude or denounce his aspirations as some reviewers did on those of Jane Eyre some years earlier. For the anonymous reviewer in *The Christian Remembrancer* writing in April 1848, *Jane Eyre* 'burns with moral Jacobinism': ' "Unjust, unjust", is the burden of every reflection upon the things and powers that be' (Anon, rpt. in Allott 1973, 58). And in her notorious commentary for the *Quarterly Review* in December 1848, Elizabeth Rigby pronounced at length on *Jane Eyre's* revolutionary and anti-religious stance:

> No Christian grace is perceptible upon [Jane Eyre]. She has inherited in fullest measure the worst sin of our fallen nature – the sin of pride ... she looks on all that has been done for her not only as her undoubted right, but as falling far short of it ... the autobiography of Jane Eyre is pre-eminently an anti-Christian composition. There is throughout it a murmuring against the comforts of the rich and against the privations of the poor, which, as far as each individual is concerned, is a murmuring against God's appointment – there is a proud and perpetual assertion of the rights of man, for which we find no authority in either God's word or God's providence.

She ends her rhetorical opprobrium by associating the novel with 'Chartism and rebellion', with the French revolution as the ghost at the feast (Rigby in Allott 1973, 71–2).

This view might seem strangely old-fashioned – positively 'Victorian', indeed – but it and others like it have persisted in slightly more moderated tones well into the twentieth-century critiques of Brontë's fiction. For Virginia Woolf, for instance, writing in 'Women and Fiction', lamented that in *Jane Eyre*, 'we are conscious of a woman's presence – of someone resenting the treatment of her sex and pleading for its rights', a presence she identified as a weakness in the writing (Woolf 1979, 47–8). And Raymond Williams, writing about *Villette* (but in a manner also applicable to *Jane Eyre*) describes the technique as 'the fiction of special pleading ... in which the only major emotion ... is that exact stress, that first-person stress: "circumstanced like me" ' (Williams 1984, 74). For Williams, the female voice overwhelms the other subjectivities in the fiction that tells her story, and overwhelms the reader in its torrent of demands and pleas to accept her story and the subjectivity that her story has produced.

It may be that in being the first to speak from the position of the orphan, *Jane Eyre* was responsible for creating a taste that did not exist when her novel was published in 1847. Or – more likely – it may be that the acceptance of the polite fiction that one should be grateful, and satisfied with one's divinely ordained lot was imposed on female characters and authors rather more forcibly than it was on male ones. Jane Eyre is 'disconnected, poor, and plain' (Brontë 1996, 183). She, like David Copperfield, is also orphaned; yet she maintains a strong sense of the rights that accrue to a woman of her class, on the borders of gentility. *Jane Eyre* additionally intervenes in striking ways in the debate that was to come to be known as the 'Woman Question' of the mid-nineteenth century, a debate that concerned social attitudes to middle- and upper-class women – ladies – who could not marry.

The 'Woman Question' was precipitated by a demographic crisis in the mid-century. The censuses of the 1840s, 50s and 60s showed that there were considerably more women than men in England, rising to around half a million more women than men by the time of the 1861 census. The period's ideology of gender presumed that the male individual would work for his living, finding a sphere of action in the public domains of the professions and economic striving and getting. Middle-class women, on the other hand, were described in terms which rendered them strikingly unfit for any economic endeavour. Their proper role was to be a home-maker, a wife and mother if possible, a nurse to aged parents if all else failed, and only in the very last of last resorts to work for a living. In a domestic economy which demanded that young ladies be decorative and useless – veritable Clara Copperfields, every one – women's education was severely limited, designed for the purpose of producing angels who conformed merely to the domestic ideal, as Elizabeth Barrett Browning's *Aurora Leigh* satirically attests. A woman is valued, in the end, according to Barrett's poem, as long as she 'keep[s] quiet by the fire, / And never say[s] "no" when the world says "ay" ' (Barrett Browning 1981, 51, ll. 427–37).

Jane Eyre is resolutely a novel that says 'no' when the world says 'ay', with its narrator identifying herself as 'a discord at Gateshead Hall' (Brontë 1996, 23); and the fires in the text are not exactly of the sort that represent cosy domesticity so much as rage. On the other hand, Jane does not especially indulge in howls of anguish except in her childhood, but attains her goals (wealth, marriage, class status) by outward compliance in the demands of the world, whilst on the inside she is feeling something quite different. She learns early lessons in self-control, for although her attack on John Reed is justified by the narrator's voice, it produces swift and terrifying retribution. It has its advantages because, like the bully he is, John avoids Jane thereafter; but it is a dangerous precedent on which to base a life. As Gilbert and Gubar have magisterially demonstrated, the passionate child Jane has her dark double in the madwoman in the attic, Bertha Mason, a doubling that is textually signalled in the imagery that surrounds them: the infant Jane is a 'mad cat' who is threatened with being tied to a chair in the Red Room (Brontë 1996, 19); Bertha Mason springs tiger-like at Rochester, and is 'mastered' only when she is tied to a chair (328). The price of a lack of self-control is insanity. When Jane makes a passionate speech about the virtue of resistance to injustice to Helen Burns, describing just how she would break Miss Scatcherd's rod of twigs if anyone threatened to use it on her, Helen calms her down with a homily on endurance and passivity in the face of fate: she, unlike Jane, accepts her place in the hierarchy as divinely ordained. But the result of Helen's ladylike submission to fate is death – hardly a great role model for our heroine. A better lesson comes from Miss Temple who, when admonished for feeding the starving pupils in her care by Mr Brocklehurst, is an example of self-control as repression of instinct:

> Miss Temple ... gazed straight before her, and her face, naturally pale as marble, appeared to be assuming also the coldness and fixity of that material, especially her mouth closed as if it would have required a sculptor's chisel to open it, and her brow settled gradually into petrified severity. (Brontë 1996, 75)

There would, of course, be no point in the headmistress resisting the fatuous hypocrisy of Mr Brocklehurst's sermon on the value of self-denial. If she spoke her mind, she would lose her job, so she accepts his admonitions in silence. The cost of repression is weighed in the balance with its benefits, and it is this balancing act, always precarious in the novel, that Jane must learn. Her subjectivity is a hard-won possession that cannot be taken for granted, a selfhood that oscillates between a quasi-autonomous self-respect which enables Jane to claim her own self-worth – '*I* care for myself. The more solitary, the more friendless, the more unsustained I am, the more I will respect myself' (Brontë 1996, 356) – and a more uncertain self-respect, one which depends on the reflections of approval from the faces of others: 'I know

I should think well of myself; but that is not enough; if others don't love me, I would rather die than live – I cannot bear to be solitary and hated' (81).

Jane's ambiguous subjectivity – her wandering 'I' – is shown in almost every episode of the text. Even 'love' itself is problematic in its alternating of subject and object positions, and in its affirmation of a self-worth that is nonetheless expressed in the language of possession by the other. At the outset of her affair with Rochester, he does not love her for herself alone, but for the fey images of sprites and elves that he weaves around her, and which Jane consistently resists, demanding instead that he accept her as a woman rather than an object conjured out of his own desires. Love does not solve the problem of subjectivity, as Lacanian psychoanalysis demonstrates. In his writings on spoken language, Lacan discusses the fundamental communicative failures entailed in speech and conversation: 'What I seek in speech is the response of the other. What constitutes me as a subject is my question. In order to be recognized by the other, I utter what was only in view of what will be. In order to find him, I call him by a name that he must assume or refuse in order to reply to me' (Lacan 1988, 94). In the case of *Jane Eyre*, there is a certain congruity between Rochester's and Jane's fantasies of each other, which speaks of their mutual attraction from the outset. If Mr Rochester 'thought unaccountably of fairy tales' (139) when he first encountered Jane after his fall from his horse, she had interpreted his dog as 'Gytrash', a mythical hound from Bessie's stories. The difference between them is that in Jane's case, 'the man, the human being, broke the spell at once' (128), whereas for Rochester, there is a consistent will to misrecognition in his dealings with Jane. He refuses at times to believe in her substantiality: 'If I dared, I'd touch you, to see if you are substance or shadow, you elf! – but I'd as soon offer to take hold of a blue *ignis fatuus* light in a marsh', he proclaims on her return from Mrs Reed's deathbed (275). But Jane insists that she would 'rather be a *thing* than an angel' (294), and is self-assertive throughout her courtship, demanding repeatedly that Rochester see her as human rather than as a figure proceeding from his over-heated imagination. The erotic attraction of his fantasies of her does not entirely compensate her for the loss of subject identity it entails. The illusion of subjectivity is more easily maintained in this structurally unequal relationship (an inequality that is also emblematic of the inequalities of Victorian society more generally) by a man than by a woman. Rochester calls Jane into a mode of being that emphasizes the insubstantiality of her subjectivity; in her reiteration of his 'master' status, however, she calls him into a mode of being that consistently recreates him as a man of substance and power. The power is at once sexy and exciting in a rather masochistic way; but it is also utterly threatening in its potential for the annihilation of Jane's hard-won identity. And this is both a psychoanalytic observation, proceeding at once from mind and body (Rochester is more experienced and physically stronger than Jane) and a materialist one, proceeding from the social structures which they each inhabit rather differently because of their relative class and gender status.

No matter how eagerly her projected marriage is desired, therefore, Jane cannot ignore the fact that her identity will be subsumed into Rochester's, and describes her discomfort at this thought in terms that derive from gothic fantasy. On the eve of her wedding, she writes:

> *I*, at least, had nothing more to do: there were my trunks, packed, locked, corded, ranged in a row along the wall of my little chamber; to-morrow, at this time, they would be far on their road to London: and so should I (D.V.),[7] or rather, not I, but one Jane Rochester, a person whom as yet I knew not. The cards of address alone remained to nail on … I could not persuade myself to affix them … Mrs Rochester! She did not exist: she would not be born till to-morrow … I would wait to be assured she had come into the world alive, before I assigned to her all that property. It was enough that in yonder closet, opposite my dressing-table, garments said to be hers had already displaced my black stuff Lowood frock … for not to me appertained that suit of wedding raiment; the pearl-coloured robe, the vapoury veil … I shut the closet, to conceal the strange, wraith-like apparel it contained; which, at this evening hour … gave out certainly a most ghostly shimmer through the shadow of my apartment. (308)

Her present self is substantial – it can be emphasized textually, as often in the text, by italicization; her future self is merely a ghostly projection. Her anxiety is of course proleptic: the wedding will not take place and Jane Rochester will remain, for the time being a fantasy figure. But this is also emblematic of a more general anxiety about the nature of female experience and subjectivity – a woman's identity is *covered* by the men in her life;[8] her status is defined by his; her freedoms are curtailed by his permissions; marriage is ownership at least as much as partnership, something made abundantly clear to Jane in Rochester's 'eastern allusion' to her as better than 'the Grand Turk's whole seraglio' (301).

Thus, whilst David Copperfield sees his marriage to Agnes as the completion of the quest of his life, Jane at this stage figures her marriage as an ending, as the termination of self-possession and of whatever individualism her education, experience and career have provided her with so far. In a quite literal sense, she will become her husband's property – a fact dwelled upon with some relish by Rochester. Describing Jane as 'a little tyrant' during their courtship, he says to her: ' "it is your time now ... but it will be mine presently: and when once I have fairly seized you, to have and to hold, I'll just – figuratively speaking – attach you to a chain like this" (touching his watchguard) ... "I'll wear you in my bosom, lest my jewel I should tyne" ' (303). In the material circumstances of Victorian England, the 'chain' is more than a mere 'figure' of speech. This novel, however, is a romance, and Rochester's joking threat is neatly reversed at the end of narrative, when, blind and maimed, he hands her his watch and chain, having 'no use for it' (495), and projects a rather different relationship in their second attempt to get married: 'Hitherto I have hated to be helped – to be led; henceforth, I feel, I shall hate it no more. I did not like to put my hand into a hireling's, but it is pleasant to feel it circled by Jane's little fingers' (496). It is Jane who becomes the active and controlling party at the end; Rochester is the *object* of her affection. As Kate Flint puts it, we should be alert to the fact that in the phrase 'Reader, I married him' (498), the grammar is active (Flint 2002, 181), rather than the more usual passive construction – he married me. In the end, Jane both gets her man and – somewhat fortuitously – retains her self-possession.

There are many coincidences and happy accidents (for Jane, at least) that bring about this dénouement.[9] But key to its realization is Jane's self-assertion; and key to her self-assertion is her preference for fantasy, derived from influential fictions, rather than cold reality. In her battle with St. John Rivers about whether her destiny is to become his wife and curate in missionary work in India, she is sorely tempted to give in: 'I was tempted to cease struggling with him', she says of their last encounter: tempted 'to rush down the torrent of his will into the gulf of his existence, and there lose my own' (465). The metaphors of a sublime landscape are very telling; they imply the utter loss of self-possession that submission to St. John would involve. It is at once dangerously attractive because it would mean the loss of uncomfortable self-consciousness and hopelessly unattractive, for precisely the same reason. When she pleads to God to show which decision she should make, she hears Rochester's voice calling her name. (No surprise this, since earlier Jane has admitted her confusion of God and man in the figure of Rochester: 'My future husband was becoming to me my whole world … He stood between me and every thought of religion, as an eclipse intervenes between man and the broad sun. I could not, in those days, see God for his creature: of whom I had made an idol' [307]. No wonder, then, that Elizabeth Rigby found the novel irreligious.) His calling, whether real or imagined, makes her assert herself: 'It was *my* time to assume ascendancy. *My* powers were in play, and in force' (467). She stands firm against the torrent of St. John's will, disguising her own desires in the matter by an appeal to preternatural forces beyond her. This sublimation of sexual desire probably fools no one, but it is a neatly satisfying ending for readers who empathize and identify with Jane's struggles.

Jane Eyre presents wish-fulfilment, fantasy and romance, and a figuring of feminine subjectivity which depends on Jane's relations with the masculine other(s), in a way that simply is not true of David. And this can be directly related to her subject formation in relation, not to family, but to fictions. The nearest thing Jane has to a mother in this novel is the nursemaid, Bessie Leaven. Bessie, we are told, '*fed* our eager attention with passages of love and adventure taken from old fairy tales and older ballads; or (as at a later period I discovered) from the pages of *Pamela*, and *Henry, Earl of Morland*' (15, my emphasis). Bessie's stories include the ballad of the poor orphan child whose 'feet … are sore and … [whose] limbs are weary' (29); and the whispered and overheard tales of ghostly visitations she shares with a fellow servant after Jane's incarceration in the Red Room: ' "Something passed her, all dressed in white, and vanished" – "A great black dog behind him" – "Three loud raps on the chamber door" … &c. &c.' (27). All of these fictions are strangely predictive of Jane's eventual fate, suggesting the ways in which her subjectivity is formed by fictional models. Her story, of course, bears an uncanny resemblance to *Pamela*, as at least one early reviewer noted with disapproval (Rigby in Allott 1973, 67). Jane, like the orphan in the ballad, will traverse dangerous territory in a state of physical and emotional collapse after her departure from Rochester. Her first meeting with Rochester is heralded by his large black dog; and Thornfield turns out to be haunted by the all-too-substantial presence of Bertha Mason, who does indeed pass Jane dressed all in white.

In addition to this oral tradition passed on by Bessie, Jane also has her own reading to support her developing sense of self. We first meet her hidden behind a curtain in the library, reading Thomas Bewick's

History of British Birds, which she devours with rapt attention, and whose illustrations fill her mind with the images of sublime nature that she will later reproduce in the watercolours she paints, pictures, incidentally, that first really capture Rochester's attention. To comfort herself after the Red Room incident, she requests *Gulliver's Travels*, commenting, that in contrast to the fairy stories she has heard:

> This book I had again and again perused with delight; I considered it a narrative of facts ... Liliput and Brobdignag being, in my creed, solid parts of the earth's surface, I doubted not that I might one day ... see with my own eyes, the little fields, houses and trees, the diminutive people ... in the one realm; and the corn-fields forest-high, the mighty mastiffs, the monster cats, the tower-like men and women, of the other. (28–9)

A sturdy empiricist in some ways, Jane has searched for fairies and found that there aren't any. But the child fantasist who takes Gulliver's satirical travel narrative as 'fact' is well armed to imagine impossible dreams for her own life.

At the same time, there are also many texts that Jane resists, including that most authoritative text of all, the Bible. When questioned by Mr Brocklehurst about her knowledge of scripture, she proves herself to be a resistant reader, announcing that she likes the visionary Book of Revelations and the adventure stories of the Old Testament, but has no time for the Psalms, which are 'not interesting' (42). Indeed, her Biblical knowledge appears very limited, to the extent that at Lowood, Helen Burns apparently tells her for the first time about Christ's message of 'turning the other cheek' (66). And the infant Jane has no time for Samuel Johnson's *Rasselas*, the book that Helen is reading when they first meet because 'I saw nothing about fairies, nothing about genii; no bright variety seemed spread over the closely printed pages' (60). (This is, by the way, a novel that argues that happiness may be unobtainable.) In other words, her preference is markedly for romance rather than realism, for passion rather than forbearance, and for self-validation rather than self-abnegation. All the same, the lessons Helen teaches through her description of Christ's teaching and her own patient example do have their effect. In contrast to the impassioned account she gives of her childhood to her schoolfriend, the account she makes to Miss Temple is far more restrained:

> I resolved in the depth of my heart that I would be most moderate and most correct; and, having reflected a few moments in order to arrange

coherently what I had to say, I told her all the story of my sad childhood. Exhausted by emotion, my language was more subdued than it generally was when it developed that sad theme; and mindful of Helen's warnings against the indulgence of resentment, I infused into the narrative far less of gall and wormwood than ordinary. Thus restrained and simplified, it sounded more credible. (83)

Repression renders her credible, and begins the process of bringing her the respect and affection of others, without which, as she has earlier declared, she cannot live. Self-respect, self-possession and subjectivity are instituted at school for Jane not so much in terms of lack and loss, as in terms of new-found and sustaining friendships. But the narrative of her life demonstrates the extent to which any subjectivity is involved in a constant negotiation with the external circumstances of its life.

Notes

1. The quotation in the quotation is from the German philosopher, Wilhelm von Humboldt.
2. I have made this argument elsewhere, in a rather different context. See Robbins 2000b, 106. I am grateful to John Stokes for his commentary on that essay when it was in the draft stage.
3. The best account of Dickens' life for sheer reading pleasure is Ackroyd 1991.
4. This fragment appears, very nearly unaltered in Chapter 11 of *David Copperfield*. Readers who want to see the points of resemblance can consult Dickens, ed. Buckley 1990, 766–72 for the full text of the fragment.
5. This term is Kristeva's development of the Lacanian subject. In French, *sujet-en-procès* designates a subjectivity that is forever in the process of 'becoming' rather than ever achieving the status of a fixed entity. In addition, there is a pun in French on the word *procès*, which also means 'trial' – thus the subject in process is also always 'on trial'. For Kristeva this means that the subject is always being tested against the norms and values of its society, and the subject experiences these tests as often coercive, just as the law is coercive. For an account of this term see Kristeva 1984; for an explanation of its implications see Robbins 2000a, 127–9.
6. The resonance of this phrase derives from Eve Kosfosky Sedgwick's book *Between Men*, in which she argues persuasively that the literary discourse of the nineteenth century is a largely masculinist construction which focuses on male–male relationships rather than on romantic love (male–female relationships), which are the novel's usual 'cover story'. See Sedgwick 1985.

7. D. V. stands for *Deo volonte*, God-willing.
8. This is a reference to the concept of *femme couverte*, or covered woman. In the law of England at the time of the novel's publication, a married woman's identity was legally *covered* by her husband's.
9. Jane's success in the novel is at the expense of just about every other female character, as I have argued elsewhere (see Robbins 2000(a), 40–7). The *locus classicus* of contemporary critiques of Jane's bourgeois individualism – the liberal feminism in which a middle-class heroine asserts her equality with her middle-class male contemporaries – is Gayatri Chakravorty Spivak's 'Three Women's Texts and a Critique of Imperialism'. See Spivak 1986, 262–80.

4   James Joyce and
Self-Portraiture

Near the beginning of James Joyce's 1916 novel, *A Portrait of the Artist as Young Man*, we come across the 'artist's' first artistic production, a limited and repetitive poem which consists entirely of the words 'Pull out his eyes / Apologise' (Joyce 1992, 4). Towards the end of the novel, an apparently more sophisticated Stephen writes another repetitive poem, this time in the form of a villanelle (Joyce 1992, 242–3). The second poem, scrawled on the back of a cigarette packet, comes to Stephen Dedalus in a moment of inspiration, which he identifies as an annunciation (236), but the transcendent moment is fleeting, and the sordid space of his room reasserts itself. The villanelle form is a technically difficult form to write, especially in English, a language with a scarcity of easy rhyme words. It consists of nineteen lines, divided into five three-line and one four-line stanzas, with only two rhyming sounds. The first and third lines of the first stanza repeat as the 'refrain' of the poem, forming the last lines of succeeding stanzas and the last two lines of the poem as a whole. Its movement dramatizes repetition with difference, for in the different contexts of succeeding stanzas, the same words come to function differently. And to this extent, the later poem and the earlier poem share something quite important: repetition and difference reiterated across the pages of the novel constitute one of this novel's major themes. They stand for the ways in which subjectivity is made: the child repeats the words and gestures of others, but his repetition is always a modification of what has gone before, refracted through his developing idiolect and increasing consciousness of his own subject position.

The first poem, for all its apparent simplicity, is a strangely over-determined production. Its immediate context is that the infant Stephen is hiding under the table for some childish infraction of household rules – an infraction that is not specified. 'His mother said: / – O, Stephen will apologise. / Dante said: / – O, if not, the eagles will come

and pull out his eyes' (Joyce 1992, 4). As a child already fascinated by
language, and already anxious to appropriate to himself the words and
cultural products he hears around him ('that was *his* story ... that was
his song' [Joyce 1992, 3, my emphasis]), the poem he produces is a psy-
chologically accurate representation of a childish strategy. He plays
with the words because he likes their sound – the fact that they rhyme.
He repeats the words, and thereby extends power over them, masters
them by rendering them meaningless in repetition. He makes something out of them which was not intended to be when they were first
spoken out of the mouths of his elders and betters. At the same time,
however, the poem, realistic representation of infant subjectivity as it
may be, is also clearly open to psychoanalytical interpretation. It
enacts a moment where the child is beginning to learn the rules of
social interaction – the prohibitions and taboos that hedge his subjectivity around. He has done something he should not have done, and
must therefore apologize. Dante's threat that if he does not apologize
he will be blinded, is certainly open to an interpretation which associates blinding with castration, the punishment posited by Freud for
inadequate repression of forbidden desires: and in his essay on
Hoffmann's 'The Sandman', 'The Uncanny', Freud makes explicit the
relationship between eyes and castration anxieties:

> the fear of losing one's eye is a terrible one in children. Many adults retain
> their apprehensiveness in this respect, and no physical injury is so much
> dreaded by them as an injury to the eye. We are accustomed to say, too,
> that we will treasure a thing as the apple of our eye. A study of dreams,
> phantasies and myths has taught us that anxiety about one's eyes, the
> fear of going blind, is often enough a substitute for the dread of being
> castrated. The self-blinding of the mythical criminal Oedipus, was
> simply a mitigated form of the punishment of castration. (Freud
> 1986, 352)

At some level, therefore, we must read Stephen's first poem as representing the institution of his subjectivity through the process of repression and fear. It is through sight that desire operates, in the Freudian
universe, hence the things and beings one loves are 'the apple of our
eye'. The 'I' of subjectivity is also a 'seeing eye', one might say, and loss
of 'eyes' entails a loss of the 'I', the loss of (gendered) identity itself. The
poem, such as it is, is also therefore, a marker of Stephen's initiation
into the trials of the Oedipus Complex, and his entry into the symbolic
order of the law of the father, both the real 'daddy' and the potent

mythology of the heavenly father and his more earthly (and earthy) hypostases. For of course, the fact that it is an *eagle* that will wreak this damage on the recalcitrant child, is also significant: one of the many social structures into which Stephen will have to insert himself in the course of his story is that of the Catholic Church, the Church of Rome. In an act of metonymy, the eagle, sign of the Roman legions of old, stands in for that Church, with its prohibitions and taboos on desire and the flesh. And the fact that Stephen is as yet too young to make this connection does not matter, for Joyce was making it, and wanted his readers to make it too. This is version of subjectivity in which the subject is *subject to* forces the child can neither articulate nor comprehend, but which are nonetheless powerfully coercive in his subject-formation.

His more technically sophisticated 'adult' poem, the untitled villanelle, represents one element of Stephen's attempt to free himself from the cultural coercions of his subject position. It is a very sensuous poem, deriving some of its imagery, as well as its form, from the writings of the 'decadent' poet of the 1890s, as Seamus Deane has noted (Joyce 1992, 320–1n). But although it is a poem about the desire to escape desire itself – a description of sensual and sexual weariness, and an attempt to say farewell to the beloved – the poem's speaker is still held by his beloved's 'gaze' and still fascinated by her looks and body (243). He may be weary of it, but he has not yet extricated himself from the woman's attraction. The imagery of the poem is largely derived from the language of Roman Catholicism, and its sexual content is barely disguised by the sacred images that are put to 'profane' usages: thus the desired woman is the 'lure of the fallen seraphim'; 'the smoke of praise' refers us to the incense of Catholic ritual; the sounds of lovemaking are a 'eucharistic hymn'; and love is an overflowing 'chalice'. If this is the sublimation of desire, its terms do not securely disguise its nature. And just as it inhabits a repeating form, the poem also describes an act of rebellion against Catholic injunctions against the sins of the flesh which is absolutely inscribed by the taboos it seeks to break. There can be no rebellious blasphemy or profanity if the structures of belief are not at least minimally still intact.

The villanelle enacts the awkwardness of the process of self-possession and self-definition. Its two-steps-forward, one-step-back structure makes it clear that Stephen Dedalus's subjectivity is produced both by, and in reaction against, the culture that surrounds him. In fact, it is hard to imagine a text more committed to expressing the impossibility of escaping the structures that constrain subjectivity than *A Portrait*. From its opening virtuoso sequence, the narrative represents for its readers all the elements that go into the making of subjectivity, from the senses, to language, from the secure structure of the family to its threatening confinements and punishments. It produces a representation of a self first of all in relation to the various sense impressions, as Hugh Kenner has noted. The child situates himself in relation to

> each of the five senses in turn; hearing (the story of the moocow), sight (his father's face), taste (lemon platt), touch (warm and cold), smell (the oil-sheet). The audible soothes: the visible disturbs. Throughout Joyce's work, the senses are symbolically disposed. Smell is the means of discriminating empirical realities ('His mother had a nicer smell than his father' ...), sight corresponds to the phantasms of oppression, hearing to the imaginative life. Touch and taste together are the modes of sex. Hearing, here, comes first, via a piece of imaginative literature. (Kenner 1998, 10–11)

The hierarchy of the senses that Kenner identifies is, of course, a reversal of the usual order. Sight is normally the most highly regarded of the senses; smell is generally relegated to a very low level indeed. But before the child learns the importance of sight (before he is threatened with 'blinding' by eagles), he constructs his own sensual universe, with his own preferences, and to some extent these idiosyncratic choices prevail throughout the text. Stephen Dedalus in the opening passage is on the cusp of leaving behind his Lacanian infancy, and is just beginning to speak. At this stage, the sense impressions are more important than their conventional ordering into a linguistically made hierarchy of significance. Moreover, it is no accident that the very first words of the novel are also the very first words of the literary genre most associated with children and primitive emotion – the fairy story. The child who lives in the story that his father tells him – Baby Tuckoo – cannot yet articulate his own name, Stephen Dedalus; but he already has a sense of himself as a 'hero', in the sense, of course, of the main character of a particular narrative, but also in the sense of someone of heroic proportions. Just like David Copperfield before him, no matter what the other differences in narrative representation between the two texts, Stephen will come to know himself in relation to pre-existing fictions, fictions explicitly associated with his father. Family relations and cultural relations slide into each other and become virtually indistinguishable. His attempt to claim language's capacity for self-expression for himself ('that was his story') will be repeatedly doomed.

For the *Portrait* presents us, *avant la lettre*, with a quasi-Structuralist account of language. Just like Carroll's Humpty-Dumpty, Stephen Dedalus begins from the assumption that words and things, and especially names, have a secure designatory function. Humpty-Dumpty knows with arrogant certainty that with a name like his, he must be the nice round shape he is: Stephen similarly 'knows' that his is a hero's name, that his name constitutes him as different from other boys and men with ordinary names like Roche, Doyle or – as in this example – Dolan, the name of the Prefect of Studies who affects not to hear what Stephen's name is, and offends him by asking him twice:

> The great men in history had names like that and nobody made fun out of them. It was his own name he should have made fun of if he had wanted to make fun. Dolan: it was like the name of a woman that washed clothes. (Joyce 1992, 56–7)

This self-conception as hero is important to the child, and he does not wish to relinquish it for it bolsters his sense of self-importance. Unlike David Copperfield, he expresses – at least at this stage – no doubts about his heroism. At the same time, though, Stephen learns very early that words and things are not intimately related, so that a hero's name need not designate a hero after all. The eagle poem shows him experimenting with language as pure sound. Slightly later, whilst doing his geography homework, he discovers that it is very difficult to learn the place names of South America. If the name and the place were really related, if sign and referent were really connected, there ought to be no difficulty: but thinking like this makes his head hurt. In an early metaphysical moment, he considers his own place in the universe, attempting to place himself securely in it, by narrating his place in the flyleaf of his geography book: 'Stephen Dedalus, Class of Elements, Clongowes Wood College, Sallins, County Kildare, Ireland, Europe, The World, The Universe' (12). What is outside the universe, he wonders? Only God can answer a question like that, is his reply; but this starts him off on another – equally frightening – train of thought, for God's name is different in different languages. And the only way to stop the terror of the slide into meaninglessness is to assert an act of faith: 'God's real name was God' (13). Although the child resists the implications of his thought, however, and although this whole sequence is presented as the slightly fevered imaginings of a little boy who is coming down with a childhood illness, the fundamentals of the Saussurean propositions are in place: language is arbitrary – the place names do recreate the places on the map in the mind of the child who tries to learn them; language is relational (there is repeated emphasis on the word 'different' in his discussion of the South American map); and language is conventional – in the Irish community he belongs to, God's real name *is* God.

Stephen is also intensely involved in the Kristevan semiotic: the language effects that have to do with sound and rhythm as opposed to semantic content. The first poem is primarily for Stephen, whatever it may suggest to the reader, about the sounds of rhyming words, the connection 'forged' between words that otherwise have no relationship. His is always, from the outset, a poet's view of language, in which sound matters at least as much as sense. He loves the sentences in his spelling book, for example, because they are 'like poetry' (Joyce 1992, 6). Other words produce sensations of displeasure and disgust, emotions that Stephen cannot, at first, analyse. When another boy calls one of his schoolfellows a 'suck', Stephen is vaguely disturbed by the word, but does not quite know why:

> Suck was a queer word … the sound was ugly. Once he had washed his hands in the lavatory of the Wicklow Hotel and his father pulled the stopper up by the chain and the dirty water went down through the hole in the basin. And when it had all gone down slowly the hole in the basin had made a sound like that: suck. Only louder. (Joyce 1992, 8)

For the adult reader, his sense that it is a 'queer' word is not merely the innocent designation of its sound. We know what Stephen does not quite understand – that the boy accused of being a 'suck' is probably involved in the homoerotic practice of 'fagging' – of gaining favour in the school hierarchy by acting as servant to older boys and teachers. But Stephen does know – physically rather than linguistically – that word has some potentially shocking content, which has something to do with the forbidden world of the body, making him go hot and cold in the memory of it: remembering the sound of the word and the sound of the dirty water, produces a bodily response that his consciousness cannot trace to its origins. The disgust for certain words, as well as his attraction to others (like the metaphors for the Virgin Mary – *'Tower of*

Ivory ... House of Gold' [35]), remains with Stephen throughout his life. And, despite their structuralist failings, they are also potent in their often-physical effects on him. On a trip with his father, visiting the university anatomy lecture room, he comes with a sudden shock on the word *foetus* carved, several times, into the wood of one of the desks. The word produces vivid imagery in his mind of the young men, students in the long-distant past, who had carved an obscenity into a desk, and he imagines especially a particular student, writing the rude word: 'He was dressed in loose grey clothes and had tan boots' (Joyce 1992, 95). His father's attempts to evoke his student days' words are less influential than a random piece of obscene graffiti, which is, of course, significant in itself. But, here, a whole scene opens up to him, which has nothing to do with the word itself – for *foetus* cannot really signify a broad-shouldered student in loose grey clothes, and wearing ill-matching tan boots.

The novel shows the extent to which subjectivity is always in a dialogical relationship with other people's words, whether lovely poetic words, or hideous obscenities. As Mikhail Bakhtin puts it:

> [T]he speech experience of each individual is shaped and developed in continuous and constant interaction with others' individual utterances. This experience can be characterized to some degree as the process of *assimilation* – more or less creative – of others' words ... Our speech, that is, all our utterances (including creative works), is filled with others' words ... These words of others carry with them their own expression, their own evaluative tone, which we assimilate, rework, and re-accentuate. (Bakhtin 1986, 89)

In Stephen's case, the reworking and re-accentuation are rendered especially acute in the context of an English language – a mother tongue – that is also an alien speech to the Irish child. To some extent, this sense of a language made by others is, of course, true for all language learners; we all insert ourselves into language communities that pre-exist us, and which subject us to rules that are not of our own making. But *A Portrait* is a very specifically Irish text. It *is* accented differently from any text written in England, with structures of speech that derive from the particular colonial situation in which it was written. The Irish language of Gaelic may have been very nearly wiped out as a result of the predations of English imperialism; but the speech patterns of Irish-English bear its traces, as well as the traces of a certain loss of confidence in fluency. For instance, the common reiteration of

Irish-English in tag-phrases such as 'so it is' attached to any simple
statement, can be understood as a defensive gesture, a speech act that
requests the auditor to comprehend a statement spoken, as it were, in a
foreign tongue. An example of that pattern appears in the very
first lines of Joyce's text: 'Once upon a time, and a very good time it
was ...' (3). It is both a loss (of self-assurance in a language which
belongs to one's community) and a gain (it adds new inflections to the
language of the other).

   Although all speech is 'acquired', inherited, learned, however, one of
Joyce's concerns in the novel is to suggest the ways in which the politics
of the English language in Ireland in the context of the Home Rule
debates and the rise of Irish nationalism, affect the subjectivities that
inhabit that foreign tongue. As John Paul Riquelme has put it: 'in
A Portrait the artist's activity is essentially rewriting. Joyce indicates
within the text the task performed by every serious writer: the act of
revision that is at once the author's writing and reading (as interpretation) of his self-made image in language' (Riquelme 1998, 90). To be the
artist of the title involves first of all an acute awareness of the problems
of language *per se*; second, an engagement or dialogue with the language practices that already exist around one; and third, a rewriting of
that language into a new form. In a key moment of the novel, Stephen
discusses the possibility of a vocation to the priesthood with an English
Jesuit convert. He discovers that the Englishman does not know the
word 'tundish' (the funnel for pouring oil into a lamp), and is shocked
that a 'countryman of Ben Jonson' is so ill-equipped to speak precisely.
It is a moment of crisis, and Stephen, in a much-quoted passage, thinks
to himself:

> – The language in which we are speaking is his before it is mine. How
> different are the words *home, Christ, ale, master*, on his lips and on mine!
> I cannot speak or write these words without unrest of spirit. His lan-
> guage, so familiar and so foreign, will always be for me an acquired
> speech. I have not made or accepted its words ... My soul frets in the
> shadow of his language. (Joyce 1992, 205)

The choice of those four simple nouns as the evidence of the foreign-
ness of English speech is fascinating in itself. In this language, the word
home becomes *unheimlich*, unfamiliar or uncanny because it sounds
so different from the way the Irish-English speaker would pronounce
it. *Christ*, who stands for religious belief, and who is supposed to be the

home of the weary soul, is shown to be a foreign imposition. *Ale*, or beer, an ordinary – homely – drink, is displaced and defamiliarized. What is at stake is *mastery* – 'The question is ... which is to be master?' as Humpty-Dumpty puts it (Carroll 1970, 269).

In Britain, accent still matters. It is not merely a question of identifying the region of a speaker's origin (I'm from the North of England, and pronounce words like 'class' with a short /a/ as in /hat/, and British people know immediately what general region I must come from); it is also a marker of socio-economic status. In *Great Expectations*, Estella knows that Pip is merely a common labouring boy not simply from the evidence of his clothing and the manual labour inscribed on his hands ('What coarse hands he has! And what thick boots!' [Dickens 1985, 90]), but because he speaks differently from her: 'He calls the knaves, Jacks, this boy!' The accent of the English upper classes – not for nothing often identified as the Queen's English – is a mode of pronunciation and intonation that implies mastery, not only of the language, but also over others who do not speak in the same way. Stephen's meditation on the sounds of these 'foreign' words, therefore, dramatizes the sense that he has no ownership over the very words that he must use to inscribe his own self-possession – he is master of nothing. Even the word 'I', which he will only really use at the end of his linguistic journey in *A Portrait*, is a foreign imposition, ensuring that even selfhood is always already estranged from the voice that says it. That Irish-English speakers were aware of the importance of accent is clear in this period: we know, for instance, that Oscar Wilde deliberately lost his Irish intonation and pronunciation almost immediately on his arrival at Oxford in the 1870s, reinventing himself as the successful impersonator the English gentleman: 'My Irish accent was one of the many things I forgot at Oxford', he said (Ellmann 1987, 37). George Bernard Shaw, on the other hand, defiantly retained his accent as a kind of political act, and even wrote one of his most famous plays, *Pygmalion* (1912) as a rebuke to English snobbery about the way other people talk. In his Preface to the play, he wrote: 'it is impossible for an Englishman to open his mouth without making some other Englishman despise him' (Shaw 1977, 327). This contempt for others' speech is even more marked in the case of those whose accents are not identifiably 'English' at all. And this is not merely an English trait: Stephen himself is 'infected' by contempt for the speech patterns of others, consistently noticing pronunciation and intonation, for instance in relation to one of his fellow university students, an Ulsterman who pronounces *science* as a monosyllable, and whose 'voice ... accent ... mind ... offended him' (Joyce 1992, 209–10).

Most importantly of all, though, is the novel's enactment of the most significant and challenging of Saussure's insights. It is not merely that language is arbitrary, relational and conventional; it is also *constitutive* of the reality it sets out to describe. The language community in which one lives, combined with the developmental stage one has achieved in one's life, constitute the kinds of thought it is possible to have, the kinds of response one might have to one's world, and ultimately, determine the subjectivity one is able to inhabit. The point about accents and pronunciation implies that subjectivity is formed in reaction against, and in impersonation of, the words of others. But despite their major importance in this book, they are less significant than either language's semantic content (what it says) and language's grammatical structures (the logical connections syntax enables one to make, as well as the connections syntax disbars). The brilliance of *A Portrait* is the extremely concise way in which Joyce was able to dramatize the limitations that speech and language acquisition more generally impose on the speaking subject. Any attempt to rewrite especially the early sequences of the text from a different perspective – for instance the omniscient anonymous third-person narrator of classic realist fiction, or the ironically distanced autobiographical voice one finds in Dickens's autobiographical novels – immediately exposes the limitations of those supposedly potent narrative modes. When Pip sits down to his fateful Christmas dinner, in a 'false position' because he has robbed the pantry to feed the convict in the churchyard, the perspective comes from an adult looking back, describing what happened, but also judging it in relation to subsequent knowledge. But the narrator is also in a 'false position' because the focalization of the scene explicitly combines the sensibility and consciousness of the child Pip with the ironic and distanced view of the adult Pip, looking back. The language, the ideas and the modes of expression – the rhetorical complications of the scene – are all forms that belong to the adult, not the child. What child could speak, for instance, of 'those obscure corners of pork of which the pig, when alive, had least reason to be proud' (Dickens 1985, 56)? There is a linguistic sophistication in Dickens' evocation of the scene to which the child Pip has no access: its comedy and timing are mature, not childlike.

In contrast, when Stephen sits down to his first 'adult' Christmas dinner, although the adults loom large in the scene, and although their speech dominates it, the narrative itself entirely inhabits the child's perspective. The child's consciousness is far more limited, hemmed in by inexperience and incomprehension of the argument about politics and religion in relation to the Church's condemnation of the Irish nationalist hero, Charles Stewart Parnell. The adult speech is reported, but not 'glossed' by the narrating voice, for the child whose consciousness that voice impersonates, does not really understand what the arguments are about. Waiting for the turkey to arrive, Stephen thinks:

> Why did Mr Barrett in Clongowes call his pandybat a turkey? But Clongowes was far away: and the warm heavy smell of turkey and ham and celery rose from the plates and dishes and the great fire was banked high and red in the grate and the green ivy and red holly made you feel so happy and when dinner was ended the big plum-pudding would be carried in, studded with peeled almonds and sprigs of holly, with bluish fire running around it and a little green flag flying from the top. (Joyce 1992, 28)

The contrast in narrative method is instructive. In *Great Expectations*, the narrator's voice is distanced from the experience he is retelling. This is the viewpoint of an adult looking back; he knows the outcome of his story, knows, therefore, what was important, the formative of his life experiences. He knows what he has become, and he believes he knows *how* he has become the middle-aged gentleman, Mr Pirrip, who tells us the story of his early life. In contrast, Joyce's technique speaks of a self that is still in the process of formation – a self, indeed, that will always still be in the process of formation, a *sujet-en-procès*. Joyce's text looks different on the page because so much of it is made up of dialogue, reported without authoritative commentary: no judgement is explicitly vouchsafed. Moreover, the speech is staccato, interrupted and slangy, not rounded, oratorical and fluent. And when we enter Stephen's own thought processes, as in the quoted paragraph above, we do so typically with the child beginning his meditation on the scene before him wondering about the arbitrary nature of the word 'turkey', which can mean both Christmas dinner and an implement for the imposition of infantine discipline. The word 'turkey' sets off a brief excursion into memories of school – no surprise, this, because for children school is a major reference point. But memory is displaced by the physical sensations of the present scene, of what it *feels* like to be in a room with roaring fire, and with hot, heavily scented foods. The description of what he *feels* is the child's own description, constructed in a syntax that dramatizes the child's lack of syntactical sophistication. What he sees, and smells, in front of him, to paraphrase is: turkey and ham and celery and plates and dishes and fire and green ivy and red holly ... This is the syntax of parataxis; it operates entirely by co-ordination, and contains no subordination – that is, the syntax eschews the grammar of causality and contrast (words like because, although, therefore, however), and of multiple tenses (past and future) in its excitement over the presence of the present moment. We are reading a child's sensory impressions – a recreation of sensory overload; but we are also reading the child's inability to process his sense impressions into narrative coherence.

The process of acquiring the capacity to create coherence is at once the general experience of language acquisition, and the special experience of learning artistry. Before Stephen Dedalus becomes a 'writer' – an artist – he is a reader (or, in that first story his father tells him, an auditor), placing himself in relation to fictions created by others. Just like David Copperfield before him, Stephen Dedalus attains subjectivity by imaginatively reliving the fictional adventures of others. Like David, his novel is the rewriting of a number of traditions of fiction in his own image. His subjectivity is also, that is, a literary fabrication. The dialogism that Bakhtin identifies in relation to speech acquisition is also at work in Stephen's attempts to find a writing voice – sometimes via explicitly intertextual references to other people's texts; and often by implication.

When, for example, Stephen attempts his first heroic act, when he complains to the Rector about having been unfairly beaten at school, the terms in which he imagines his actions are directly drawn from the books he has been reading. Similar protests against injustice, he reasons, have been 'done before by somebody in history'; if he decides to go ahead with his protest, he will become like a hero in a history book or a book of adventure that make up his staple reading matter (Joyce 1992, 54–5). He wants to behave like the people in books; he wants to appropriate the versions of heroism to be found in this rather narrowly conceived version of history for himself. And when he does so, successfully by his own lights, he is indeed treated like a hero by his schoolfriends – this time, in the slightly reduced terms of the schoolboy fiction that is presumably their staple reading matter, where heroism is measured not by territory conquered or numbers of men slain, but by the smaller measure of his school friends '[flinging] their caps into the air' and giving Stephen three cheers (60). The problem with appropriating the models of other people's writings, however, is such appropriation can rebound on the plagiarist himself. This same episode, narrated from his father's point of view somewhat later, reduces whatever heroism Stephen had achieved – cuts him down to size, one might say, in a rather different version of a castration story. Mr Dedalus 'imitated the mincing nasal tone of the provincial', and shows how the adult world sees the opportunity for 'a famous laugh' over the child's precocity (76).

In another episode, Stephen becomes obsessed with reliving the adventures of *The Count of Monte Cristo*. Like a latter-day Don Quixote, he makes the topography of Dublin conform to his imagined version of the count's milieu, turning an ordinary little house in Blackrock into the home of the lady Mercedes. He imagines himself making the grand gestures of the novel's hero and constructs a fantasy cave 'on the parlour table … out of transfers and paper flowers and coloured tissue paper and strips of silver and golden paper in which chocolate is wrapped' (64–5). The fragility and the gaudiness of this self-making are, of course, imaged in the flimsiness of the trashy materials he has to hand. His obsession with the life models he finds in books continues throughout his life. When he repents the sins of the flesh, he uses the works of the Catholic divines to construct a model for the life he will lead: 'Sunday was dedicated to the mystery of the Holy Trinity, Monday to the Holy Ghost, Tuesday to the Guardian Angels' and so on (Joyce 1992, 159). But despite the authority of the church, this is equally insubstantial, and a vocation is turned into both dull routine and a nursery rhyme – like 'Solomon Grundy' or 'Monday's child is fair of face'. When he gives up piety and turns to aesthetics, far from being original, he draws his ideas from a great tradition of Christian divines – Augustine and Aquinas – and from an equally great, though differently construed, tradition of poets and writers – Flaubert and Baudelaire. This subjectivity is paper thin, a house of cards. What Stephen's story shows is the extent to which, as Roland Barthes puts it in 'The Death of the Author' 'a text is not a line of words releasing a single "theological" meaning … but a multi-dimensional space in which a variety of writings, none of them original, blend and clash. The text is a blend of quotations drawn from the innumerable centres of culture' (Barthes 1977, 146). The novel in which he appears might be original, but Stephen most certainly is not.

The attempt to author one's own subjectivity, Joyce's texts shows, is doomed. Whatever path one takes towards it – whether one accepts the

limitations of one's culture, or whether one rebels against it – the milieu
is inescapable. The most that Stephen can hope for is that his own
chosen rebellion, his *non serviam* and his strategies of 'silence, exile
and cunning' (Joyce 1992, 269), will not be merely banal and total
repetitions of the arguments and strategies of others, but they will be
repetitions. The terms of his rebellion – his rejection of family, country,
language and religious conviction – are, of course, determined by the
particular family, country, language and religion he was born into.
Reacting against them does not undo the relationship he has with
them, for as his friend Cranly says to him: 'your mind is supersaturated
with religion in which you say you disbelieve' (261). And as Stephen
himself says: 'This race and this country and this life produced me ...
I shall express myself as I am'; this is not the statement of autonomy
that it might first appear. It comes in the context of Stephen's nationalist friend Davin attempting to persuade him to join the republican
cause, and the Celtic revival, by learning the Irish language, an invitation he refuses, identifying nationalism, Irish revivalist culture and
Catholicism as traps: 'You talk to me of nationality, language, religion. I
shall try to fly those nets' (Joyce 1992, 220). But Stephen Dedalus, son
of Simon Dedalus, is Icarus. Every attempt to fly will bring him back
down to earth with a bump. His subjectivity will always be *subject to*
those structures which formed it; and even the vocation of an artist will
not free him.

5 In Prison and in Chains: Oscar Wilde's *De Profundis* and Brian Keenan's *An Evil Cradling*

It is, of course, always the case that subjectivity is under pressure, powerfully *subjected to* influences outside itself and beyond its control, with the individual often reduced to an *object* in the plans of others. The narratives that arise from very extreme experiences, however, and the subjectivities that these narratives relate, are necessarily rather different from the autobiographical text produced as somehow typifying more general experience, even if that typicality is also a marker of the exceptional status of 'genius' or artistry. The two texts that make up the material for this chapter both narrate the extreme experience of imprisonment, though they do it rather differently, and from different perspectives in relation to that experience. For Wilde, the text we now call *De Profundis* was written in the very midst of his imprisonment following his trial on charges of gross indecency. Brian Keenan's *An Evil Cradling* was written after the events it narrates, with the 'benefit' of hindsight, though the narrative itself recreates the confusions of the situation he found himself in, in which the experiencing subject did not know how his story would end. In this, it differs significantly not only from Wilde's text, but also from the other narratives produced by the Beirut hostages, such as John McCarthy and Jill Morrell's *Some Other Rainbow* and Terry Waite's *Taken on Trust*. The latter examples dispel the atmosphere of claustrophobia that Keenan carefully recreates, presenting narrative structures that alternate between the experience of imprisonment and the more general autobiographical issues of the life before and outside kidnap experience. In McCarthy's case, the narrative is also shared with his then partner, Jill Morrell, with two narrators explaining their own experiences alternately, providing relief from imprisonment in the story of Morrell's campaign for McCarthy's release.[1] In the cases of Wilde and Keenan, however, both retell experiences that are extremely raw, and both focus on the fact that the material conditions out of which these narrative performances were produced is formative of the selves each narrates.

In this argument, I am drawing on the work of Regenia Gagnier in both *Idylls of the Marketplace* (1987) and *Subjectivities* (1991). In the latter book, through the examination of several hundred nineteenth-century autobiographies by marginal or excluded subjects largely from the British working classes, Gagnier argues that subjectivity is very strongly formed in relation to material pressures; these material pressures have a *determining* influence on the shape of the narratives, and on the self-conception of the narrators. She demonstrates the extent to which the traditional generic markers of autobiographical writing with their appeal to the shaping coherence of realist fiction are inadequate for describing lives which do not fit the patterns which it inscribes. All autobiographies are 'rhetorical projects embedded in concrete material situations' (Gagnier 1991, 40), and those material situations differ from person to person.

> The classic realist autobiography includes such elements as remembered details of childhood, parent–child relationships, the subject's formal education, and a progressive developmental narrative of self culminating in material well-being and 'fame' within a greater or lesser circle ... Most workers' autobiographies deviate from this narrative pattern for fairly obvious reasons. (Gagnier 1991, 43)

In the case of the working-class autobiography, these reasons include an extremely shortened childhood, for Victorian labouring-class children began to labour early; there was – certainly before the 1870 Education Act in Britain – very little in the way of formal education for such children; and their stories generally do not accommodate a narrative of material success. The trajectory of such narratives, therefore, is rather differently conceived than that of more materially privileged contemporaries, and cannot be easily shaped according to an upward curve of progress. What is important to me about Gagnier's arguments in this chapter, however, is the sense that experiences understood as extreme by a bourgeois cultural hegemony, will necessarily be rather different from those that neatly inhabit that dominant framing social and material milieu. This will be the case not only for working-class writers, but for the educated and middle-class figure who finds him/herself, for whatever reason, outside the mainstream of experience. Different narrative structures have to be found for different experiential terms, for as Gagnier puts it:

> ... the body, so common that everyone ha[s] one, under conditions of deprivation [becomes] the most private and alienating aspect of identity ... subjectivity cannot exist without intersubjectivity, whereas bodies in pain exist only as bodies in pain. (Gagnier 1991, 83)

Wilde's *De Profundis*: an experiment in autobiography?

The unwary reader who comes fresh from *The Importance of Being Earnest* to confront the text now known as *De Profundis* in the expectation that the wit and sparkle of the former will be replicated in the latter is in for deep disappointment. The stereotypical view of Wilde – the wit, the dandy, the *flâneur* – appears to find no expression in this, his most nearly autobiographical text. That sense of disappointment is possibly one of the more charitable explanations for the critical vitriol which has been poured out on Wilde's prison letter. For Graham Hough, for example, the text is dismissed as 'emetic posturing' (Hough 1983, 202); and there is an evident distaste in Hough's description for what he euphemistically terms 'Wilde's *mésaventures biographiques*', as if he cannot quite bear to describe what those 'misadventures' consisted. Written in 1949, however, perhaps it is no surprise that distaste for Wilde's homosexuality overwhelms sympathetic interest. But even more sympathetic critics such as Jonathan Dollimore, are disappointed in its making. Dollimore for instance is concerned that *De Profundis* stands as a 'conscious renunciation of [Wilde's] transgressive aesthetic and a reaffirmation of tradition as focused in the depth model of identity'(Dollimore 1991, 95). The 'depth model' Dollimore refers to here is the sense of subjectivity as a deep and interior structure, the preferred model of the Romantic and Victorian traditions against which most of Wilde's works stand. He argues that Wilde's usual mode of thought depends on the reversal of the hierarchy of values represented in any moral schema of selfhood: Wilde's writings generally prefer, for example, surface to depth, lying to truth, persona/role to essential self, insincerity to sincerity, artifice to authenticity, and so on (Dollimore 1991, 15). *De Profundis*, he suggests, represents a retreat from this subversive mode, a retreat he figures as the defeat of aestheticism brought about by the forces of ideological coercion that had been brought to bear on Wilde through his incarceration.

It is not, though, quite as simple as that. For after all, *De Profundis* is not like Cecily's diary, in *The Importance of Being Earnest* – 'a very young girl's record of her own thoughts and impressions, and consequently meant for publication' (Wilde 1994, 393). Although he clearly intended that it should survive into posterity, and be published, leaving careful instructions with his friend Robert Ross about what should happen to the letter, immediate publication was not Wilde's aim. Nor is it strictly speaking 'autobiography' in the terms of the genre as it is usually defined, for instance by Philippe Lejeune as 'a retrospective prose narrative produced by a real person concerning his own existence, focusing on his individual life, in particular on the development of his personality' (Lejeune 1989, 44). For one thing, it is not exactly retrospective, having been composed *in medias res*, in the midst of the event (his imprisonment) which is also its *raison d'être*. Indeed, perhaps it is closer to the genre of *apologia*, a word which hovers uncomfortably between *apology* ('an explanation with expression of regret; a regretful acknowledgement of a fault') and a defensive strategy which sets out to justify the speaker's position and actions. Moreover, *De Profundis* has a complicated history which has probably had an effect on the way that it has been read. Its first appearance in public was in a severely edited form, and the full text of the letter was not published until 1962. The text that we now have entitled *De Profundis* was written by Prisoner C.3.3., one Oscar Wilde, in Reading prison between January and March, 1897, in the form of a letter to Lord Alfred Douglas (Bosie), his former lover and erstwhile friend. I want to consider this text as an example of the sense of self being rewritten, under particular pressures, as an act that seeks to reaffirm the subject and resist the structures of subjection that are implicit in any prison regime. And I want to suggest that far from being a renunciation of his previous views about life, art, personality, Wilde is, in fact, at considerable pains to reconfigure himself in precisely the terms he had used in his past.

When Wilde was sent to prison in May, 1895, as Gagnier shows, it was under the rules of what was called penal servitude (as opposed to simple 'imprisonment'). Under the rules of imprisonment, a prisoner could be sentenced to any term between three and five years. He would be kept in solitary confinement for the first nine months of his incarceration; but after that period he would be allowed to associate with other prisoners, work with them, talk to them, and receive a certain amount of education. Under the rules of penal servitude, on the other hand, a prisoner would be sentenced to a maximum of two years with hard labour. But the whole of that period would be spent in isolation, with severe penalties if, during the one hour of exercise allowed per day, he spoke to any other prisoner. The prisoner's existence was one monotony and silence, with a rigidly regulated regime of daily life, spent largely in a tiny cell, with a window placed so high above the ground that no prisoner could look out of it.

> No personal possessions were allowed in the cell, which included only a plank bed, a blanket, a hard pillow, and a small table. Each morning on pain of punishment, the prisoner would arrange these items symmetrically for inspection. ... One letter could be sent and received per quarter for the 'purpose of enabling [prisoners] to keep up a connection with their respectable friends and not that they might be kept informed of public events.' No books were allowed the first month, during the second and third only a Bible, a prayer-book, and a hymn-book. Afterwards, one book a week from the prison-library was permitted. (Gagnier 1987, 185)

The regime of penal servitude was so extreme that many prisoners preferred to serve longer sentences under the rules of imprisonment; and, indeed, the monotony, silence and solitude were known to be prime causes of insanity amongst the prison population. The food was also extremely bad; and Wilde suffered – as almost all prisoners did – from diarrhoea for the first few months of his imprisonment; the unpleasantness of the condition was exacerbated by the fact that prisoners were locked into their cells for most of the day. Wilde wrote movingly of the appalling conditions in two letters he sent to the *Daily Chronicle* about prison reform after his release (see Wilde 1979, 269–75 and 334–8). Prisoners who had hard labour attached to their sentences had to pick oakum (separate strands of rotten rope) or turn the crank or operate a treadmill. These were all useless forms of labour with no end product: work figured merely as punishment. On the first day of his sentence, Wilde was also forced to bathe in dirty water that had been used by other prisoners, had his hair cut, and was put into a prison uniform (Ellmann 1987, 450–1). So alongside the sheer tedium of an unhygienic regime, there were also assaults on the bodily dignity of the prisoner, rituals of humiliation and alienation from the image of the former self. For a man like Wilde, whose image had been a very large part of his public (and private) persona, this was a profound humiliation.

These physical constraints were not the only constraints on Wilde as he composed the letter. The act of writing was supposedly forbidden to prisoners under Home Office regulations, except for the quarterly letter to one's respectable friends on the outside. But when Wilde was eventually moved to Reading, having served part of his sentence at Pentonville, the liberal governor, Major Nelson, made special provision for Wilde to be allowed to write, and to have more books than the official allowance. His reasoning was that this would enable Wilde to continue his career as a writer on his release. But Wilde was still a prisoner, and therefore could not be allowed to do just what he pleased; and in a letter to the Prison Commissioners, Major Nelson explained: 'Each sheet [of paper] was carefully numbered before being issued and withdrawn each evening at locking and placed before me in the morning with the usual papers'. Wilde, that is, was given one quarto sheet of paper per day. He had to hand the paper in at the end of each day, and he was not supposed to be given access to sheets that he had already written. It seems likely that Major Nelson did allow Wilde to see and correct his previous pages, for as Rupert Hart-Davis notes, the manuscript contains evidence of annotation and change, and some sheets are fair copies of earlier drafts (Wilde 1979, 152–3n). Nonetheless, Wilde was clearly working under very severe restraints, and under these conditions, it should come as no surprise that *De Profundis* is not a seamless whole.

When Wilde was eventually released from prison in May 1897, he sent the manuscript of his letter to his friend Robert Ross, having previously written to him explaining what it was, and what Ross was to do with it. Wilde's instructions were that two typewritten copies were to be taken from the manuscript, and that the original was to be sent to its addressee, Lord Alfred Douglas. In the event – probably wisely – Ross kept the original, and sent one of the copies to Douglas. Wilde wrote further:

> As regards the mode of copying: of course it is too long for any amanuensis to attempt ... I think the only thing to do is to be thoroughly modern,

and to have it type-written. Of course, the manuscript should not pass out of your control, but could you not get Mrs Marshall to send down one of her type-writing girls – women are the most reliable, as they have no memory for the important – ... to do it under your supervision. I assure you that the type-writing machine, when played with expression, is not more annoying than the piano when played by a sister or near relation. Indeed many, amongst those most devoted to domesticity, prefer it ... If the copying is done at Horton Street, the lady type-writer may be fed through a lattice like the Cardinals when they elect a Pope, till she comes out on the balcony and say to the world, '*Habet Mundus Epistolam;*' for indeed it is an Encyclical Letter, and as the Bulls of the Holy Father are named from their opening words, it may be spoken of as the *Epistola: In Carcere et Vinculis*. (Wilde 1979, 241)

The importance of this letter is twofold. In the first place it shows Wilde reasserting his guise as a wit. There is the joke about women, and – in an echo of *The Importance of Being Earnest* – the commentary on type-writing having a similar aesthetic value to the domestic accomplishment of lady-like pianists. In the second, it gives his prison letter both a genre and a title – it is a papal bull (though there's more than a whiff of another kind of bull about the tone), and it is to be called 'Letter: in prison and in chains'.

The title *De Profundis* is in fact Robert Ross's invention, and in some ways it does not serve the text particularly well. In giving it this title, Ross was doing a number of things. *De Profundis* is a quotation from the opening lines of Psalm 130 in the Vulgate Bible: 'Out of the depths have I cried unto thee, O Lord. Lord hear my voice ... ' The Vulgate is a Roman Catholic version of biblical scholarship, and its use here explicitly – and justifiably – associates Wilde with Catholicism (as Ross knew, Wilde became a Catholic on his deathbed, and had flirted with the possibility of conversion, significantly known as *perversion* in the late nineteenth century, for many years). In giving it this title, however, Ross places the text in a particular generic position, effectively describing it as a kind of confession, and consequently associating it with what Dollimore calls the 'depth model' of personality. This leads to a perceptual problem for readers of the text, for we have a particular genre signalled by the title, which is belied by the content. For whatever else it is, *De Profundis* is a divided text, oscillating between its explanatory or defensive functions in describing Wilde's conduct, and its attempts to reconstruct a positive image of Wilde for himself and for others: it certainly does not have the structure of a confession. It wavers between a properly Christian spirit of self-abnegation and a highly 'inappropriate' self-assertion and self-affirmation, which is at odds with the title under which it is published. The explanatory part of the letter largely consists of blaming Lord Alfred Douglas – Bosie, the letter's addressee – for what happened to Wilde; the reconstruction of self hood largely consists of Wilde's grandiose assertion of himself as a Christ-like figure. The text is split between inscribing its protagonist as victim and as hero.

The traditions of discussing autobiography, however, especially in the nineteenth-century 'great tradition' of the mode, ideally presume a model of subjectivity in which the self is presented as coherent. Although in Lejeune's formulation there is an emphasis on the *development* of personality, there is also a presumption in favour of the autobiographical subject as a complete package, available to narration as a composite and consistent totality. Thus one of the effects of Ross's title is that it sends confused messages to the public. A confession is supposed to be sincere; a cry from the depths implies not only a cry from the lowest point of emotional distress, but also a cry from the bottom of one's heart, relatively unmediated and certainly not crafted by the aesthetics of self-conscious writing. Sincerity is presumed to be straightforward, but whatever else Wilde's message in *De Profundis* might be, it is not a straight text, in any sense of that phrase. It glories in a construction of self hood which is double, if not exactly two-faced, and which functions in relation to subjectivism and relativism as strategies to produce an alternative interpretation of the self to oppose to Wilde's fear that he had become the mere catspaw of fate.

In a passage which is clearly derived from the writings of Walter Pater, author of *Studies in the History of the Renaissance* (1873), whom Wilde greatly admired, Wilde writes in *De Profundis*:

> Modern life is complex and relative; those are its two distinguishing notes; to render the first we require atmosphere with its subtlety of *nuances*, of suggestion, of strange perspectives; as for the second, we require background. That is why sculpture has ceased to be a representative art, and why music is a representative art, and why literature is, and has been, and always will remain the supreme representative art. (Wilde 1994, 1012)

This passage sets up a relationship between perspective or point of view, and context, named here as background. The complexity of modern life, Wilde suggests, demands a point of view in which one views the world, as it were, aslant, or sidelong, or in any case, somewhat indirectly. Part of the reason for this peculiar glance is precisely that it is also necessary in Wilde's formulation to look at the background as well as the foreground – focus is something of an issue. In an auto-biographical text, one might well expect that 'background' implies a particular set of narrative possibilities – elements such as parental influence and upbringing, educational opportunity, and key moments from the emotional life. Readers of Wilde, however, know perfectly well that this has not been his usual habit in representing the personae who inhabit his fictions. When Wilde does touch on these elements, noting the great family name his parents bequeathed to him, for example, it is in the service of recreating himself as the hero of a Greek tragedy, to whom the gods had given everything (Wilde 1994, 1017). There are two basic strands to Wilde's letter – a strand which accuses Bosie of being the author of Wilde's misfortunes (the metaphor is deliberately chosen), and a strand in which Wilde re-authors himself, detaching himself from the past by reference to an ideal future with Christ at its heart. The two strands, which sometimes shade into each other, appear to be absolutely at odds with any notion of coherence, and with any sense that what Wilde is producing for us is the spectacle of an explanation. What is particularly interesting about Wilde's position, however, is the extent to which his notion of the Self is discursive, a self created through language; and a self, therefore, which is contingent rather than essential.

That the self is not 'essence' is something that Wilde had constantly reiterated throughout his writings, in particular his sense of the dis-tinction between the mask and the person that stands behind it. The particularity of the prison situation, makes this even more an acute revelation. Who is Oscar Wilde when: his name has been taken away from him? (He is called C.3.3. after the number on his cell door.) Who is Oscar Wilde when his status as a writer has been dismissed, and his name has been removed from his plays in the West End? When his chil-dren have been removed from his jurisdiction by court order? When his mother has died, and he has been unable to go to her funeral because he is in prison? When all his goods have been sold in order to pay for his bankruptcy? When his image and clothing have been taken away from him? In other words, what does a self whose markers of identity have been removed consist in? In all the terms of the world, Wilde has become nothing in his prison guise – except a prisoner, defined entirely by his crime and his punishment. As a man, as a father, as a husband, a son, an economic entity, a writer, an image, he has been collapsed into the image of the prisoner with no name except his number, C.3.3. These external props make the performance of selfhood possible: without them, Wilde fears he has been reduced to a vulnerable nakedness: 'Behind Joy and Laughter,' he writes, 'there may be a temperament, coarse, hard and callous. But behind Sorrow there is always Sorrow. Pain, unlike Pleasure, wears no mask' (Wilde 1994, 1024). But he wishes to aestheticize pain – to turn it into 'the type and test of all great Art' (1024) – and thereby to *form* it into an artistic performance.

In the special circumstances of imprisonment, for Wilde the self must be made to reside elsewhere than in the present, in the here and now of the 'house of detention'. His subjectivity is therefore created in relation to memory (the past) and desire (the future). He posits a self which exists in memory which was hopelessly implicated in the self of the Other, Bosie, and a self which may exist perhaps in the future through an act of imaginative resistance to the position of the prisoner, as he identifies himself with Christ. Of the two selves, critics have disliked the vitriol addressed at Douglas, who represents in the text Wilde's past self; and they have disliked also the hubris of a self-identification with Christ. But they have seldom seen that the two selves arise directly out of the conditions in which Wilde found himself.

Most of the first part of *De Profundis* consists of a minutely detailed rendition of Wilde's life with Douglas. It includes a wealth of financial detail; lists of what they did and where, very carefully recorded with dates recalled exactly as possible; specific incidents in which Bosie misbehaved; and a precise record of the consequences of Wilde's relationship – including his bankruptcy, his projected divorce, the loss of his children and his current position in the 'house of detention'. Regenia Gagnier describes this minutiae as the attempt to pose 'a total imaginative world against the frozen time and alien space of imprisonment. ... Wilde forces the presence of Douglas in the prose in order to make the pre-prison Wilde a reality' (Gagnier 1987, 187); she also notes however, that the present insistently intrudes on these imaginings, in that Wilde structures his memory in three-month blocks; 'three months go over' and its synonyms are a constant refrain in the early part of the letter, because the prisoner Wilde measures out his existence in three-monthly intervals in relation to prison regulations, so that the past is utterly infected by the material conditions of the present. What becomes clear from this wealth of detail is that for Wilde to 'know himself', as he puts it, he must also recall Bosie's self: there is a profound identification between the two men in the text which dramatizes the position that to know oneself one must also know the other – indeed, that the *self* may be entirely dependent on the *other* for its definition. Hence the proposition that the self is at once what the other is not, and the other is whatever is 'not-self'. In the oscillation between these two binary poles Wilde presents a version of self that deconstructs. For, as Jacques Derrida argues, one cannot create a self without a notion of not-self, or other. And the self is therefore relational rather than fixed, deferred rather than knowable:

> There is not narcissism and non-narcissism; there are narcissisms that are more or less comprehensive, generous, open, extended. ... without a moment of narcissistic reappropriation, the relation to the other would be absolutely destroyed, it would even be destroyed in advance. The relation to the other – even if it remains asymmetrical, open, without possible reappropriation – must trace a movement of reappropriation in the image of oneself for love to be possible, for example. Love is narcissistic. (Derrida 1995, 199)

The force of this statement is that any binary opposition is never just a single or simple opposition. Definition – including self-definition – is necessarily relative and open ended. The self must act and define itself by appropriating the other to a greater or lesser degree, and self affirmation depends on that appropriation of the other. Wilde, in telling Douglas's story, appropriates events and Douglas's personality for his own purpose: in telling his own story he is also always telling the other's story.

The confusion between self and other becomes particularly acute in the sustained grammatical contortions of Wilde's narrative in which the subject and the object of the sentence (roughly equivalent to Wilde and Bosie) collapse into each other.

> I will begin by telling you that I blame myself terribly ... I blame myself for allowing an unintellectual friendship, a friendship whose primary aim was not the creation and contemplation of beautiful things, entirely to dominate my life ... I blame myself for having allowed you to bring me to utter and discreditable financial ruin ... But most of all I blame myself for the entire ethical degradation I allowed you to bring on me. The basis of character is will power, and my will power became absolutely subject to yours. (Wilde 1994, 981–4)

Grammatically, Wilde signals that subject and object are the same; that self and other are inseparable; that there is a sense in which Wilde became Bosie, and Bosie became Wilde.

To be Bosie, however, is clearly not a desirable thing to be. Bosie is selfish, extravagant, rude, unsympathetic, non-intellectual and wasteful. To attach one's own self to Bosie's self/other is to risk becoming all of those things. Wilde, therefore, proposes an alternative imaginative version of the world and the self in the figure of Christ. Christ has many advantages here: 'There is something so unique about Christ' says Wilde in a litotes which is typically satirical, but which also borders on the profane. One advantage is that he represents a figure of forgiveness (hence Ross's use of a psalm about forgiveness as his title for the work), and if Wilde is to cease to be Bosie he has to detach himself from Bosie's self by means that Bosie himself would not use: Bosie is an unforgiving figure and Christ is the supreme figure of forgiveness in Western culture. Inside his autobiography, Wilde writes other biographies of both Bosie and Christ – where Bosie represents all that is ugly and painful, and is a bar to Wilde's art, Wilde's Christ is an aesthetic figure, a supreme artist in his own right. Norbert Kohl has suggested that for Wilde, Christ is the paradigm figure of the suffering artist (Kohl 1989, 278), and he identifies him as a poet. Indeed, as Richard Ellmann notes, the one aspect of Christ that has no significance in Wilde's account is his divinity – precisely the aspect of Christ which ought to be most important in conventional religiously inspired readings of his meaning (Ellmann 1987, 483). For Wilde, Christ's story ends with 'the stone rolled over the door of the sepulchre', not with divine manifestation of the Resurrection.

Wilde's Christ is an erotic figure, with a sexy compelling personality. His narrative insists that Christ's most important value is that he exemplified imaginative sympathy with suffering, something that Bosie is incapable of. (Wilde continually castigates Bosie for his empathetic failures, both in the past, and – in Wilde's imagination – in the present, to feel what Wilde is feeling now.) Christ's sympathy made his life into a work of art, into 'the most wonderful of poems'. His miracles have nothing to do with divinity. They are dependent on his 'fascinating' personality.

> His miracles seem to me to be as exquisite as spring and quite as natural. I see no difficulty in believing that such was the charm of his personality that his mere presence could bring peace to souls in anguish, and that

those who touched his garments or his hands forgot their pain; ... or that when he taught on the hillside the multitude forgot their hunger and thirst and the cares of the world, and that to his friends who listened to him as he sat at meat the coarse food seemed delicate, and the water had the taste of good wine, and the whole house became full of the odour and sweetness of nard. (Wilde 1994, 1029)

What Wilde is describing as Christ's personality, is of course, very close to the common perception of his own personality. His conversation acted like a charm on those who heard him. Even his greatest enemy, the Marquess of Queensberry, when he met Wilde for the first time, was charmed, writing to Bosie: 'I don't wonder that you are so fond of him. He is a wonderful man', and the poet W. B. Yeats recorded his awe at Wilde's 'perfect sentences' (quoted Ellmann 1987, 393, 37). In this text then, man is not made in the image of God; Christ is remade in the image of Wilde.

Paradoxically, it is partially the invocation of Christ that enables Wilde to avoid the confessional mode. He does not confess past faults, except inasmuch as he 'blames himself' for his friendship with Bosie, thereby rendering Bosie the cause of his misfortunes. The conventional narratives of confession, and of crime and punishment are invoked but not produced. So, for example, Wilde produces a list of things that are supposed to help the fallen sinner, but which do not help him. 'Neither Religion, Morality nor Reason can help me at all' (1019). But he also says, 'I don't regret for a single moment having lived for pleasure. I did it to the full, as one should do everything that one does. ... But to have continued the same life would have been wrong because it would have been limiting' (1026). Repentance becomes merely another experience rather than a distinctively moral choice. The ghost of Lord Henry Wooton (in Wilde's *The Picture of Dorian Gray*) refracted through Pater's *Renaissance* speaks here. And he speaks of himself as a 'born antinomian ... made for exceptions, not for laws' (1019).

There is, throughout *De Profundis*, a resistance to conventional narratives of the self, which is why I would argue that far from being an unconsidered trifle and in opposition to the rest of Wilde's oeuvre, it is a central restatement of the positions he adopted throughout his life. Not only is modern life complex and relative, so too is the modern narrative that attempts to record it; and its complexity is borne out of Wilde's conviction that selfhood is not a deep structure, securely possessed as unique individuality by anyone. Throughout his writing career he made capital out of the distinction between the mask – usually of 'social manners' – and the person who stands behind it. But in Victorian psychological thought the social mask and the essence of self were very often regarded as a seamless whole. As William James put it in his *Principles of Psychology* (1890):

> it is clear that between what a man calls *me* and what he simply calls *mine* the line is difficult to draw. … *In its widest possible sense … a man's Self is the sum total of what he CAN call his*, not only his body and his psychic powers, but his clothes and his house, his wife and his children, his ancestors and friends, his reputation and works, his lands and horses and yacht and bank-account. All these things give him the same emotions. If they wax and prosper, he feels triumphant; if they dwindle and die away, he feels cast down. (James I 1950, 291–2, emphasis in original)

'Only the shallow know themselves', Wilde wrote in his collection of epigrams, 'Phrases and Philosophies for the Use of the Young' (Wilde 1994, 1244). But selfhood can be known to some extent through material objects, as James implies. When those objects are removed, the subject has to find another place from which to construct itself. In the end, for Wilde, subjectivity is performance not essence.

This sense of subjectivity as a series of roles is indicated in Wilde's typical vocabulary. He eschews the language of character, which, as I have argued elsewhere, is a term better suited to fictions than to real people (see Robbins 1996; and see also Rylance 2002). The English word character has its origins in the Greek word *kharakter*, meaning something impressed or stamped. It implies stability and knowability. Character is stamped or impressed through the individual: inside and outside match. It is a word therefore better suited to fictions than to real people whose knowability and stability must, after all, always be open to question.

Personality, Wilde's preferred term, on the other hand comes from a Latin root, *persona*, meaning in the first instance 'actor's mask', and then increasingly the sense becomes the public face, the face that one presents to the world, which may not quite be the same thing as one's reality. The difference between the two terms is that personality refers not the essential being, the inner core of self, but to a role which can be adopted and put aside at will. Consequently a self figured as personality is potentially inconsistent, and knowable only in a conditional way, for the moments during which that particular mask is being worn. Wilde comments in *De Profundis*: 'Behind Joy and Laughter there may be a temperament, coarse, hard and callous. But behind Sorrow there is always Sorrow. Pain, unlike Pleasure, wears no mask.' And there is a sense in which that statement stakes a claim for the authenticity of emotion and sincerity of expression of *De Profundis*. But in speaking of the mask, Wilde also implies that even though the naked face is sincere, it may yet reassume its disguise. So that whilst on the one hand he asks his addressee to see him unadorned – naked, as it were – and is thus risking his self, making himself vulnerable, he also dramatizes in *De Profundis* his unwillingness to occupy this position for long. He reassembles a personality which he then associates implicitly and explicitly with the personality of Christ, replacing himself in the process on the artistic pedestal from which scandal had removed him: this matters, for Douglas had told Wilde that when he was not on his pedestal he was not 'interesting' (Wilde 1994, 993). In remounting the pedestal, Wilde is also restoring his sense of himself as a loveable being – as an erotic personality who might once again seduce his petulant lover. The maskless face of sorrow is not a permanent condition. It does not reveal character – essence – but is an alternative persona which is soon rejected.

So, if the letter is inconsistent in that it is not merely a humble con-fession, nor just the letter of an injured lover, nor a therapy, nor an autobiographical explanation, it is at least consistent with Wilde's view that each of these alternatives is just one possibility amongst many. A self may write (or be written into) all of these genres in turn. Life is not something that can be seen steadily and whole, as it 'really is'. It has to be read instead sequentially as a series of possibilities. The biogra-pher or critic who seeks a single or simple explanation for any life is treacherous. Wilde's view is that lives, even narrated lives, must resist the closure of *the* authoritative interpretation. The self is always multiple, and therefore knowledge of it is always deferred. And the self is always a performance, at least as much as it is an expression of any stabilized identity.

Brian Keenan's *An Evil Cradling*: telling and restoration

In thinking about Keenan's narrative *An Evil Cradling*, I want to think first about the comparisons we might draw between his imprisonment by Shiite Muslims in Lebanon from 1986–1990 and Oscar Wilde's period of imprisonment in Wandsworth, Pentonville and Reading at the hands of Her Majesty's Government between May 1895 and May 1897. My primary source of comparison arises in a consideration of the operation of the law. In Chapter 1, I quoted Hayden White's assertion that '[t]he reality that lends itself to narrative representation is the conflict between desire and the law. Where there is no rule of law there can be neither a subject nor the kind of event that lends itself to narrative representation' (White 1987, 12–13). Its application in relation to the fictional character of *Pamela* is relatively straightforward; in the case of Keenan, White's comment points out a particular problematic at the heart of *An Evil Cradling*'s narrative structure. In the lawless world into which Keenan was plunged, it becomes clear that subjectivity is pressurized almost out of existence, and coherent narrative is in some sense impossible. Wilde and Keenan were also both Irishmen – though Wilde often strategically forgot that fact, giving his solicitor his word as 'an English gentleman' that he was not guilty of the crimes of which he had been accused. And both might well have argued that they were unjustly imprisoned because of the policies of a British government. But there are also fundamental differences between them. In particular, the circumstances of Keenan's imprisonment were far more brutal than what happened to Wilde, and it is in relation to the abused body that one of the key contrasts between them arises. I want, therefore, to think about what imprisonment does to the body and to the subjectivity that inhabits the body. In brief, then, Keenan's text raises questions about the legal subject and the narrative sentence, about national identity and about the subjected body as an object in other people's plans.

Whatever one might wish to say of the laws under which Wilde was imprisoned, Wilde was at least afforded his day in court. He was not sent to prison until the due process of the law had been played out in public. He knew why he was in jail; and he knew exactly, to the minute, the precise term of his imprisonment. So what was played out in the courtroom where he was convicted was a narrative of cause and effect which had utterly predictable consequences. His prison letter, as we have suggested, poses an imaginative response to a situation which was intensely real. He creates new versions of his self in order to assert his own existence. But bad as Wilde's conditions were, they were at least ordered by the narrative of crime and punishment, and by the monotonous but steady regime of prison life in which time could be measured in blocks of three months.

Keenan's situation, on the other hand, taking place as it did in a lawless world, demands a different kind of narrative response. If, as White has suggested, narrative and the subjectivity of narrative demand a sense of the desiring self in conflict with law – rules and prohibitions which can be understood – that Keenan managed to write anything, managed to make any sense of his imprisonment through its narrative is a remarkable achievement. This could have been a narrative which simply reiterated that life is not fair or just, and that the world is absurd and chaotic, but that is not what *An Evil Cradling* presents us with. The world into which Keenan and his fellow hostages were plunged implied, through the confrontation with people who shared no value systems in common, that selfhood, when it is unsupported by the other people reflecting back on it, depends on the forging of one's own values and meaning. It forced, that is, a confrontation with what is meant by the category of the human; and in particular, it forced the recognition that the category of the human is culturally constructed rather than naturally determined. Wilde said that reason could not help him because his reason told him only that the laws under which he had been convicted were unjust. Keenan has to recognize that there is no law current in that place and that time which protects his notion of his own humanity: the sense of the self, therefore, has to come from within. In order to reconstitute his Western notion of self, he writes a narrative which appeals to laws which his captors could not understand. This is something he can only do retrospectively rather than *in medias res*. Writing during his imprisonment was nearly impossible – physically (for most of the time he had no writing materials), but also mentally, since the structures of narrative imply a knowledge of the end, which during his imprisonment Keenan did not have. There could be no teleology, only diurnality whilst he was still *in carcere et vinculis*. Narrative would not have made sense of something that had no end, and could not have created patterns out of the random until the end had come.

Autobiography as genre is often used as a discourse of self-restoration – meaning both the restoration of the self to and for that self, and the assertion of selfhood in situations which do not recognize it. *In extremis*, it becomes, therefore, the art which is performed in order to shore up the uncertainties of identity. The autobiographical story becomes therapy, which is what Keenan himself suggests is his motivation for writing in the preface to *An Evil Cradling*: 'I think it was

D. H. Lawrence, speaking about the act of writing, who said that writers throw up their sickness in books. So it is with this work. It is the process of abreaction in art form, both a therapy and an exploration' (Keenan 1992, xiii). Lawrence actually said that 'we shed our sickness in books', meaning that writing as a process is therapeutic, but also that writing allows one to transcend the conditions of sickness by transforming them into something else, an artwork for example. Abreaction refers to the psychological process of resolving a neurosis by reviving – or reliving – the events which caused it; in the process of reliving the trauma, through narrative, the therapeutic subject is enabled to take control of the traumatic events, editing the experience, choosing what to include and what to omit, and shaping the narrative to produce an ending appropriate for the suffering subject. What Keenan seeks to do therefore is to 'imprison' (xiv) his experience on paper; but what we are to read is an edited account, not structured by chronology and deliberately elliptical in its relation of torture in a refusal to 'feed the voyeuristic vulture' (xiv). He relives his trauma by recounting it, but in the narrative, he also controls that trauma by constructing and reconstructing the value systems and the sense of self which imprisonment damaged in the first place. Making those events coherent shores up the sense of identity which the trauma fragmented in the first place, and it reconstitutes the self as a subject within narrative frames of the generic category of law.

Unlike Wilde's text, which examined not the minute detail of the here-and-now of prison existence so much as the concreteness of pre-prison existence, Keenan minutely examines the conditions of his imprisonment, and the effects on the sense of self of their existential challenge. He uses his text to consider what strategies are available to the self under pressure – and one of the strategies is, of course, the book itself. At many points in the text, Keenan is poignantly aware that the composite self could slip away from him easily, and leave him in madness. To re-possess himself – and to regain his self-possession – whilst he is imprisoned, Keenan takes a great risk to write about himself in his Lebanese cell, and to review his state of mind every few days. On a few scraps of paper, and with the remnants of a pencil from the briefcase he was carrying when he was kidnapped, he begins to record 'the minutiae of [his] existence', not editing or structuring it, but simply recording. At intervals, he would:

> read over what I had written ... How could I make sense of it? ... To see all the fissures and fractures, to throw light into dark cavities, to see the

landscape of a mind and recognize no part of it but know that it is yours is a fearful and disturbing thing. ... Eventually it came to me that here in these pages there was something ... some threads running through and holding it together like the veins that carry blood to the living heart. ... [S]ome veins of life held everything together ... in these strange pages was a whole human being. (Keenan 1992, 80–1)

The self-possession he regains through writing in the formlessness of free association is tenuous in the extreme. Writing demands order; reading functions as the interpretation of that order. Where there is no ordering of thoughts into articulacy, Keenan, both the writer and the reader of his own text here, confronts a fragmented self that cannot be rendered whole by hermeneutic enterprise. The picture of the complete human being can only be dimly perceived and with effort, and indeed, is almost figured as a Frankensteinian monster, with its veins showing through its barely containing skin. Keenan speaks of the fear that his writing might actually destroy his sense of self, since he cannot organize his writing into a coherent structure. He is disturbed that he cannot recognize himself, and that he has been dispersed into 'confusing ideas ... abstract thinking ... religious mania ... longing ... grief'. Narrative does not make for coherence except in the most attenuated way. And at this point, still writing in the prison cell, Keenan could not even make art transcend his experience. He also wrote poems in this period – poetry usually being a mode of supremely ordered articulation (the word poetry, remember, derives from the Greek word *poesis*, meaning 'craft' or 'skill'). But as with the documentary record, when he reviews them, the poems are also crazily incoherent: they are a 'body of work which I could not believe was any part of me. It was as if I had seen my face again in the spoon and had failed to recognize it' (Keenan 1992, 81). The conditions in which the poems were produced are reproduced in the poems themselves, suggesting the extent to which the speaking/writing subject is contextual rather than essential. The poems provide not an escape from insanity, but a dramatization of it. But the particularity of this situation also masks a more general point about the contingency of language itself. If the 'craft' of the poems Keenan has written is an assertion of self expression, it is also a commentary on the 'impersonality' of language. In the metaphors of the 'body of work' and a distorted facial image in the concave mirror of a spoon, Keenan is forced to confront the ways in which language is always already implicated in systems of misrecognition: there is a separation between the 'I' that speaks, the 'eye' that sees, and the self. Subjectivity becomes an act of literary impersonation: the self is someone else.

Because the events that Keenan recounts take place in a context of lawlessness with no predictable narrative structure, language can only reconstitute his subjectivity conditionally and vaguely. As a teacher of English, his profession depends on the ideal of language as a medium of communication. But, as he notes repeatedly, his captors do not share the same relationship or assumptions about language, and are incapable, at least in his reconstruction of them, of abstract conceptual thought. For them, language is not man-made but comes directly from God through the mediation of Gibreel and the prophet Mohammed. Language is the concrete expression of the existence of Allah. Ideas that do not refer back to this conceptual framework are incomprehensible to them. Although both Keenan and McCarthy, and the other hostages try to keep lines of communication open both with their captors and with each other, something is lost in the process of translation. It is a kind of commonplace that the category of the human depends on the use of language. But if language does not communicate, then the notion of a common humanity between prisoner and guard is difficult to maintain, and the prisoners feel themselves to have been relegated to the condition of animals. Keenan writes often of his resistance to this alternative insulting categorization, and of his strategies to defeat it. He and McCarthy laugh hysterically about their situation, and use humour to diffuse their pain – laughter, of course, being one of the other things that differentiates the human from the animal. They also use language abusively, insulting each other with inventive obscenity:

> The rich elaborations that we slung at one another endlessly with childish competitiveness intoxicated us. It was heady, monstrous and foul. But it was also gloriously imaginative and unfettered ... the laughter pushed back the crushing agony of the tiny space. (Keenan 1992, 126–7)

This bad language operates on many levels. Because it breaks the bounds of expected polite behaviour, it is an imaginative resource against the physical bounds of close incarceration. It provides entertainment, and work for the brain, in that the two men had to work hard to invent different modes of insult. But it also acts as a displacement of violence. In ordinary contexts, such language could be regarded as aggressive, hostile or violent. In a situation where physical violence always threatens to become a reality, to use linguistic violence is an assertion of one's own power over the situation. This is a place where the normal rules do not apply, and where, therefore, the speaker need not stick within the codes of linguistic good behaviour. You can break social laws when social laws have been broken against you.

Keenan's own pronunciation, contrasted with his fellow hostage, John McCarthy's 'clipped' English speech, is of course, recognizably Northern Irish. In other circumstances, it is highly unlikely that these two men would ever have met. But Keenan's Irishness is also a disputed identity, deliberately chosen by him. From his birthplace in Belfast, he is British; but he travels to Beirut, we are told, on an Irish passport, signalling a particular political positioning as well as a notion of identity that is relatively autonomous rather than being imposed from the outside. The Conservative British government of the 1980s, despite many other divisions, were united in a notion of Britishness as an intelligible core for identity. The rhetoric of Tory politicians stressed homogenization: we are British because we share a set of assumptions (democracy and free-market trade), a common history (or heritage), a culture (Shakespeare, football and cricket). It is clear that this rhetoric is deeply old-fashioned, masculinist and profoundly embattled: one would not need to assert a national identity if everyone really did share it. The rhetoric of national identity, that is, only exists in Britain because we can all see that in fact Britain is culturally, historically, economically, politically and ethnically diverse. Northern Ireland in this period of the extremities of 'The Troubles' demonstrated the heterogeneity of British national identity very acutely.

The relationship between personal identity and national identity is very important to Brian Keenan's narrative. From the outset, he is sensitive to the ways in which national identities may be deployed in constituting the sense of the Self and the sense of the Other. For Keenan, Irishness is a chosen identity. Born a British citizen, he claims Irishness rather than having it thrust upon him. In the early stages of his narrative, he clings to this national identity because he believes that here in Beirut – unlike anywhere in the UK or Ireland – his Irishness asserts neutrality in relation to the political situation of Lebanon; that is, Ireland, unlike Britain, is not implicated in the crisis which precipitated the taking of hostages. Britain's strong identification with the United States is what makes British subjects easy game. The Irish would appear to be unimportant here. In the period immediately after his capture, Keenan then draws on his Irish identity and his interpretation of it as politically neutral to shore up his optimism and his hopes of an early release. But as the time in captivity grows longer, the chimerical nature of this view becomes more apparent. The hostage takers see no difference between a Brit and an Irishman, nor between a Frenchman, a Belgian or an American and an Irishman: to them, Westerners are all the same – they look the same, and they stand for the same eroded cultural values. So a notion of national identity which starts for Keenan as a matter of political convenience becomes increasingly important and operates as a different kind of construction by the end of his captivity.

To the outsider, there are parallels between the situations in Belfast and Beirut. Both are disputed territories, torn by internal and external strife, and subject to fundamentalist forms of religious and political belief. Before Keenan goes to Beirut, he is warned by his London friends to be careful, to which he responds: 'I come from Belfast. I know how to be careful' (Keenan 1992, 18). He believes that he understands the historical parallels between the culture which sustains terrorism in Northern Ireland, and that which pertains in the Middle East. As his imprisonment continues, he draws on his knowledge of how Republican prisoners in Northern Ireland have responded to their own subjection to British laws and penal systems. He speaks explicitly of the potency of the hunger strike as a weapon to be used by prisoners against the system which imprisons them. It is a non-violent assertion of will or choice, and is powerful precisely because it calls into question the rights of the guards to hold one captive as if one were animal: will is something which returns one to the category of the human from the category of the subhuman – and it is largely effective in this captivity, because, after all, a dead hostage is worth nothing.

> Hunger-strike is a powerful weapon in the Irish psyche. It overcomes fear in its deepest sense. It removes and makes negligible the threat of punishment. It powerfully commits back into the hunger-striker's own hands the full sanction of his own life and of his own will. (Keenan 1992, 55).

He also teaches John McCarthy about the historical and existential importance of the H Block dirty protests in the Maze prison, which took place in the late 1970s and early 1980s, where prisoners deliberately lived amongst their own detritus and excrement, refusing to clean themselves or their cells in non-violent dissent against their incarceration. Keenan sees this example as significant when he seeks to resist being forced to wear new clothes because such a capitulation would seem like accepting the possibility of a longer term of incarceration. But Keenan is also aware of the dangers of mythologizing his Irish past, making his existence in Belfast into the kind of epic romance in which he is a hero. He derives strength from its examples, but also chooses the pragmatic route for survival rather than the route of martyrdom in his dealing with his Lebanese captors: he wears the new clothes, he submits eventually to having his head and beard shaved, and he does not starve himself to death.

These are significantly choices Keenan makes because of the effects that such actions might have on McCarthy, and then on the other hostages. The hunger strike would be an imposition not only on his own body and resources, nor just on the guards: it is also an imposition of his will on his fellow hostages, and he decides not to go through with it because of what it might do to them. His sense of an Irish national identity in these moments is tempered by his sense that identity is a symbiotic thing. The upper-class English ex-public school boy and the working-class protestant Belfast teacher each define themselves against the other, as well as defining themselves against their common captors and situation. The nationalist rhetoric of resistance that Keenan invokes cannot speak precisely to McCarthy because he doesn't share its context; hunger strikes and dirty protests do not have the same meaning for him in shoring up his own sense of identity. In the end, Keenan's Irishness is something he holds onto, but he invokes it only for specific situations, as a pragmatic gesture against the particular moment, not as a solution for all the problems of captivity.

If identity depends on the *other* – myself *is* whatever the *other is not* – Keenan has also to be careful of identifying too closely with the contexts in which terrorism arises. He does not, after all, want to be like his guards. He has to resist the totalitarianism of the fundamentalist positions which bring about violence in both North of Ireland and in Lebanon. So he returns over and over again to a western, liberal humanist position; and although he is agnostic/atheist, he draws strength from the Christian traditions of a God of Love as opposed to a God of power, implicitly contrasting 'Allah, the God of retribution and judgement' (Keenan 1992, 147) with the New Testament tradition of a God of love, which figures 'power' as an embrace rather than as a destructive force:

> For them, the relationship with God was one of complete submission and man should not question the words of the Koran. I could not abide their abject surrender. How can one submit to what one does not understand? Their submission to God was an act of repression. Their God was a God of judgement and of vengeance and they were afraid of this God. ... [Their religion] held them in bondage. These men existed in their own kind of prison, perhaps more confining than the one that held us. (Keenan 1992, 187–8)

These are uplifting notions of what power might mean: that power is positive and loving (it 'embraces'); and there is also a powerful rhetoric which implies a transcendence of the conditions of imprisonment – if the guards are more prisoners than the prisoners themselves, then what price their power? But these transcendent moments of language are almost always undercut by a return to the reality of the situation: that a prisoner can be beaten, starved, left in the dark, crawled over by cockroaches, threatened with guns. Any transcendence is momentary. Keenan's narrative structures refuse a sweep in a single direction. If there are highs there are also very definitely lows.

Keenan's version of Irishness is not simple or inclusive: indeed it is structured on significant gaps and silences. He lays claim to a slightly romanticized Irish identity: an amalgam of the qualities of creativity, stubbornness, passionate resistance and a touch of the blarney that constitute a literary appropriation of Irish identity. Sharp divisions of class, or of religious and political affiliation are elided in this retelling of Irishness – it is a version which is a powerful fiction. What emerges from it is the desire to move away from political frameworks in the construction of selves and meanings. Politics is what got Keenan into this mess in the first place. Politics apparently offers no solution to the mess. In the course of the narrative, a politicized (though also pragmatic) Irish identity becomes something else instead – an idealized, mythologized, romanticized version rather than a political reality. 'Politics can only be a small part of what we are', says Keenan in the Preface. 'It is a *way* of seeing, it's not all-seeing in itself' (Keenan 1992, 3).

In many ways what most shocks the reader of this text are the insults offered to the bodies of those imprisoned. The food is monotonous and sometimes scarce; the electricity supply is uncertain, and they are occasionally left in darkness for days at a time; they have no occupations except for the ones that they can dream up for themselves, or make using the debris from their diurnal existence; it is not always possible to wash or go to the toilet at will; McCarthy and Keenan are forced to share a physical intimacy which is remarkably close to that usually associated with lovers – but as they are not lovers, the lack of privacy, the fact that one may occasionally have bodily needs that cannot be denied, is particularly painful. Keenan narrates, for example, what it feels like to defecate in front of another person, and to have to live with the consequential stench in a very confined space. He writes of the dysentery he suffered from, and its real physical effects, as well as of McCarthy's nursing of him through this his own pain and disgust. And of McCarthy trying to help him to pee after he is chained upside-down for resisting the will of the most brutal guard, Said. He also speaks of an effect of impotence after his first few weeks of solitary confinement, when his body refuses to be aroused through masturbatory fantasy. Powerlessness over bodily functions – shit or sex – is one of the aspects of the book which asks us to think through the category of the human. Like language, the possession of the *logos*, the idea that man is not merely an instinctive animal is one of the ways in which that category is defined. Man is not supposed to foul his own space; man is supposed to be able to choose the moments of his sexuality. When the body lets you down, there is fear. Keenan uses the word 'abject' to describe his captors; but his experiences are closely involved in what Julia Kristeva, in *Powers of Horror* has called *abjection*. She argues that the body, with its urgent instincts and waste products, is one of the key sites of disgust. We shudder and turn away from our bodily mess because it reminds us that, far from inhabiting the mind alone, far from residing in pure subjectivism, we are also objects in the world. Corporeal necessity over-rides mental will: subjectivity (mind) and object (body) collapse as structuring binaries and selfhood is forced to confront loathing and disgust (Kristeva 1982, 1–32). In Keenan's narrative, however, we are also shown how fear and loathing and disgust can become something else. When both men have shat in the corner of their cell out of dire necessity because they have been forgotten for three days, Keenan comments that 'we were now, and would always be somehow without shame or guilt before each other' (115). In breaking taboos and in the vulnerability they share, there is gain as well as loss.

The hostages were also chained for the last three years of their captivity. They were only let off their chains to wash and to exercise,

just like dogs. As Keenan comments, if they kept pigs in Muslim
Lebanon, they'd be better treated than the prisoners. But the abuse of
the body is most explicit in the beatings they receive because it is
within the power of the guard to beat them if he chooses. Keenan
explicitly identifies these beatings as a form of sexual abuse, in a
chapter entitled 'Rape'. The violence is sexualized partly because it is
an assault on the masculinity of those who are beaten, and partly
because it is undertaken in order to assert the masculinity of those who
do the beating: '[Said] was attempting to make himself a man. He
thought by beating and brutalizing us, that his manhood was assured'
(Keenan 1992, 208). This interpretation of sexualized violence is perhaps
particularly satisfying to the hostages because it implicates their captors
in a sexuality that their belief-system would not tolerate – homosexual
sadism. But Keenan is also struck by the implications of that violence,
and its sources in Western movies such as the *Rambo* and *Rocky* series.
Western entertainment, just as much as fundamentalism and
ignorance, has played its part in the creation of the mindset of the
guards. Violence is not a displacement of repressed sexuality only in
fundamentalist Beirut where the cinema audiences of young Arab men
'would groan and moan in a kind of ecstasy, crying out the names of
the weapons ... "Kalashnikov, Kalashnikov, Beretta, Beretta" ... The
cinema rang with a chant of excited worship' (Keenan 1992, 133). The
message of violence as a form of sexual potency is *in* the films
themselves, and rebounds back on western identity as liberal, tolerant
or humane.

   Writing of the humiliations that were suffered by his body, Keenan
refuses the category or status of victim. He regards self-pity as destructive, and as a sign of defeat. Resistance is not futile, though it may be
dangerous. The body is natural, and has its instincts. It is by accepting
that the body is also part of the category of the human that Keenan was
able to produce a sense of self when all other markers of identity were
taken from him. The body is the site of subjectivity as well as of
subjection; it is by dramatizing that belief that the narrative seeks to
transcend the conditions which provoked the narrative in the first place.

Note

1. The marketing of these other texts is also significantly different from
   that of Keenan's narrative. Both were published by popular mass market

paperback publishers, with author photographs on the front, and with glossy production values (indeed, Terry Waite's name appears embossed in gold). Both also reprinted photographs of the authors, and their friends and family as part of the text itself, breaking up the narrative of confinement with images of happy families, life at work, ordinary experience. McCarthy and Morrell's text, in particular, was marketed as a love story above all, though the 'happily ever after ending' of marriage and children, did not in the end occur in life beyond the narrative. These autobiographies were marketed as the triumphant reassertion of normality after the extremity of appalling experience. There is, on the other hand, no author photograph of Brian Keenan in the first paperback edition of *An Evil Cradling*. And the cover refuses the 'documentary' marketing cliché of the 'real-life story' as presented by mass market paperback production associating the story instead with the more 'highbrow' and 'quality' productions. The cover image is an illustration by Brian Cairns, showing, emblematically rather than realistically, a seated naked man, his knees drawn up to his face, and his head hidden – a man whose adoption of the foetal position illustrates his physical humiliation and his mental distress. No reassertion of normality on this cover – and that maps very neatly the fact that the book itself does not suggest that normality is reassumed, with its last words emphasizing that 'freedom comes slowly at first' (Keenan 1992, 296). The cover messages of these various texts situate them very neatly in relation to their proposed audiences, though the marketing does not really do justice to either McCarthy and Morrell or to Waite, whose texts are rather better written and thought out than their tabloid styling implies.

6 Talking Properly: Class Acts in Carolyn Steedman and Alan Bennett

> Mental life flows from material conditions. Social being is determined above all by class position – location within the realm of production. Consciousness and politics, all mental conceptions spring from material forces and the relations of production and so reflect these class origins. (Alexander 1984, qut. Steedman 1989, 12)

In Richard Hoggart's 1957 tome, *The Uses of Literacy*, a foundational text for what is now called 'cultural studies', Hoggart investigates the meanings of working-class life in the early and middle years of the twentieth century in relation to the narrowed views available to people who were both only marginally literate, and who lived within a more or less subsistence economy – certainly not, that is, within a realm of material privilege and plenty. This is a world in which the menfolk work long hours for low pay in heavy, dirty industry, and where the women 'get by' on what their husbands can earn; a world of anonymous streets of identical red-brick terraced houses; the lives here are not understood as 'individual lives' at all, but are instead figured as typical, or even stereotypical – or, more crudely, as the life of the herd, hemmed in by both material circumstances and the limited vocabulary for emotions and thought that are the consequence of poor education. In setting out the working-class life that he himself experienced as a child, Hoggart was acting in good faith, I believe. He thought that he was telling a kind of truth about lives lived in scarcity, want, hardship and sorrow; these were also lives in which deprivation was not always experienced as deprivation. His analysis of this kind of life is one that associates it strongly with the lives of the non-literate peoples analysed by Walter Ong in *Orality and Literacy*. 'Life', for these people 'is very much a week-by-week affair, with little likelihood of saving a lump sum to fall back on', and no possibility of planning for – or even imagining – a better future (Hoggart 1992, 44). It is a life of monotony and sameness, week-in, week-out, with each day measured by the task it requires (wash day, ironing day, cleaning day, shopping day). It is also a life constricted by the limited consciousness that limited material conditions produce and reproduce. Acceptance of one's lot, cheerfulness in the face of adversity, proverbs, stock phrases and attitudes expressed in the language of previous generations, Hoggart suggests, are features of a life that is utterly *subjected to* the conditions the people live in. Their subjectivity resides in clichés, repetitive verbal gestures which are comforting because they are predictable in a world where so much can and does go wrong. Thus, writing of the popularity of *Peg's Paper*, a weekly magazine aimed at a working-class readership in the 1920s and 30s, Hoggart observes:

> If we look ... at the stories [in the magazine], we are reminded at once of the case against 'stock responses': every reaction has its fixed counter for presentation. I run through the account of a trial: the mouths are 'set', the faces 'tense with excitement', tremors run down the spines; the hero exhibits 'iron control' and faces his captors with a 'stony look'; his watching girl-friend is the victim of an 'agonized heart' as 'suspense thickens in the air'. But what does this indicate? That the writers use cliché and that the audience seems to want cliché, that they are not exploring experience, realizing experience through language? (Hoggart 1992, 128)

The 'case against' the stock response is the literary or aesthetic case: cliché masks feeling rather than expressing it, is the argument. But Literature and Art (the capitalization is important) are not the possessions of these subjectivities, whose self-possession is apparently blunted by dis-privilege. Aesthetic or literary values belong to a world of material privilege in which, as the Eagleton quotation I cited in the Introduction suggests, someone else is doing the donkeywork. In the apparently anonymous working-class districts of northern England, however, the point is, precisely, that nobody else is doing the donkeywork, and consciousness is therefore confined by the demands of daily experience. Thus, as I suggest above, Hoggart's analysis of working-class speech patterns and the consciousnesses those patterns express maps closely onto Ong's analysis of oral peoples and the ways in which they transmit their important stories and their hard-won practical knowledge, also in terms of cliché, for oak trees always need to be sturdy and warriors always brave to fix both the emotional repertoire and the knowledge it contains in place (Ong 1980, 9).

As Carolyn Steedman's *Landscape for a Good Woman* attests, however, there is also a 'case against' Hoggart's view of the labouring classes – along with the views of other writers who focus on the same social groupings. For, in its own way, it is also a stereotype, masking the differences between people who lived this kind of life, and denying them the specificity and individuality that more materially privileged people are usually accorded. Moreover, the stories of working-class escapes from sameness and dis-privilege documented, in the wake of the early novels of D. H. Lawrence, in the so-called 'Angry Young Men' writings of the 1950s, are masculine stories, which make no place for the young women who also sometimes 'escaped'. As Steedman puts it: 'Women are ... without class, because the cut and fall of a skirt and good leather shoes can take you across the river and to the other side' (Steedman 1986, 15–16). The 'stepping stones' of her escape, she writes, were 'clothes, shoes and make-up' (15) – the assumption of a disguise and the performance of a certain classed (classy) version of gender.

In a very different context, discussing the diaries and correspondence of middle-class Victorian women such as Elizabeth Barrett Browning and her circle, Liz Stanley makes precisely the opposite case – the case against a focus on individualism in the recuperation of the stories of nineteenth-century middle-class women. Discussing Margaret Forster's biography of Elizabeth Barrett, she comments that it is, in the terms that it sets itself, an excellent biography, true to the sources of the archive materials. At the same time, though, 'from other more renegade sources a different picture can be assembled', and she suggests that it might be better to treat this particular biographical subject less as an individual than as an example of a socially constructed figure, inhabiting networks of influence and discussion. The suggestion that there might be a different picture of the subject if different resources are called into the narrative, is not, Stanley argues, a criticism of Forster's methodology, but it does point out that:

> *all* biographical research involves making choices about what counts as 'knowledge' about the subject ... These are *epistemological* choices, which result in a particular construction of the subject and the social world. It is not possible to avoid making such choices. My preferred – anti-spotlight, feminist, constructionist – approach equally excludes

some things from consideration as well as highlighting others; however, I find focussing on networks and relationships better fits my concern with the social. (Stanley 1992, 215–16)

It is certainly true that different foci in describing the construction of subjectivities will produce different narrative accounts of the process and radically divergent emphases about the importance of different elements. I am, however, especially struck by two observations that arise from Stanley's suggestion about a different approach to biography through a collective lens rather than an individual one. The first is that it points out the extent to which individuality is apparently securely possessed by the nineteenth-century middle classes (even the women). Individual biography is the usual method of approaching these figures. And by extension, it implicitly argues that individuality is not securely possessed by the working classes – male or female – at all. The collective biography has, in fact, been the 'usual' method for producing narratives of working-class subjectivities, at least in those accounts of it which were originally produced by (middle-class) social investigation in the nineteenth century and beyond. As Peter Keating has suggested, the social investigators often figured themselves as individuals who explored the masses, quasi-heroic figures who journeyed into 'an alien culture and offer ... the detailed results of [their] findings' (Keating 1976, 13), rather than as class representatives who investigated the representatives of other (economically and socially lower) classes. That this culture *is* alien to the privileged observer is dramatically articulated by what Steedman identifies as Henry Mayhew's bafflement in his confrontation with the Watercress Seller in the series of interviews he conducted for a daily newspaper that were eventually collected as *London Labour and the London Poor* during the 1850s and 60s. Mayhew, Steedman argues, cannot 'place' the watercress seller, has no category to fit her into: 'He was attracted to her, and repelled by her at the same time', Steedman observes, because when he spoke to her as a child, 'she would not be treated as a child' (Steedman 1986, 128). Mayhew's confusion arises from the facts that, first, she looked like a child, but had an adult attitude to her labour and its economic value to her poverty-stricken household; and second, that all her personal relationships were 'bound by [her] economic vision' (Steedman 1986, 135). She exemplifies a kind of category error – for nice middle-class children (the sort that Mayhew presumably knew best) did not have to work for a living, so this child is not a child. By the same token, nice middle-class people of whatever age, living in a realm of economic privilege, do not notice the privilege they inhabit, and therefore narrate their personal relationships in terms other than purely economic value with abstract words like love and affection. The little girl's subjectivity is conditioned by material circumstance to be necessarily an intersubjectivity. The child is primed by her situation to recognize her interdependence on others (and theirs on the few shillings she makes in a week), so that her individuality is distinctively and explicitly also a *connectedness* to those others, figured in the terms of her economic contribution which she exchanges for love and affection.

What is important about Mayhew's interviews for Steedman, however, is precisely the fact that he interviewed *individual* subjects, *particular* examples of the socio-economies he investigated. Thus, although he is baffled and cannot always interpret what he sees and hears in the terms of the models he already inhabits (these are not stories like David Copperfield's), he does at least provide examples of labouring people speaking on their own behalf, though they are also, presumably speaking in response to the (often slightly off-target) questions that he asks. The water-cress seller's account of her own life requires a different kind of reading practice, Steedman suggests, because her desperately impoverished lot undermines our normative responses to narrative. In comparing and contrasting her story with that of Freud's Dora, narrated in 'A Fragment of An Analysis of a Case of Hysteria', she points out the ways in which the little girl has a sound grasp of her own situation, and demonstrates mental health and coherence. But her story 'does not fit: all its content and its imagery demonstrate its marginality to the central story, of the bourgeois household and the romances of the family and the fairy-tales that lie behind its closed doors' (Steedman 1986, 139). The dominant narrative models do not fit the subjectivities of those who are excluded and marginalized.

The two texts I consider in this chapter, Alan Bennett's *Writing Home* and Steedman's *Landscape for a Good Woman*, are both, amongst other things, descriptions of the effects of class positioning on subjectivity, especially the effects of the labouring class's marginal position in relation to a dominantly middle-class culture. Steedman, however, is also anxious to state the case of gender in relation to class – and to focus on differences between people rather than on their sameness. She argues for a version of subjectivity that is, if not absolutely determined by class position and material circumstance, is nonetheless strongly conditioned by it. But individual working-class people experience their subjection individually, uniquely. To serve as an illustration of this fact, she inserts part of her own autobiography, alongside her mother's biography, into her more general historical observations, for she was brought up by her mother, a woman who worked outside the home rather than labouring entirely within it, as Hoggart's narrative suggests was 'always' the case; and her father 'wasn't a patriarch', all-powerful within the domestic space as a compensation for his powerlessness outside it. Her point is to 'particularize ... not in order to find a description that can be universally applied (the point is *not* to say that all working-class childhoods are the same, nor that experience of them produces unique psychic structures)', but to enable a mode of historical inquiry that permits the 'people in exile' from mainstream accounts to begin to use the 'autobiographical "I" ' (Steedman 1986, 16). In other words, her project demands that working-class narratives (and narratives *about* the working classes) be emancipated from stereotypical structures so that the subjectivities within this class grouping can inhabit – and be represented as inhabiting – individuality. The fascination of her account is that she must also do so in relation to typicality – the general and the particular emerge as mutually determining categories for the making of selfhood.

The trajectory of Alan Bennett's *Writing Home* is, in one important sense, precisely the reverse of Steedman's view. For Bennett, the class origins he describes in his text, working-class and northern, have deprived him of social confidence. Instead of wishing to 'stand out' from his background, to dominate his own particular landscape with figures,[1] he seeks instead to blend in, to fit in, to disappear. *Writing Home*, therefore, is a hybrid text that combines the highly personal writing of autobiographical fragments and excerpts from Bennett's diaries with samples of the works he has written for public consumption, screenplays, occasional journalism, obituaries, reviews and other more idiosyncratic pieces. The personal revelations of this text are carefully modulated, for, as Bennett puts it: 'authors resent the knowledge of themselves they have volunteered to their readers' (Bennett 1994, 321). He chooses carefully what to reveal, and leaves a great deal carefully concealed, refusing to assert any kind of individualism, though that is not to say that he is not an individual. On the other hand, he too resists the stereotyping of working-class subjectivities, particularly the literary uses to which such stereotypes have been put. In a skit he originally wrote in the early 1970s, and which he reprised in 1981 for *The Listener* magazine, he parodied the very idea of the writer's 'roots' in Northern England, in the pastiche of an interview between a journalist and a northern working-class author:

> We were all miners in our family. My father was a miner. My mother is a
> miner. These are miner's hands. But we were all artists, I suppose, really.
> But I was the first one who had this urge to express myself on paper
> rather than at the coalface. But, under the skin, I suppose I'm still
> a miner. I suppose, in a very real sense, I'm a miner writer. (Bennett
> 1994, 383)

This could be a Monty Python sketch, and there is a wonderful dramatic
irony in the fact that 'miner writer' can scarcely string intelligent sentences together. In his commentary on this sketch, Bennett suggests that
he objects to the cliché of the northern writer who goes back to his roots,
who falsifies his own history by claiming at once that his early life was
hideously squalid and remarkably transcendent ('we were all artists ...').
And he comments that he dislikes this kind of self-dramatization
because it partakes of the falsifications of nostalgia. Although he was
born and bred in Leeds in what he 'supposes' must have been a working-
class family, 'it all seemed perfectly satisfactory at the time', and the only
deprivation he appears to have suffered is that he got no material for
writing from his childhood because he did not, in fact, suffer from a
deprivation that felt like deprivation during the experience (Bennett
1994, 385–6). Actually, though, *Writing Home* is filled with the materials
of his past, slightly uncomfortably poised between precisely the very
nostalgia he disparages and the disparagement of it. More importantly,
however, Bennett is also concerned with category errors, from the
unwittingly revelatory incongruities of (overheard) everyday speech to
his own 'inability' to 'read' social situations and nuances. And as with
Steedman's text, this is an issue to do with class as a broad category as
well as with individual temperament and preference. *Writing Home*
is fragmentary in construction, but not incoherent for all that; it focuses
attention on the conceptual lacunae that come from class positioning,
as well as on the strategies for dealing with them – and the fragmentation
is part of the process of resolving social awkwardness.

Carolyn Steedman's *Landscape for a Good Woman*: between history and autobiography

> All happy families are alike, but an unhappy family is unhappy after its
> own fashion. (Tolstoy 1954, 13)

Carolyn Steedman is a professional historian, a Professor indeed, of history and education at the University of Warwick. Amongst the many things that her book is about, it is above all, about the writing of history itself, and the necessary compromises that such writing entails for both readers and writers of history. The point of historical writing, she suggests, is to provide explanations for historical events, but the process of telling – the choices about what is included or excluded in the process of telling – mean that it is only a temporary explanation that 'will do' for now (Steedman 1986, 22). But along the way, she undertakes a number of interesting meditations on the nature of story-telling and their effects on the subjectivities they document and on the subjectivities of those who read them. *Landscape for a Good Woman* considers the tensions between autobiography (personal and private narratives) and history (official and public versions of the past), and her text represents a critique of the usual historical methodologies because of their blindness to both gender and class. It also offers a critique of the explanatory mode of history-writing, the connections that are 'forged' between disparate events in order to produce an interpretation of them. The risk of explanation is that it totalizes and homogenizes; and it risks 'explaining away'. And yet this is also in some sense the obligation of narrative, whether historical or autobiographical. The tensions between the will to tell an authentic story, and the necessity of moulding the story into coherence are what *Landscape for a Good Woman* examines. Additionally, it also focuses attention on the subjectivities that do not fit the normative patterns of the particular genres of history and fiction. Her argument concerns the fact that narratives have real effects: readers seek themselves in the stories (and histories) they read; they empathize and identify with the characters (and historical personages) they encounter in texts; they measure their own achievements and failings against those stories and histories. And the problem with this is that some kinds of experience are actually absent from the very narratives where the reader has most right to expect their presence.

Steedman, writing in the 1980s, is able to take it for granted that history does not consist merely of the biographies of 'great men' as Thomas Carlyle had put it in the nineteenth century. Her professional career began in the period when labour history (the history of the working classes), inflected by Marxist approaches to what history might mean, became almost the dominant mode of historical inquiry. But, despite her own working-class origins, she argues that stories like hers are still absent even from the new canon produced by the different perspective the labour historians presented – an absence she figures in terms of gender. At the same time, whilst academic history was revolutionized by the emphasis on social history in the 1960s and 70s, Steedman was also living through another revolutionary movement: that of academic feminism, which brought gender to bear on a variety of discourses, including history. But, again, although this new perspective also had its importance for her thinking, she argues that she was excluded from the mainstream stories about gender oppression because of her class. She read classic feminist accounts of coming to female consciousness, or of women's relations with their fathers, and felt 'the painful and familiar sense of exclusion from these autobiographies of middle-class little girl-hood and womanhood, envy of those who belong, who can ... use the outlines of conventional romantic fiction to tell a life story' (Steedman 1986, 17). The dominant explanatory frameworks of, for instance, psychoanalysis, she suggests, were written for and by the middle classes, as if they were universal stories, when in fact they are blind to their own social exclusions. This affects working-class men and women in particular ways; they are not part of the story, even *the* story of familial relationships outlined by Freud and his followers. Their subjectivities are ignored and misunderstood by the very discourses that are alleged to bring them to light.

Steedman's epigraph to the book, taken from John Berger's *About Looking*, sets up the frames within in which she is working. Berger writes:

> The present tense of the verb *to be* refers only to the present: but nevertheless with first person singular in front of it, it absorbs the past which is inseparable from it. 'I am' includes all that has made me. It is more than a statement of immediate fact: it is already biographical. (Berger qut. Steedman 1986, 3)

This statement is significant in general for the understanding of subjectivity in that it states that selfhood is the result of the accretion of experiences: I am what I have been, or even, I am what I *think* I have been. But it is especially important for historical narratives in that it at once establishes the necessity for the study of history (the present absorbs the past and is inseparable from it which is why the study of history is necessary); and it also establishes what we might call the impossibility of history as an objective discourse. For if all statements of being are always already implicated in the past, what we look for in history reflects our own present much more than it reflects the past *per se*. Indeed, the past is in some senses always altered by the concerns of the present – history is not what it used to be, one might say, precisely because of the intervention in the past of present concerns with class and gender, *inter alia*.

These new emphases have dismantled history's claim to be a supremely empiricist and objective discourse, in which the written record was supposed to have some relatively transparent relationship with lived reality. The object of its study was the remains – the memorials – of the past that are enshrined in official documents and records. But those remains, like the remains of a long-dead body, represent only very partial evidence. As Catherine Morland comments about the discourse of history in Jane Austen's *Northanger Abbey*: 'Real solemn history, I cannot be interested in … The quarrels of popes and kings, with wars or pestilences on every page; the men all so good for nothing, and hardly any women at all' (Austen 1972, 123). Official history, that is, is exclusive. It excludes all men who are not 'great' (and who judges greatness, what are its standards, as Virginia Woolf might have, but did not ask), and it excludes virtually all women. It produces an objective and universal truth that is not objective (since it serves the interests of 'great men'); which is not universal (for there are hardly any women nor labouring-class men at all), and which probably therefore isn't 'true'. The concentration of traditional history was on 'fact', derived from written records. The 'facts' found there are taken more or less uncritically 'as read'.

'Fact' however is a problematic term. The traditional, empiricist historian must seek facts and events using a properly constituted 'historical' method. S/he must approach primary sources and refer to them extensively in order to prove the rigour, originality and 'seriousness' of his/her project. The sources must be cross-referenced for accuracy and representativeness. There must be a due respect shown for the origins of sources: when, where, why, how was the text produced, what appears to be its intended audience, what sources has it used in its own formation, and so on. Personal or subjective accounts are examined in the interests of comprehensiveness, though they must, of course, be treated suspiciously as partial and selective, ignoring the fact that 'official' documents are also partial and selective in who and what they represent.[2] The development of feminist and labour history are two of the responses to gaps and blindnesses in the empirical historical record, and the problem that Steedman identifies is that these two new ways of seeing history were not combined, did not, as it were, speak to each other, nor to the official histories of the past.

Steedman's *Landscape* is written very much out of this context of rethinking history as an academic discourse. As Laura Marcus has put it, it is written at 'the intersections of biography and autobiography, case-history and social history, psychoanalysis and oral history' (Marcus 1994, 275). In telling the interlinked stories of her mother and her own childhood, alongside accounts of one of Freud's most famous patients and Henry Mayhew's uneasy interview with a labouring-class child, the little Watercress Seller, she mounts a critique of the various historical narratives which exclude stories like her own. In addition, in publishing autobiographical material alongside historical medita-tions, she is also polemically focusing our attention on the processes of history-*writing*, on forms as well as on content. This subjective focus opens up an arena for speculation rather than insisting on the rigours of interpretation. Thus, whilst Steedman is broadly in sympathy with the impetus to open up the discourse of history to marginalized groups that both labour history and women's history initiate, she actually very strongly disapproves of the totalizing narratives of gender and working-class lives that these writers present us with. 'It will not do', she argues, 'to describe working-class childhood as a uniform experience, and to reserve the case-studies for the children of the upper classes' (123). Such narratives are a kind of dehumanization of the people whose sto-ries these are: to historians, even those who come from working-class backgrounds, the working class all look the 'same', are an undifferenti-ated, unindividuated mass. Her own story is *eccentric*, outside the cen-tre, at the margins even of the margins. It does not fit into the paradigms of working-class life that Hoggart *et al.* have produced: hers was not a life in which father worked in heavy industry, and mother stayed home to mind the house and children in some northern town where there were rows of terraced houses that all looked the same, and all housed remarkably similar families. Steedman's mother was clearly immensely powerful in the home, not least because her father was such a repressed and virtually absent figure. But it was not a power based on affection, such as that narrated by the male working-class writers against whom Steedman measures her own account; when they talk about their own working-class mothers, 'our mam', they rep-resent them with a blindness to the particularity of their experience as gendered experience.

Thus, this is not only a narrative of class, but also one of gender, since mothers and daughters might be expected to have very different relationships from mothers and sons. 'All women become like their mothers, that is their tragedy. No man does, that is his', says Algy Moncrieff in Wilde's *The Importance of Being Earnest* (Wilde 1994, 371). This is rewritten by Steedman in her comment that she ended up 'believing that my identification was entirely with [my mother], that whilst hating her, I was her' (55). The concentration on female relationships in a quasi-historical document unsettles the accounts that history offers of human relationships by refocusing attention, from the public to the private sphere, and from explanatory narrative to experience. One of the significant things that Steedman's text does, therefore, is to resist the very power of narrative in history, whilst at the same time producing a narrative which she openly admits is partial and subjective. But for her, it is nonetheless important for being a story told in a personal voice.

The central focus of Steedman's text is in the space between experience as lived, and experience as remembered and retold. At several points in *Landscape*, she emphasises that the narratives provided by both history and literature leave their traces on memory, and modify the remembered events. For that reason, her first chapter is called 'Stories', and it expresses why the stories that a culture tells about itself are insufficient to express individual experience. She tells us that the book is about 'lives for which the central interpretative devices of the culture don't quite work' (5). Literature and a certain type of history tend to suppress the eccentricities of an individual experience in the service of producing a coherent and stable narrative that acts as a catch-all explanation for most people's lives. 'Personal interpretations of past time', Steedman writes, 'are often in deep and ambiguous conflict with the official interpretative devices of a culture' (6). She goes on to argue that even the relatively new discipline of working-class history, arising of history's confrontation with Marxist theory, actually suppresses the stories of large numbers of people: 'The problem with most childhoods lived out by social class III (manual), IV and V parents is that they are simply not bad enough to be worthy of attention'. Her own childhood was 'not only ... not very bad', but it was experienced by her as '*ordinary*' (Steedman 1986, 9). Material and emotional deprivation were not experienced at the time as deprivations. Steedman and her sister knew, because they had been told, that they were lucky: 'she was a good mother; she'd told us so' (1). Like all children, knowing no other life apart from her own family, as a child she had been unable to place her experience in the terms of the wider world. It's for that reason that she was able as a child, looking at her mother's elegant 'New Look' clothing in the early fifties, to decide that her family must really be middle class, despite the lack and longing all around her. 'I ... reflected very precisely on my mother's black, waisted coat with the astrakhan collar, and her high-heeled suede black suede shoes, her lipstick. She looked so much better than the fat, spreading South London mothers around us, that I thought we had to be middle class' (37).

Indeed, it is only when she came to compare her own childhood to those of the other women that she knows professionally, and then to the lives of her sister's children, that her own deprivation became clearer. If working-class stories exclude her because her life was not bad enough or because their focus is on male subjectivity, reading middle-class autobiographies of family life is similarly disappointing. Steedman cannot use what she calls 'the outlines of conventional romantic fiction' to tell her own story (17). Middle-class women writers, says Steedman, in an interestingly paradoxical formation, are caught in 'an exclusion from the experience of others that measures out their own central relationship to the culture.'

> The myths tell their story ... the psychoanalytic drama was constructed to describe ... middle-class women ... The woman whose drama psy-choanalytic case-study describes ... never does stand to one side, and watch, and know she doesn't belong. (Steedman 1986, 17–18)

In other words, Steedman argues that her own experience is served neither by the paradigms of literature (fairy-stories, conventional romance, myth), nor by those of history (working-class, but male, or traditional and utterly exclusive).

At the same time, because lived experience is all we have to measure memory, literature and history against, it is difficult to judge the pre-cise order of experience: there is no meta-experience, as it were, which transcends the experience of living. As Steedman comments, it was a 'joyless childhood', 'But I don't *remember* the oddness; it's a reconstruc-tion' (Steedman 1986, 44). The layer that narrative – the re-ordering of experience when it is told as a story – necessarily places over experi-ence is the historian's problem. It cannot be escaped.

Moreover, it is not just telling an experience that modifies it. There is also the problem of reading about experiences other than your own that shifts the focus of one's own memory. If Steedman argues that her own story does not measure up to the grim narratives of poverty produced in working-class autobiography or the happy-ever-after of fairy-tales of some middle-class narratives, she is nonetheless interpellated into such narratives, forced to see herself through the narrative positions that such stories imply. When she thinks about the time when her mother kept a kind of theatrical boarding-house, she writes of the treachery of a memory overlain with literary models – memory interpellated (called into the position of) the models of literary culture.

> I like the idea of being the daughter of a theatrical landlady, but that enterprise, in fact, provides me with my most startling and problematic memories. The girl from Aberdeen really did say, 'Och, no, not on the table!' as my father flattened a bluebottle with his hand, but did he *really* put down a newspaper at the same table to eat his breakfast? I remember it happening, but it's so much like the books that I feel a fraud, a bit-part player in a soft and southern version of *The Road to Wigan Pier*. (Steedman 1986, 35)

In passages such as these, Steedman expresses the layering of experience once it has been exposed to narrative. It's not just her own memories that count, but also the reading she has done. The 'idea' of being the daughter of a theatrical landlady is a literary idea as well as a description of fact. Certain picturesque things really happen which speak of the traditional representations of working-class life, such as her father's use of a newspaper instead of a cloth, but they become fraudulent or clichéd because they have already been represented in working-class history elsewhere. She dramatizes, as well as describes, the interplay between texts: the script you lived and the script you write or read about living.

After her mother's death, Steedman discovered that her mother and father had never married, and that therefore she and her sister were both illegitimate. 'We have proper birth certificates, because my mother must have told a simple lie to the registrar, a discovery about the verisimilitude of documents that worries me a lot as a historian', (40) Steedman comments. The remark is a mere aside, but the text as a whole is a very serious assault on the authenticity of documents that must worry not only historians, but all readers and writers. In the later part of the book, when she is talking about the stories of Henry Mayhew's Little Water Cress Girl and Freud's Dora, she insists that history, far from being a totalising and coherent narrative, must instead inhabit disruption and dislocation (127). And this connects to her own narrative method in *Landscape* where events are not placed in chronological, causal sequences, but are recalled in a seemingly random way. The relationships between events and her responses to them are not precisely causal. They are implied by juxtaposition, not stabilized by a grammar of causation, of the words 'because', 'however', and 'therefore'. In the terms of traditional history or traditional autobiography, this is an incoherent story, and, as Steven Marcus suggests, 'a coherent story is in some manner connected with mental health' (quoted Steedman 1986, 131). But the judgements of health or otherwise come from elsewhere, from a cultural centre from which Steedman's family is marginalized, as witnessed in the short scene narrated about the visit of a health visitor, shortly after the birth of Steedman's sister. Steedman describes a vignette with her mother weeping at the bare window of a Streatham house, pained by the judgement of the health visitor who has proclaimed ' "This house isn't fit for a baby" ... And then she stopped crying, my mother, got by, the phrase that picks up after all difficulty (it says: it's like this; it's unfair; I'll manage)' (Steedman 1986, 2). The health visitor's damning comment is the voice of the cultural centre, which decides on health and fitness, on insanity. Thus, one of the things that text charts is the stand-off between being both absolutely visible and absolutely invisible to official culture. In one sense, the working-class family is very well known to organs of officialdom. Health visitors can pronounce judgement on Steedman's mother in a way that they never could on a middle-class mother. The doctor who wrote in a character reference that Steedman's mother was 'clean' is also making a judgement that he would not make on someone of his own class (34). Since Mayhew was writing in the 1840s and 50s, and before that too, the working population has been an object of study for official bourgeois culture. But observing a group of people as a group, and understanding that the group is made up of unique individuals are two quite different things. The stories of working-class life that middle-class culture tells are an attempt to fit one group into the terms of reference of the other. Since the middle-class officials have the power to label, the power over language ('this one's got an inferiority complex'), the weaker group is categorized and fixed. And yet, Mrs Steedman also represents a heroic resistance of this fixity: 'she got by'; she coped, she managed, just as earlier generations had done in the face of official incomprehension. Her endurance was an act of defiance, like tearing up the ration books, or throwing back an inadequate tip in the face of a wealthy client. Her very existence as a character in a story, or as a figure standing out from a landscape, as an alternative representative of the performance of representation, tears holes in the seamless narrative that homogenizes the working class and makes it possible to fix and judge them. At the same time, though, for all the valiant effort of this story, the mother will retreat back into the background. On Steedman's last visit to her mother, she notices a print by L. S. Lowry hanging over the mantelpiece. Lowry's paintings, which enjoyed immense popularity as reproductions in the 1970s, documented a version of working-class life in Northern England that was then passing away in unemployment and economic depression. They are – oddly – nostalgic images of stick-like figures milling around their northern townscapes, on the way to and from work at the mill, painted in muted colours; the figures have no individual faces. The nostalgia is odd because the lives these images document were harsh; as Steedman puts it, 'Why did she go out and buy that obvious representation of the landscape she wanted to escape?' (Steedman 1986, 142). She does not know the answer to that question.

In the end, then, Steedman's narrative has a very serious purpose, which must be seen as a political purpose. Those who hold the power of representation hold real power over real people's lives and their capacity to inhabit a subjectivity of their own choosing. The obligation on those who represent others' lives is to ensure that their observations are accurate rather than stereotyped. Steedman's argument throughout her book is that there is no best-fit paradigm in narrative to describe experience. Narrative is always contingent, and the truths that it tells are only ever partial. History depends on the 'making' of it, its practices of formation, rather than on the facts. And the obligation on historians is towards a more careful reading of their sources, and towards a narrative that makes space for the exceptions as well as for the rules.

Bennett's *Writing Home*

> Every family has a secret, and the secret is that it's not like other families.
> (Bennett 1994, 35)

For Steedman, one of the defining moments of her narrative is her memory of a dream in which her mother is wearing – for the first time – a New Look coat, a lavish and expensive fashion statement of the early 1950s, a shake of the fist against rationing and wartime austerity. In the dream, her mother

> wore the New Look, a coat of beige gaberdine which fell in two swaying, graceful pleats from her waist at the back (the swaying must have come from very high heels, but I didn't notice her shoes), a hat tipped forward from hair swept up at the back. She hurried, something jerky about her movements, a nervous agitated walk, glancing round at me as she moved across the foreground. (Steedman 1986, 28)

This coat contained the meaning of romance for Steedman; it was a fabulously extravagant gesture requiring twenty yards of material; it also meant her mother's resistance to her role as drudge – for in the dream she has the coat, even if she also has 'two living barriers' in her daughters to the wealth of material it would have required to make it (30). Two other coats make similar – though also rather different – appearances in Bennett's *Writing Home*. In the Introduction to this collection of occasional writings of various kinds, Bennett describes his own experience of what we might call heteroglossia, his sense of being split between two modes of language (Northern speech with its flat vowels, and 'talking proper'), two modes of writing (writing as Art and writing as sincerity), and the sense of impersonation that haunts him. The impetus for this mediation is an anecdote of life back home in Leeds, where his father was a butcher, and where he was sometimes a butcher's delivery boy. One of their customers had a daughter who eventually became T. S. Eliot's second wife, Valerie. For years, he thought that his only connection to culture would be that 'I had once delivered meat to T. S. Eliot's mother-in-law' (Bennett 1994, ix). Some years later, his mother met Mrs Fletcher, the former customer, walking in the street with – it turns out – her famous son-in-law. Bennett was unable to get his mother to understand the momentousness of her encounter, that she had actually met Eliot, the winner of the Nobel Prize for Literature. ' "Well", she said, with that unerring grasp of the inessentials which is the prerogative of mothers, "I'm not surprised. It was a beautiful overcoat" ' (x).

In a second coat-related episode, Bennett, who owns an apartment in New York as well as homes in Yorkshire and London, describes an encounter with a New York mugger. The episode has the quality of a dream, dislocated in time and place, and in grammatical tense, as dreams often are. Bennett is wandering in an unfamiliar part of the city, and has just made a rapid retreat from a group of derelicts when he is 'confronted by a young man in a smart cavalry-twill coat, the coat slightly too big for him'. The man demands money, and realizing that Bennett has more cash on his person than he is giving away, 'he suddenly has a knife in his hand which he is holding before my face'. Bennett's gloss on this encounter is that he has been 'misled' by the coat

> into thinking him a better class of person. Suddenly I see why the coat is too big – because that too is stolen. I look into the face of this cold-eyed runt and see as I wake and die that I will perish because I have been a snob. (Bennett 1994, 120)

These episodes are what might be called 'allegories of misreading'. Clothing is a semiotic system – but like any other system, its meanings are arbitrary and open to misinterpretation. Clothes are a mask or performance of a particular social self, a signifier not a referent. Steedman's mother's New Look coat is the literally fabricated evidence of middle-class status. T. S. Eliot's lovely coat might be an 'inessential' in an understanding of who Eliot was, but they provide for Bennett's mother a reassurance of a social standing and respectability; in another context, though, a coat can both literally and metaphorically 'cloak' 'real' meanings, disguising and obfuscating interpretation in ways that might just literally prove fatal to the observer.

Alan Bennett's *Writing Home* is fundamentally about the negative meanings of what might be meant by 'self-consciousness'. In his partial self-revelations, he focuses on the semiotics of class, which remain important even though 'class isn't what it was' (Bennett 1994, 46). The misreadings of social situations that he suffers are the precise analogues for what he calls 'the treachery of books' (3); and, like Steedman, there is a persistent awareness through this text of a subjectivity that does not find its reflection in the cultural texts that surround it. Bennett's childhood did not match up to the stories he read. When he was briefly evacuated to a farm outside Leeds at the beginning of the Second World War, his parents presented the move in the manner of an adventure, and promised a picnic, 'something I had hitherto only come across in books'. His excitement about doing something that happened in stories meant that he missed the portentous announcement of the beginning of the war itself; and the picnic did not live up to the images the stories provided: it 'wasn't eaten as picnics were in books, on a snowy tablecloth set in a field by a stream, but was taken on a form in the bus station at Vicar Lane, where we waited half that day for a bus that would take us out of the supposedly doomed city' (Bennett 1994, 3–4). The fictions of middle-class Edwardian childhoods in the South of England were a fantasy of escape, a fantasy that reality never could live up to, even when the Bennett family briefly decamped to Guildford in Surrey where 'there were thatched cottages and mill-streams and children who called their parents "Mummy" and "Daddy" – the world I had read about in my books, and the world Mam and Dad had read about in theirs' (7). The experiment was not a success, and the family soon trailed back to Leeds. The problem, presumably, is that the stories are as 'classed' as real life itself; they contain no appropriate measure of the subjectivity of those others who do not share their implicit class positions. And this is not just a matter of minor, unimportant disappointments: if all the stories tell the same story of a particularized set of possibilities for selfhood, when one's own story does not match up, the presumption is, argues Bennett throughout *Writing Home*, that the fault is your own, not the fault of the stories' misrepresentations.

His disjointed autobiographical narratives are, in one sense, a representative or a shared story. Bennett, like many others from working backgrounds, was the beneficiary of the 1944 Education Act, the act which established universal secondary education, and which made it possible, via a system of scholarships, for children from poorer backgrounds to gain entry to the academic 'grammar-school system', to 'stop on' at school for much longer periods, and, eventually, for some of the them to enter the university system.[3] But each individual who went through this system experienced the same dislocations differently, uniquely. Bennett makes the point very forcibly that the working class itself is not a homogeny, where everyone really was the same, despite the uniformity of houses and occupations. His parents differed from those of his school friends because they were more shy and socially timid than other people were, or appeared to be; he experienced his schooldays as a period of partial isolation, in which his acutely felt difference from his contemporaries made him a loner rather than part of a group. Recalling a poem by the Leeds poet, Tony Harrison, for instance, he focuses on Harrison's deliberate recollection of the dialect word 'tusky', meaning rhubarb.

> I recall [the word] too, reading his poem, but cannot remember when I was a boy in Leeds ever calling it that myself. Other boys did, I remember.

> Other boys nicked rhubarb from the field's edge. Though I did it too, it was more fearfully than the others. They were part of the gang as I never was, quite, and not being part of the gang (the last to be picked, the first to be turned out) I never felt easy using the language. So with me it wasn't 'tusky'; I stuck to 'rhubarb'. In later years, and for the same reason, I never said 'bird' or 'screw', and today hearing myself say 'guy' I winced and felt it an imposture. (Bennett 1994, 160–1)

The language he was speaking, he is almost saying, was theirs before it was his. He is not at home even in the very dialect of the place that he comes from; unlike Joyce, this is not a matter of cultural imperialism, though, so much as a matter, Bennett argues, of temperament. That temperament makes him, if not a barbarian, at least someone whose language is foreign even to his own 'kind', a literal 'rhubarb, rhubarb', one might say.

Trying to make a coherent wholeness out of *Writing Home* is futile, for it is precisely about the tensions between revelation and concealment, private life and public persona, performance and sincerity. Near the end of the text, Bennett reprints a review of Andrew Motion's biography of Philip Larkin, in which he meditates on Larkin's public persona as a man who hated publicity, and the tensions that being a poet (and therefore what Yeats called 'a *public* smiling man') and being shy and socially inept (a private man) erect.

> Peter Cook once did a sketch in which, dressed as Garbo, he was filmed touring the streets in an open-topped limousine, shouting through a megaphone: 'I want to be alone!' Larkin wasn't quite as obvious as that, but poetry is a public-address system too and that his remoteness was so well publicised came about less from his interviews or personal pronouncements than from the popularity of [the] poems ... which located Larkin, put him on (and off) the map, and advertised his distance from the centre of things. (Bennett 1994, 367)

In autobiographical writings that focus on more extreme kinds of experience, self-revelation and self-expression function as modes of reassurance – for both reader and writer – that the writer still has a self to express and to reveal, despite all that has happened. But in stories of more 'ordinary' lives, the trajectory of the narrative is necessarily rather different. The will to communicate exists in dialectical relation with the will to conceal the self through the performance of a self that is not quite one's real self (whatever that might be). Unlike more conventional autobiographies, Bennett's text is less concerned with forging an identity in writing. This text does not chart his struggle towards individuated self-expression so much as it documents its attempts to disguise his subjectivity – he is more concerned with belonging, with fitting in than he is with standing out from the crowd. Bennett has a very well-developed public persona, representing himself as a shy and diffident man who nonetheless has an extremely weather eye for incongruity and absurdity – pleasures he quietly shares with readers and audiences. He speaks in a recognizably northern accent, though it is certainly not a broad accent. He is quietly spoken. That public image is fostered by the publicity photographs that adorn his various publications, which always represent him as a man of a certain age (which is fair enough – he *is* a man of a certain age), formally dressed in a jacket, pullover, shirt and tie, almost resembling a parody of a provincial schoolteacher from some 1950s grammar school. There is a semiotics of that imagery which is relatively legible to a British audience: this man is mild-mannered, he won't hurt you, he won't be cruel or violent. And the photographs are part of the text of *Writing Home*, part of the process of self-representation the text offers its readers. But are we in fact being provoked into our own version of the mis-reading of signs that nearly proved fatal to Bennett himself in his confrontation with the mugger?

We are warned against simple readings in the introduction. Bennett describes himself as a man who lives with conflicting tendencies – to be sincere, but not to give too much away. The dialectic of concealment and revelation is established in two phrases that he learned from his parents. In her fleeting encounter with T. S. Eliot, Bennett imagines his mother 'trying to "speak properly", though without "putting it on" – "putting it on" being one of the several charges Dad had against my mother's sisters ... [who] nursed pretensions to refinement'. His Mam and Dad had a faith that Bennett's superior education would enable him to square the circle of social performances enacted with sincerity – a faith in the possibility of 'being yourself'. They believed that 'education was a passport to social ease and had they been able to "stop on at school", everything would have been different ... Funny and voluble on their own, the slightest social pressure sent them into smiling, nodding silence. But it was different for me, they thought. I was educated; I could be myself; I had a self it was not embarrassing to be' (Bennett 1994, x). Of course, it is not so: in the minutiae of every-day life, almost any self can potentially be a site of embarrassment, and the gradual realization that everyone might feel this does not make the embarrassment go away. The text is thus structured around repeating incidences of the idea that other people are always – naturally – more self-confident, self-assured, self-possessed, than Bennett is (than I am), an idea that is continually deflated and disproved. The reality of his continuing shyness and diffidence is set up in tension against our narrative expectation that (as stories usually show us) we expect experience to change people, we 'know' that events alter consciousness.

The embarrassment Bennett inhabits is the result of a combination of class, region and temperament. The narrative that tells the story of Miss Shepherd, 'The Lady in the Van' who camped out for nearly fifteen years in a series of battered vehicles in the garden of Bennett's London home, is above all, a narrative of ongoing, persistent social embarrassment. This prolonged episode, as with so much else in *Writing Home*, is a relocation of the genre of the comedy of manners. A comedy of manners is a comic mode that presents society as a series of complex codes of behaviour; it is usually set in the upper-echelons of fashionable culture, and it insists that appearances count more than morality. Its heroic focus is generally on the unscrupulous exploiter of the code – the men or women who get what they want by playing on the social and moral vulnerability of others. In Bennett's version, of course, the 'hero' is not the unscrupulous exploiter, but the 'victim' of the code. By turning the genre's lens to another focus, he exploits it for rather different purposes. Part of his ability to 'speak properly' with which his education has furnished him is that he has privileged access to literary codes and sophisticated understandings of their meanings. The apparent randomness of *Writing Home* is testament to the extent to which this highly literate individual learned the rules of the games that originally left him foundering, and adapted them to different uses.

The gift of texts such as Steedman's and Bennett's, alongside their intellectual content and commitment, is the gift of social embarrassment. It might not sound like much of a gift, but it is all the same an important offering. Both texts unsettle comfortable assumptions about the class 'system', showing that it is an imposition, and also that it is neither impenetrable nor entirely inescapable. In the dramatic monologues Bennett wrote for the BBC in 1988 and 1998, entitled *Talking Heads*, the striking generic effect of this form has full rein. The viewer or reader of these scripts/texts eavesdrops on the mutterings of the individual speaker, often a working-class speaker, an older under-educated woman. Audiences experience a doubled relationship with that speaker in which one both simply listens to (or reads) a flow of words, and simultaneously 'judges' the subjectivity that produces them by reading between the lines of the words that are actually enunciated. This is a more humane process than it perhaps sounds because it requires close attention on the speaking subject; and like psychoanalysis, it requires that you pay attention to the gaps, the ellipses and fractures of the discourse. This process concretizes – makes real – the issues of class and subjectivity. Audiences are placed like social investigators, overhearing discourse that is not meant for them; but because this discourse, inconsequential and disordered as it often seems, is nonetheless 'aestheticized', the discomfort of the voyeur's positioning is made to function as a positive example of a necessary inter-subjectivity. We may be placed so that we can judge; but the judgement rebounds on us. Rather than charting self-development as a narrative of progress – as the genre of the middle-class fictions and autobiographies tend to do – Bennett's method in both dramatic monologues and more personal writings is to demonstrate that personalities develop, but not necessarily in progressive ways. He offers one alternative model of a subjectivity in writing such as Steedman's text demanded. And both writers show us that mental life is not absolutely determined by material circumstance, for both writers mounted reasonably successful escape bids, and mastered the discourses of their alleged social superiors.

Notes

1. This phrase is taken from Hoggart's *The Uses of Literacy*. He describes the social milieu he wishes to analyse as a landscape with figures. The force of Steedman's title, presumably, is that she is engaged in a rewriting of the kind of cultural history that Hoggart inaugurated.
2. This part of the argument was developed in collaboration with Dr Karen Sayer for a joint conference paper we delivered together in 1996. I am grateful to Dr Sayer for her input into my thinking here.
3. This story of state-sponsored opportunity has particular resonance for me, because it is in part my story: not mine directly – I'm actually too young; but both my parents were 'grammar-school' children, who passed the eleven plus examination and thereby gained access to a greater level of education than would have been easily possible for working-class children in previous generations. This was a mixed blessing. My father, much the same age as Bennett, though from a very different region and from

a background with considerably less privilege, won a scholarship not to a state grammar school, but to a British public school (which in Britain, means a private school). With a regional accent that marked not only his provincialism but also, very strongly, his class, the school offered both a remarkable opportunity and a real degree of personal misery.

7   China Women: Jung Chang's *Wild Swans* and Maxine Hong Kingston's *The Woman Warrior*

The past is a foreign country: they do things differently there. (Hartley 1958, 7)

In the attempt to work out who one is, one must also work out who one has been. In order to answer the question, 'who am I?' one is necessarily involved in the question 'how did I get to be who I am?' Who I am, in addition, is not merely a question of my personal past, the particularity of my own auto/biography. It is also implicated in the past as both wider history and culture: a context that is more collective than purely personal. If the cultural stories can exclude some subjectivities on the basis of class, then the strangeness of the past, figured by L. P. Hartley as a foreign land, is perhaps even more acutely realized by those subjectivities who have literally left their past behind, in foreign countries, as migrants, refugees and exiles. A central question in any discussion of subjectivity that suggests it is culturally derived rather than naturally occurring is about the extent to which subjectivity is therefore culturally specific. In other words, is the self-figuration that one finds in autobiographical writings dependent on a particularly western model of self-identity? Is autobiography itself a thoroughly western idea? In this chapter, through reading two very different autobiographies from ethnically Chinese women writing in the west, but with their ethnic identities always firmly in mind – with the presence of their personal and cultural pasts making the narratives what they are – I want to examine these questions. The two texts at issue are Jung

Chang's *Wild Swans*, first published in 1992 and Maxine Hong Kingston's *The Woman Warrior* first published in 1977.

The fundamental differences between them are extremely important for the arguments I want to make. Jung Chang's story of 'Three Daughters of China', as her subtitle has it, is a history of China in the twentieth century at least as much as it is a personal story. It places Jung Chang's family against the backdrop of the often violent and always dramatic political events that brought China – a feudal society at the beginning of the century – through a rapid political and industrial revolution, and made it a 'modern' communist state by its end. Her method partakes of documentary history and realism, discourses that she uses because her story is the story of a subjectivity learning the meaning of the very individualism that these discourses (history and realism) were developed to describe, even though she comes from a culture where individualism is radically repressed. Maxine Hong Kingston, on the other hand, presents a subjectivity in conflict both with the dominant models of western individuality and with the usual methods of representing them; her text eschews the realist conventions of chronology and factuality in favour of a writing that is fluid, fantastic, mobile and unstable – her form is a dramatization of some of the problems encountered through ethnic and cultural difference. Kingston herself is not a migrant but was born in the US of first-generation migrant parents. She writes of the hybridity of identity, while Jung Chang attempts to write of, and thereby to construct, its stabilization.

Wild Swans

I want to begin with the end, for the kind of subjectivity that Jung Chang proposes in her narrative is one predicated on the idea of retrospection; moreover, the fact that she can write it at all, depends on looking back on her life from a position of relative safety. She can revisit the past – now literally a foreign country – mentally, at least, and her journey is the testament of her survival of the bad times. In the Epilogue to the text, Chang writes:

> I have made London my home. For ten years I avoided thinking about the China I had left behind. Then in 1988, my mother came to England to visit me. For the first time she told me the story of her life and that of my

grandmother. When she returned to Chengdu, I sat down and let my own
memory surge out and the unshed tears flood my mind. I decided to
write *Wild Swans*. The past was no longer too painful to recall because
I had found love and fulfilment and therefore tranquillity. (Chang
1993, 673)

The love, fulfilment and tranquillity are not part of what she narrates,
but they are an essential foundation for the narrative she produces. It
would not have been possible, the book tells us, either materially or
culturally, to write *this* story in China itself. She recreates the history of
her family and country from a Western perspective, in a Western form,
and her story is 'complete'. The person she now is, is her final word on
the subject, paradoxically rendered stable by the ellipsis with which
she ends: 'reader, she married him', but as that is the story we already
'know' from our perspective in the West, the love story does not
belong here.

When, however, the narrative of *Wild Swans* is analysed, it becomes
clear that any view of stable identity is simplistic. This autobiographical text is taken up for half of its narrative space with the lives of two
people who are not its autobiographical 'I': Jung Chang's mother and
grandmother. In placing their personal stories squarely against the
backdrop of the public events of official 'history', Chang shows that
subjectivity may well have meant something different in China, partly
because China is figured as a place in which 'individuality' is not valued – and especially because the individuality of women is particularly
problematic, for women are figured not as subjectivities, with values
and ideas, wishes and desires of their own, but as objects of exchange
in a patriarchal culture. The narrative structure also suggests that
Chang is only able to examine her own identity when she has left
behind the forces that made it. It is only the distance between past and
present, and between here and there, and her exposure to cultural
difference that enables her to rethink those things she saw as 'natural'
in her home climate. And in telling her story for a Western readership,
she asks us to make the same journey. There is cross-fertilization, if not
exactly hybridity at work here. She works from the stereotypes to a
different kind of knowledge – which is both a fascinating and a risky
strategy, for the Western and White conception of China is often a
barely disguised racist and 'orientalist' view:[1] China is exotic and
erotic; and the Chinese all look the same to Western eyes. Turning the
realist mirror back on the West, she points out that for her, during her

childhood, the West was similarly presented in reductive and simplistic ways as a 'miasma of poverty and misery, like [the representation] of the homeless "Little Match Girl" in the Hans Christian Andersen story' (Chang 1993, 326). And the fact that China was a closed society meant that there was no opportunity to discover any corrective to this vision:

> My image of a foreigner was more or less the official stereotype: a man with red, unkempt hair, strange-colored eyes, very, very long nose, stumbling around drunk, pouring Coca-Cola into his mouth from a bottle with his legs splayed out in a most inelegant position. Foreigners said 'hello' all the time, with an odd intonation. I did not know what 'hello' meant; I thought it was a swear word. When boys played 'guerilla warfare' ... their version of cowboys and Indians, the enemy side would have thorns glued onto their noses, and say 'hello' all the time. (Chang 1993, 327)

This is the mirror image of orientalism. It is a fascinating corrective to the defective vision of a Western culture that too often reduces individual Chinese people to typecast villains such as the 'wily oriental' of the popular fictions and cinema, and which refuses to see the differences between individual Chinese people. This fantasy West, however, only becomes visible as fantasy when she leaves behind the context that constructed it.

Autobiography divides, perhaps, into several different strands. There is the confessional mode in which the speaking persona is anxious to assert that the identity s/he inhabits has value; there is a 'historical' mode, in which autobiographical narrative places the speaking subject into a context which explains it. And there is a performative mode, in which the self is a series of masks and public gestures rather than a function of essence. No form is precisely 'pure', and there are overlaps between motivations in most autobiographical texts. *Wild Swans* is a book that places itself clearly in the historical mode, and which argues strongly for the view that one cannot separate the personal from the historical. It does this precisely because the culture of which it writes has little conception of the value of individuality, an absence from the lexicon of identity that is as true of pre-Communist China as it is of the post-revolutionary period.

The central paradox of life under Mao in China is expressed in the chapter which describes 'The Cult of Chairman Mao'. Chang discusses the contradiction of a leadership based on Mao's personality cult in the context of the loss of personality of the mass of the population in her evocation of the fictional Maoist hero, Lei Feng. Lei Feng, Chinese schoolchildren were told, 'was a soldier who … had died at the age of twenty-two in 1962. He had done an awful lot of good deeds – going out of his way to help the elderly, the sick, and the needy. He had donated his savings to disaster relief funds and given up his food rations to comrades in the hospital' (Chang 1993, 339). This paragon of virtue was paraded as a moral example to the first completely communist gener-ation; schoolchildren were encouraged to 'do good deeds like Lei Feng', as the slogan had it, though as Chang puts it, the boy-soldier was at first merely the purveyor of 'boy-scoutish good deeds' (340), and his example merely meant helping people met by chance in the streets to carry their shopping or their water supplies. Gradually, however, the use of Lei Feng began to change. The emphasis shifted from an active – if ineffectual – attempt to make people do good things to the use of the myth for the purposes of complete self-sacrifice. In the wake of Lei Feng, schoolchildren vowed to 'go up mountains of knives and down seas of flames', to 'have our bodies smashed and our bones crushed to smithereens' in acts of obedience and love of Chairman Mao. But as Chang notes, this strategy of impersonalizing or depersonalizing the masses in the service of the revolution can only ever be partially successful. As a teenager, despite her enthusiasm for Lei Feng's cult, and her desire to do the right thing for Chairman Mao, Chang could not identify the class enemy – had no visual or other clues to interpret what the phrase might mean: 'class enemies … remained abstract, unreal shadows. They were a thing of the past, too far away. Mao had not been able to give them an everyday material form. One reason, paradoxi-cally, was that he had smashed the past so thoroughly' (Chang 1993, 346). This inability to distinguish between good and bad people puts a stop to her do-gooding – for she can hardly ask the people she wants to help if they are class enemies.

Life under Communism is also a life of rigorous and continual self-censorship: the speaking subject here is absolutely a split subject, and the Western mantra 'Know thyself' is alien; indeed, it would be too dangerous to 'know' and it was, on the contrary extremely important not to know. Children were kept ignorant of their extended families, for example, just in case they let slip something from family history that should not be generally known. The importance of this ignorance is acute in the case of Chang's own family, which – just one generation in the past – contained a 'class enemy', a Kuomintang general; and two generations back her great-grandfather was a warlord. These family connections have played their part both in keeping her parents safe at different points of Chinese history, and in placing them under suspicion. Hence, Chang tells us that she did not really know her mother's and her grandmother's story until she was safely out of the country, and her mother was able to narrate it following a slight liberalization in China, following the death of Mao and the fall of the Gang of Four. But 'not knowing' extends to all kinds of knowledge, beyond the personal and the familial. Academic or intellectual knowledge, for instance, is a dangerous commodity in the midst of a revolution that figures itself as a peasant revolution, and which insists that the peasants 'know' more of life's essentials than any intelligentsia: 'The more books you read, the more stupid you are' is the slogan that circulates to establish the falsity of intellectual knowledge.

Self-knowledge is a particularly dangerous possession under a totalitarian government, Chang suggests. Like her father, she takes great pleasure in the discipline of writing self-expressive poetry in the forms of Classical Chinese literature. She identifies the composition of her first good poem as having taken place on her sixteenth birthday, at the height of the Cultural Revolution. The poem, written whilst her parents were both in detention (despite their high-official status, they were both denounced as class enemies), was an expression of the confusion that she felt now that she could no longer believe that the system by which she had been indoctrinated was good or right. She 'subconsciously avoided Mao' as a subject for criticism because he had been 'the idol, the god, the inspiration' of her childhood:

> Although his magic power had vanished from inside me, he was still sacred and undoubtable. Even now I did not challenge him. It was in this mood that I composed my poem. I wrote about the death of my indoctrinated and innocent past as dead leaves being swept from a tree by the whirlwind and carried to a world of no return. I described my bewilderment at the new world, at not knowing what and how to think.

'It was a poem', she writes, 'of groping in the dark, searching', activities that the certainties of the regime could not tolerate (Chang 1993, 487). She has just completed the poem when the house is raided by the people who had denounced her father. She dare not allow the poem to be found, lest it be used in evidence against him, or to begin the process of denouncing her as well. When her father's love poems to her mother had been found, they had been interpreted as counter-revolutionary in intention, and had caused the process of recrimination to become even more severe. This tentative moment of self-expression is literally, therefore, flushed down the toilet. The nature of life in this communist world is – not surprisingly – communal. There is very little space for privacy or interiority; indeed 'there are no exact words' for privacy and private space in Chinese, Chang observes (338); that did not stop her from yearning for them, though only now, in the West, can she identify and articulate what she yearned for.

The contemporary Western model of the self is one, which insists that the individual is the product of social and material circumstances and of experience. 'The Child is father to the Man', wrote Wordsworth in his epigraph to the *Ode: Intimations of Immortality*. The kind of person one becomes is a very direct result of the childhood one lives through. And in our post-Romantic and post-Freudian sensibilities, the role of family in the making of subjectivity is difficult to overstate. For Jung Chang, however, whatever the affection she feels for her parents, her relationship with them is modified by the Communist context: 'Father is close, mother is close, but neither is as close as Chairman Mao', as one Maoist slogan had it. Chang narrates how, in 1965, she made a new year's resolution with the traditional phrase, 'I will obey my grandmother', a phrase that simply meant a promise to behave well; her father tells her that she should not make this promise, but 'only say, "I obey Chairman Mao" ' (Chang 1993, 348). In the uncertainties of the Cultural Revolution, moreover, the family itself was attacked as a Western bourgeois concept, and a serious effort was put into dismantling its competing power for a person's loyalty. Chang's relationship with her father, a Communist-party official and committed Communist (he had participated in the Long March on Peking in the 1930s), is generally very good. He shows her affection and gives her time, playing with her when she is a small child, and taking a real interest in her studies. She notes, however, that his relationship with his sons is very troubled, depending on autocracy and violence: 'My parents thought only their sons should be scolded and hit', she writes (331). But although she never suffers from this violence, she is increasingly aware of the formality of her relationship with her father in particular. This is both a cultural issue – fathers and daughters, she suggests, are not supposed to show each other physical affection in Chinese society, and also a personal one – her father is physically imposing and forbidding. When her father, denounced and disgraced, is ordered to burn his books, and weeps as he does so, her gesture of affection, her attempt to express it, is stilted and awkward (Chang 1993, 439). The 'something that had happened in his mind' after this episode is the onset of a schizophrenic episode. The dismantling of the certainties of the Communist system to which he was so committed, as well as the repeated humiliation of public denunciation, drives him mad.

Wild Swans insists on the continuity between the Feudalist forms of oppression and the particular expression of Communism in the Chinese context. The era in which Chang's grandmother grew up was one which enforced a rigid obedience to parents and feudal masters. Familial affection is marked by its total absence, and the Western reader is shocked by the grandmother's easy sale into concubinage by her own father, a corrupt and alcoholic local official. The Communist regime, once fully established, insists on uniformity and condemns individuality as a Western bourgeois concept. For a brief moment, before the stranglehold of Maoist politics takes hold, Chang's mother, De Hong, is able to experience a freedom from the strict imposition of social roles and rules, in the anarchy of the years leading up to Mao's Long March and the Japanese occupation of Chinese territory during the Second World War. This anarchic political context renders that individuality, though liberating and exciting, also provisional, dangerous and unstable. Chang's mother lived briefly with the relaxation of the rules, seeking self-expression in such simple gestures as wearing bright clothes and in expressing the ambition to become a doctor. During the communist takeover, however, she rapidly adopts the Communist Lenin uniform, cuts her hair, and disguises her individuality in the safety of uniformity. In Chang's account, Chinese society more generally also rapidly accommodated itself to the imposition of a new set of Byzantine rules. The specificity of Chinese Communism is derived from the fact that it is based in part on the only recently departed feudal past. For her grandmother's generation, the personal was radically excised from life: ideas such as 'falling in love' were considered 'shameful, a family disgrace … because young people were not supposed to be exposed to situations where such a thing could happen … and … marriage was seen above all as a duty, an arrangement between two families' (Chang 1993, 29). In her mother's generation, marriage is less to do with dynastic considerations than with ideological ones: the marriage of two minds is in fact the marriage of two identical political belief systems, and the Party replaces the patriarch in the regulation of private relationships: in either case, the rules rebound particularly hard on women. The connection between feudalism and

Communist regulation is made explicit in a brief episode where, in the third (modern) generation, Jung Chang is accused of flirting with foreign sailors in the open port city of Zhanjiang. In her attempt to learn English, Chang chats with the sailors, but is accused of frater-nization with the enemy and required to undergo official criticism sessions at the hands of the party, because 'much of Chinese society still expected its women to hold themselves in a sedate manner, lower their eyelids in response to men's stares, and restrict their smile to a faint curve of the lips which did not expose their teeth. They were not meant to use any hand gestures at all' (Chang 1993, 649). The continu-ity of Medieval attitudes – figured especially as the curtailment of individual freedoms in the service of either party on dynasty – is an ongoing theme of Chang's narrative.

Her story, on the other hand, evinces some ambiguity about the necessity for regulation. All the men in her family are effectively system-bound autocrats: her great-grandfather, who sells his daughter into sexual slavery, is simply obeying the prevailing conventions of his era; her adoptive grandfather, Dr Xia, the Manchu doctor, sticks so rigidly to the Manchu rituals of his caste that he inadvertently causes the death of his son; her own father, Shou Yu, is described as in one of the chapter titles, with an ironic reference to Robespierre, as the 'incor-ruptible', and sticks so firmly to Communist party legislation that he will not allow his wife, eight months pregnant, a brief ride in his official car, and thus is responsible for a late and dangerous miscarriage. Although she certainly wishes us to read the latter two cases sympa-thetically – that people do stick to the rules in a world which is so filled with corruption both minor and major, is a testament to their virtues and principles – the focus on rules is not without its disadvantages. Chang's story insists persistently on the failure of the conventions and rules properly to account for human relationships. And it is to a kind of humanism that she turns for the values that she propounds in the text.

It is no surprise, then, that her chosen mode for this narrative is the realist mode, for the position she wishes to take up is one that validates Western concepts of selfhood and subjectivity – identity as individuality – a version of selfhood that is, in these circumstances, particularly hard won. Because of the vicissitudes of achieving individuality, because she enlists her readers' sympathies with the plight of her family in the various horrific passages of Chinese history, we are perhaps less inclined to read suspiciously. I am not for a moment doubting the veracity of this account; I'm merely suggesting that we should also read the manner of its telling as well as its content to get a full enough picture for appropriate interpretation. Although this is not a 'literary' autobiography – in other words, not a narrative that asks its readers to focus on the manner of the writing, but rather to be attentive to the story's content (the what, not the how is the ostensible point of the narrative) – it participates in the literary discourse of realism. It disarms critique, as realist fiction also does, by focusing on the individual, and creating the possibility of empathy on the basis of a shared humanity. Thus although the communist state offers material conditions for existence that are radically different from those experienced by most people living in the privileged West, Chang makes consistent appeal to the aspects of personality that we share, rather than emphasizing the utter difference and strangeness of her experience compared to that of her audience.[2]

Maxine Hong Kingston's *The Woman Warrior* and hyphenated identity

When we turn to Maxine Hong Kingston's *The Woman Warrior*, there is a specificity to American identities that has to be confronted. There is a sense in which American identity is always, as it were, a hyphenated identity. One is always simultaneously from the US and from somewhere else, somewhere alien or 'other'. Black, brown, yellow people, living in a culture dominated by a white hegemony, perhaps have to think about such issues, and have to think about them especially because not only is their ethnicity visible, their status as relatively recent immigrants often means the pull of two often-opposing cultures and world views, is powerfully experienced. It is, of course, that clash, that Maxine Hong Kingston's *The Woman Warrior* investigates. As she comments:

> Chinese-Americans, when you try to understand what things in you are Chinese, how do you separate what is peculiar to childhood, to poverty, insanities, one family, your mother who marked your growing with stories, from what is Chinese? What is Chinese tradition and what is the movies? (Kingston 1981, 13)

Kingston's book is based on the ambiguity of living on the borderlands, or the frontier between cultures. It is written from a place which is not grounded in a detailcd historical or cultural knowledge of either of its two geographical bases. And that confusion over its orientation is equally mirrored in the confusions of its genre(s). Is this autobiography or not? This is a question raised in an essay by Sau-Ling Cynthia Wong. Wong describes how many Chinese-American authors were disturbed by the implication of the autobiographical label. As Wong puts it: 'The most fundamental objection to *The Woman Warrior* concerns its generic status: its being billed as autobiography rather than fiction, when so much of the book departs from the popular definition of autobiography as an unadorned factual account of a person's own life' (Wong 1999, 30). The problem is one of authenticity, then. A similar point is made much more forcibly by Frank Chin, who argued that it was a travesty of every-thing that is authentic and particular about Chinese and Chinese-American experience (Chin 1999). And a visiting professor from China wrote about her sense of insult and about the mistreatment of the myths and stories of her homeland in *The Woman Warrior*:

> [*The Woman Warrior*] did not appeal to me when I read it for the first time, because the stories seemed somewhat twisted, Chinese perhaps in origin, but not really Chinese any more, full of American imagination. Furthermore, some of Kingston's remarks offended my sense of national pride as well as my idea of personal discretion. (Zhang 1999, 17)

Zhang's view of the book is one predicated on the idea that autobiogra-phy and authenticity are related concepts. It is a somewhat naïve view of both autobiography (how authentic can autobiography ever be?) and of the oral story-telling tradition which tells the myths of Fa Mu Lan (oral stories change in the telling; it's only writing which fixes things). On the other hand, the US critics – especially those who call themselves Chinese-American – think that the book is not representa-tive enough of a paradigm of Chinese-American experience: it's not Chinese-*American* enough.

But there are other ways of viewing *The Woman Warrior*. It is a book precisely about hyphenated identity, about living on the border between cultures, and about exploring possible meanings of identity in two very different cultural models. As such it broadens Western definitions of the autobiographical narrative – that straight-line story which begins with birth and ends with the completion of identity. Its structure is not linear but a collage-effect, or a patchwork quilt (to borrow a very specifically American metaphor). So how does it work?

The first words of the narrative are a command not to repeat the story that is about to be told, an invitation to silence rather than to speech:

> 'You must not tell anyone,' my mother said, 'what I am about to tell you. In China your father had a sister who killed herself. She jumped into the family well. We say that your father has all brothers because it is as if she had never been born.' (Kingston 1981, 11)

From the bald and horrible story told orally of the unknown Aunt's illicit pregnancy and suicide, Kingston's narrative imagines proliferating possibilities that might explain the story of her unknown, unknowable Aunt. It is a fairy story in the same way that Little Red Riding Hood is a fairy story: a tale told to warn girls about not straying from the paths of propriety and righteousness, or away from convention and tradition. The moral of the story, as the mother tells it, is: 'Now that you have started to menstruate, what happened to her could happen to you ... You wouldn't like to be forgotten as if you had never been born' (p. 13). And yet, despite the strong moral, we know from the outset that Kingston has broken the injunction not to tell – has strayed from conventions of silence in order to tell us, in her writing, the orally transmitted wisdom of her mother. In the retelling of the story, however, she changes it. Brave Orchid's version is horribly straightforward; it is linear and leaves no space for the imagination or for alternative endings or interpretations. Kingston's version, in contrast, is multilayered and indecisive, an open-ended story, rather than a closed, fixed one. As Zhang puts it, 'a Chinese writer would have told it differently, without the imagined situations'.

The 'imagined situations' though are precisely what Kingston has to focus on, not least because the bald facts of her aunt's story need imagined embellishments in order for them to function as a story. Traditional Chinese culture is one that is based in part on ancestor worship. Traditions are maintained by families who retain a close relationship with their pasts, figured in the facts that photographs and pictures of deceased relatives are turned into home shrines, and offerings of fake money, paper flowers and food are made to them at certain times of the year. But for the Chinese-American, the tradition of ancestor worship is remote and exotic; different from what one's neighbours do, and hard to make sense of when you have to forge a new identity out of the old models. As Kingston comments, 'Unless I can see [my aunt's] life branching into mine, she gives me no ancestral help' (Kingston 1981, 16). She therefore tries to make the story comprehensible to herself, and significant for herself, by imagining various possibilities of what the real story might have been. In one version – probably the most likely version – the Aunt is a rape victim, turned into an object by a man who 'was not, after all, much different from her husband. They both gave orders: she followed' (14). But for Kingston, that version, even if it is true, is no help in trying to become a Chinese-American. After all, she is living in the most individualist society in the world, and the horrible typicality, not to say stereotypicality ('it could have been true in old China', comments Zhang [Zhang 1999, 17]) of the story of a passive and utter victim, does not hold out much hope for her own future. This is a particularly acute feeling in the book, because Kingston's parents, for most of its duration, still think of China as their real home, and dream of an eventual return to the old China where daughters can be sold, and only sons are valued. The Aunt's passivity is a lesson therefore that Kingston does not wish to learn.

So she imagines instead, a more romantic story, in which the aunt is an individualist, a woman interested in both her own appearance and in the potentiality of her sexuality. In other words, Kingston reads a kind of Americanized dreaming into the outlines of the Chinese story, using the culture she does know (from the movies) to read the culture she does not know, and giving an improbable or impossible version: 'Imagining her free with sex doesn't fit' (16), but it might well be a necessary imaginary act to recuperate a story that cannot fit the Americanized part of Kingston's life. The ambivalence of the act of telling is summed up in the final section of the first chapter. It is an act of disrespect, even of violence, against her family for the words of the story 'are so strong and fathers so frail that [the word] "aunt" would do my father serious harm' (Kingston 1981, 22). It is a story that is not supposed to be told, and for many years, Kingston argues, she has participated in that prohibition. Now she is telling the story, and it is a kind of ancestor worship; but it is a new kind of ancestor worship, based not on the old traditions of paper money and origami flowers, but on paper written with Chinese-American-English words, which disrupts the old tradition. (Kingston 1981, 22)

This personal or family story produces one kind of objection to the *The Woman Warrior*; it is too revelatory of a shameful personal history for the Chinese reader such as Zhang, too bound up with misreading a Chinese heritage for the Chinese-American. But it was her rewriting of the story of Fa Mu Lan to which both Chinese and Chinese-American readers most objected. This is the force of Frank Chin's powerful attack on Kingston and writers like her, who provide a new (and, he suggests, inaccurate) version of the old story. But just as with the personal story of the No Name Woman, Kingston needs to adapt the tale of the woman warrior, or else she will find herself being trapped in the old story. At the beginning of the chapter which details this myth, she describes her mother's transmission of the oral tradition of Chinese mythology, recalls listening to the adults around her 'talking-story', and comments on Brave Orchid's bedtime stories: 'I couldn't tell where the stories left off and the dreams began, her voice the voice of the heroines in my sleep' (Kingston 1981, 25). In other words, not only is the subjectivity that is being evoked here dependent on the stories that are spoken to Kingston as a child, they are also indistinguishable from her own reality. As well as the adults telling stories, the children also receive their Chinese culture from Chinese films, where marvels are presented as perfectly ordinary. The realist mode has no force here, and therefore the text will not enact subjectivity in its terms. The stories, whether in the movies or in the house, are enchantments, memories of the past, intended to bind the listeners to the tradition they describe. At their heart, however, there is a contradiction. The main message of oral transmission for Brave Orchid's daughters is one of feminine submission and propriety. The chant of Fa Mu Lan, on the other hand, a revered story, is also a story of feminine power, which is also transmitted from mother to daughter:

> I heard the chant of Fa Mu Lan, the girl who took her father's place in battle ... as a child I had followed my mother about the house, the two of us singing about how Fa Mu Lan fought gloriously and returned alive from war to settle in the village. I had forgotten this chant that was once mine, given me by my mother ... She said I would grow up a wife and a slave, but she taught me the song of the warrior woman, Fa Mu Lan. I would have to grow up a warrior woman. (Kingston 1981, 25–6)

In retelling the story, Kingston places the two traditions, the movies and the oral stories, in each other's contexts. Martial arts films from Hong Kong, for example, often focus on the incredible feats of training undertaken by the novitiate in the process of achieving enlightenment. The woman warrior in Kingston's version lives out a martial arts train- ing from the films, before going on to perform the acts of her own life story pretty much in relation to the traditional telling of the story.

Again, hybridity is central to the story which blends traditional and new elements. It is likely that the movies Kingston saw as a child in the Confucian church on a Sunday afternoon usually represented masculine heroes, not women warriors. But as an American child, she enters the world of the stories through emotional acts of identification with the heroes, and thus sees them as female: 'on Sundays ... we went to movies at the Confucius Church. We saw swordswomen jump over houses from a standstill; they didn't even need a running start' (25).

The woman warrior's training regime is one based on utter physical control of all desires and needs; she sleeps on a narrow plank bed; she learns to breathe silently; and when she goes on her expedition, she learns to manage corporeal needs such as hunger, which makes her other senses even more acute: 'Hunger also changes the world – when eating can't be a habit, then neither can seeing' (31). This is a way for Kingston to try to understand the difficulties of being a Chinese-American. In the United States, a land of relative plenty, Brave Orchid remains obsessed by food and its rituals, living out of what is basically a peasant mentality of the fear of scarcity. But then, unlike her children, she has experienced hunger, and knows its distorting effects. In other words, Kingston's retelling of her mother's stories is an attempt to explain where the ethos behind the stories comes from, as well as an attempt to understand their effects on the self she became. Similarly, when the woman warrior returns to her village to take vengeance on old feudal China, her mother and father write their grievances on her back with a knife. The calligraphy is exquisitely beautiful, but also desperately painful to endure. The scars that the woman warrior carries on her back – with their beauty and their pain – are metaphors of the scars of hyphenated existence. There is beauty in old Chinese traditions, but they are a pain in the back(side) to live with in twentieth-century conformist American society.

Kingston needs the story of female emancipation and power because her own part of Chinese-American culture is so keen to denigrate femininity. 'My American life has been such a disappointment', she says – her point being that it has not been nearly American enough to tolerate her individualism, nor Chinese enough to knock that individualism out of her. There are multiple instances of the denigration of the female child, spoken in the proverbs that the other Chinese repeat: 'Better to raise girls than geese ... When you raise girls, you're raising children for strangers' (48). There are also different rituals and rites of passage for girl children and boy children, who are greatly favoured in the traditional community. Most important of all, the very language in which she speaks – her specific dialect of Chinese – renders her identity as null and void: 'There is a Chinese word for the female *I* – which is "slave". Break the women with their own tongues!' (49). As Bella Brodzki notes, this is 'the gender-specific prison house of language' (Brodzki 1998, 156–7). These different modes of discrimination against femininity are both generic to femininity *per se*, wherever it is, and take specifically Chinese forms as well.

In telling the story of her mother's life, Kingston sets out to understand the nature of the difficulties Brave Orchid confronted, and in understanding them, she expects to be able to forgive what she often experienced as maternal brutality. From the stories of her training as a doctor and from the evidence of her diplomas, it is clear that Brave Orchid has come down in the world in coming to America; her American life is also a disappointment. In China, she was well qualified and powerful. In the US, she is a manual labourer in the laundry, or a seasonal worker in the fields. She does nothing but work, and even at nearly 80 years of age, she does not retire.

The training that Brave Orchid undertook as a doctor is also an interesting instance of hybridity: a mixture of Western scientific medicine and Chinese herbal traditionalism attached to Shamanism, a training undertaken back in China itself. On her first day at college the tutors addressed their students:

> They told the students that they would begin with a text as old as the Han empire, when the prescription for immortality had not yet been lost. Chang Chung-ching, father of medicine had told how the two great winds, *yang* and *yin*, blew through the human body. ... After they had mastered the ancient cures that worked, they would be taught the most up-to-date western discoveries. By the time the students graduated ... their range of knowledge would be wider than that of any other doctor in history. (Hong Kingston, 1981, 62)

The complexity of this knowledge – its blending of Chinese traditions with Western scientific epistemology – is the root of its power. Brave Orchid may be a good student in terms of academic knowledge – the knowledge of the West – but she is also very strong when it comes to battling with and exorcising ghosts, because she does not leave out any aspect of knowledge, whether rational or spiritual. Kingston, as always, is highly ambivalent about the story her mother had told her. On the one hand, it is a powerful, potentially feminist example of emancipation and power coming out of a surprising context. On the other, it is caught up in the illiberal tradition of China. In America, Brave Orchid cannot quite adapt to the new possibilities of plenty because she has lived so long amongst poverty and loss. This is the force of the fact that the Hongs clearly ate what the West sees as inedible foodstuffs – 'racoons, skunks, hawks, city pigeons, wild ducks, wild geese, black-skinned bantams, snakes, garden snails, turtles that crawled under the pantry door, catfish that swam in the bathtub' (85) – out of the peasant mentality of fear of starvation. But it is also a sign of cultural power: in the mythology in which Brave Orchid is immersed, whatever you can eat, you can master.

'The Woman Warrior' chapter tries to reclaim a positive feminist message from the Old China. 'Shaman' is about the relative success of living between two worlds. Moon Orchid's story, narrated in the next chapter, however, demonstrates perhaps, that not all hybridity is a good thing, and that only the very strong can survive the competing pulls on their split identities. Moon Orchid is not fit to live in America. As Brave Orchid tells her in a devastating phrase, which makes use of an anti-Chinese racism: 'You're so wishy-washy' (116). (Wishy-washy is the name of a Chinese character, working in a Chinese laundry, in the pantomime *Aladdin*). Moon Orchid does not have the drive to live out a proper life in the US. This is partly a function of experience, since she has lived most of her adult life in the privileged space of Hong Kong, where she has had adequate money for a nice flat and servants. She has never had to work for her living, never had to assert an individuality separate from the passive acceptance of the status quo favoured in Chinese femininity. But this is also a function of Brave Orchid's misreading of the situation of her sister. She believes that the old Chinese rules can be made to apply in the new situation in the US. She weaves around her sister several possible narratives of how she will regain her 'rightful' position as the first wife of her successful doctor-husband. But none of these narratives, of course, could possibly come true. They are stories from the Old China, and they are inappropriate for San Francisco.

The mark of Moon Orchid's alienation is in her inability even to understand her own sister's family. They seem utterly strange to her, both in terms of their speech, and in terms of their culture. Nor does she have any of the work ethic which has sustained the family in its early immigrant years. Brave Orchid suggests that her sister could get a job to support herself, working as a hotel maid, or a waitress or in a canning factory, but it is immediately apparent that this is utterly impractical, witnessed by her inefficiency in the laundry:

> 'You should start off with an easy job,' [Brave Orchid] said. But all the jobs seemed hard for Moon Orchid, who was wearing stockings and dress shoes and a suit. The buttons on the presses seemed too complicated for her to push – and what if she caught hands or her head inside a press? She was already playing with the water jets dancing on springs from the ceiling. (124)

In these circumstances, it's no surprise that the meeting with the first husband is a farce, one which would be simply funny if it were not for the tragic consequences it sets in train. In preparing her sister for her encounter with the husband, Brave Orchid has obsessively 'talked story' about how the meeting will progress. When it comes down to it, however, the errant husband has a more powerful talk-story: he explains why he never sent for his wife in talk-story terms: 'It's as if I had turned into a different person. The new life around me was so complete; it pulled me away. You became people in a book I had read a long time ago' (139). Brave Orchid's fictions are no match for the brain surgeon's fictions. He is off the hook because he has fictionalized his China life, and thinks only of his American life. Moon Orchid is fixed in the old stories, and cannot adapt to the new ones. As she descends into madness, what is lost is variety – adaptability. (143) And that is, of course, the reason why it is necessary to change the stories, and not to keep repeating the same old versions. Kingston's narrator is extremely aware of her own fabrications and additions, but is also aware of their necessity.

The book's final chapter begins with a recantation of the story that has just been told about Moon Orchid's encounter with her husband. Everything that has been presented as an eyewitness account is, in fact, an invention. The bare bones of the story – as with the No Name Woman story – are all that the eyewitness has told, and Kingston has fleshed out those bones.

> In fact, it wasn't me my brother told about going to Los Angeles; one of my sisters told me what he'd told her. His version of the story may be better than mine because of its bareness, not twisted into designs. The hearer can carry it tucked away without it taking up too much room. Long ago, in China, knot-makers tied string into buttons and frogs, and

rope into bell pulls. There was one knot so complicated that it blinded the knot-maker. Finally an emperor outlawed this cruel knot, and the nobles could not order it any more. If I had lived in China, I would have been an outlaw knot-maker. (147)

Knots, of course, are metaphors for textuality and textual organization. The very word text, deriving from the Latin *texere*, alerts us to the 'weaving' and the 'fabrication' of written stories: a *dénouement* in a story is literally its unravelling or 'unknotting' (from the French word *noeud*, knot). The text here acknowledges its fabrications of authenticity, its embroidery of the facts. Complicated knots, like the Gordian knot of Greek mythology, have to be cut, rather than untied. And this thought is contained in the next episode that Kingston offers – that her mother cut loose her tongue so that she would be able to speak. This is yet another act from her mother that she does not know how to interpret, and she cannot even be sure really happened. The phrase 'tongue-tied', after all, is *just* a figure of speech, and cutting the 'tongue strings' sounds like the kind of thing that facetious adults habitually say to children: the English equivalent is something like the question, 'has the cat got your tongue?' Moreover, even if this event really happened, Kingston cannot work out if it is something that Chinese parents habitually do, or whether it was just a one-off in her case; nor does she quite know if it is to be understood as an act of violence against a defenceless baby, or as an act of love, to free that baby to live adequately in the strange American world.

In any case it doesn't work. Kingston has already told us that the voices of the Chinese in the States are too loud, too much. Speech is the fundamental problem she suffers with, perhaps because she has no 'mother tongue'. Her mother's kind of speech is precisely the kind she resists. She hates being made to translate her mother's haggling and bargaining in the inappropriate space of American department stores, and loathes the loudness and assertiveness of it that seems to go against everything defined as feminine by Americans, and which marks her family out not just as immigrants, but also as peasants: 'Why is it', Kingston's father asks, 'I can hear Chinese from blocks away? Is it that I understand their language? Or is it they talk loud?' Kingston notes with pain the contempt with which Anglo-Americans, white ghosts, observe the Chinese community: 'You can see the disgust on American faces looking at [Chinese] women like that. It isn't just the loudness. It is the way Chinese sounds, chingchong ugly, to American ears' (Kingston 1981, 154). The ambivalence towards speech is brought out most forcefully in Kingston's apparently autobiographical memory of her torture of a fellow Chinese-American girl, a child who will not speak. Speech is both necessary, but also a trap, since it points out differences between people, differences of class, origin and education. The scene with the other girl is horrible, greatly protracted and violent. But it is also horrible because it is a torture inflicted by Kingston at least as much on herself as on the child she bullies. She clearly recognizes herself in that child, and is disgusted and guilty with herself, retreating also into a silence of eighteen months of psychosomatic illness.

Words hurt. If, to become a subjectivity one must become a *speaking* subject, the problem of language is always acute. It is much more acute, however, when neither the English language of the majority population, nor the Chinese language of home, is really a native tongue. Moreover, the Chinese language Kingston's family speaks is a highly localized dialect, incomprehensible not only to Anglo-Americans, but also to other Chinese people who originate in different areas (Kingston 1981, 183). And, in the material context of a hostile immigration situation, the children are kept in partial ignorance of the very cultural traditions they are also supposed to uphold, so that festi-val meals, for instance, turn up suddenly, without explanation. The multiple significance Kingston ascribes to the Chinese word *Kuei* – ghost – is another example of the inability of language to fix identity. It can mean ghosts in the traditional English sense of hauntings by ancestors or strangers – the incursion of the past into the present embodied by a disembodied spirit. In *The Woman Warrior*, it clearly also refers to the sense of being haunted by traditions which have lost their potency in the alien culture of the US, but which are still com-pelling and terrifying. Thus the story that Brave Orchid tells about the baby born without an anus, which is left to die may not literally be a ghost in Kingston's own narrative; but it certainly haunts her dreams, making her afraid to go to the bathroom in the dark. But the word is also used to mean simply anything that is foreign or strange:

> America has been full of machines and ghosts – Taxi Ghosts, Bus Ghosts, Police Ghosts, Fire Ghosts, Meter Reader Ghosts, Tree Trimming Ghosts, Five-and-Dime Ghosts. Once upon a time the world was so thick with ghosts, I could hardly breathe. (Kingston 1981, 90–1)

And even the first-generation children of the migrant population are also 'ghosts' to their parents' generation. The point of the word seems to be that the ghosts are those which a given culture cannot see properly because of the blindspots in its own conceptual universe. It is also a political naming of those others who have othered Chinese-Americans. The Chinese-Americans have often been a silent and invisible ethnic minority because their own culture has not mirrored the dominant modes of interaction of white society. Kingston's use of the word ghost, then operates as what Foucault calls a reverse discourse (Focuault 1984): it turns the tool of the oppressor back onto himself, and refuses visibility to those who hurt the oppressed. But it is also used woundingly by Chinese immigrant parents of their own children, proliferating their sense of alien identiy.

The Woman Warrior is not a book without hope, however, for the subjectivity that inhabits the borderland between cultures. The last story in the book is a story that melds Brave Orchid's family lore with a traditional story about a woman kidnapped by barbarians: it is another example of Kingston's adaptation of her mother's oral tradition to focus on present needs. The beginning of the story, she tells us, is her mother's, 'the ending, mine' (184). The kidnapped woman survives by singing among the barbarians, and lives to be ransomed and returned home. On her return, twelve years after the original abduction, she 'brought her songs back from the savage lands'. One song in particular, translated back into the language of her own native people, 'Eighteen Stanzas for a Barbarian Reed Pipe' 'translated well' (186). Presumably this is supposed to be read as a story supporting the possibility that the hyphenated, alienated identity can also become a homelike place with compensations as well as discomforts and horrors. The creative appropriation of the old stories and the creative misuse of the laws of genre are both dramatized in The Woman Warrior, and hold out a speculative and tentative hope for a subjectivity that is less subjected to forces outside its control. Its form, which refuses totalizing explanation and demands creative reading, mirrors its content.

Notes

1.   Orientalism is a term coined by Edward Said to describe the panoply of Western discourses and forms of representation that are applied to non-Western cultures. His argument is that these representations serve the culture that produces them and do an immense disservice to the cultures that

are thus represented. The exoticism of non-Western peoples and places is, he suggests, hardly a recompense for the material and political oppressions it disguises. See Said 1991 and 1993 for his elaborations of the power relations inherent in conventions of representation.

2. The book is aimed at a Western audience; it was in fact, banned in mainland China on its first publication.

8 Death Sentences: The Sense of an Ending? Living with Dying in Narratives of Terminal Illness

When Roland Barthes announced the *death of the author*, I think it is safe to assume that thanatography (death-writing, or writing about the process of one's own dying) was not quite what he had in mind. It is perhaps ironic that the theoretical implications of his statement find one of their greatest challenges in narratives of terminal illness. Theory itself – a word that means 'way of seeing' – with its attendant implications of the distance, objectivity and perspective that will enable us to see things clearly, clashes with life and death with their intimacy, their messy contingency and their nonetheless urgent significance. Life/death and theory seem inappropriate partners in some ways because of what Paul de Man, writing of autobiography, has called life's 'incompatibility with the monumental dignity of aesthetic values' (de Man 1984, 68). Autobiography traditionally makes sense of life, aestheticizes it and organizes it, explains it: but in giving a life something of the 'monumental dignity' of aesthetic value, it also turns into *A Life*.

Autobiography, however, in whatever forms it takes at once resists and demands theory. Its resistance comes from the implicit demand it makes of its reader to suspend critical judgement – a suspension that is more difficult to evade in narratives that focus on very extreme experiences. The written trace of the speaking voice that says 'these things happened, and they happened to me: you have to *trust me*' is an urgently insistent and seductive voice that constructs its readers to be complicit with its urgings. And precisely because the narrative voice *constructs* its reader in this way, autobiography *demands* theory; it requires us to be suspicious and wary of the text's seductions. But reading written subjectivities is never a simple operation. In practice, the reader's – *this* reader's – response to narrative voices is rather difficult to police. In this chapter, in readings of a thanatographical narrative of terminal illness, I want to propose a test case for a reading that is both suspicious (theoretically inclined) and also humanistic (a reading that suspends hostilities between reader, writer and text). Gillian Rose's *Love's Work* offers an opportunity to think about subjectivity in terms I want to describe as a 'strategic humanism'.

This is a dangerous game, of course. The word humanism is both hotly disputed and strongly disavowed by the theoretically inclined literary critic. To be 'accused' of residual humanism is an academic insult in some parts of the academy. As Tony Davies observes, humanism 'has been denounced as an ideological smokescreen for the oppressive mystifications of modern society and culture, the marginalisation and oppression of the multitudes of human beings in whose name it pretends to speak, [and] even ... for the nightmare of fascism and the atrocity of total war' (Davies 1997, 5). To invoke humanism at all, therefore, is risky. At the same time, though, in reading narratives like Rose's, the anti-humanist gestures of much contemporary theoretical thought *feel* (I use the word deliberately) inadequate. Thanatographies are texts that literalize (and render literary) the death and the dying of their authors; and in doing so, they suggest that whilst Barthes' rhetorical flourish in his announcement of the author's demise is intellectually satisfying, it is also incomplete.

For the philosopher Emmanuel Levinas, the ethical relationship is a *face-to-face* relationship (see Eaglestone 1997, 121–2; Levinas 1991, 39–42), and although Levinas did not mean this as literally as I am going to take it, an ethical reading might well best be performed in conditions where the reader seeks to literalize the metaphor of the *face-to-face* encounter. I began this book by talking about the Lacanian Mirror Stage, and the misrecognitions at the heart of the encounter with the reflected signifier. Here, though, the (still-Saussurean) sign is differently inflected. The misrecognition is not a mistake – a category error – so much as a necessary step on the road to facing both the demands of the other and their implications for the self. My suggestion is that it is both ethically and emotionally unsatisfactory to reduce a narrative about the confrontation of mortality, and thence, by extension, any narrative, to the merely hollowed out, repetitive gesture of writing itself; and whilst it is clearly the case that language, written or spoken, cannot express subjectivity in any unmediated way, that it is always a kind of mimicry of previous writing or speech, that its apparent self-expression is impersonation and fabrication, to stop at that position is reductive. If humanism risks being a totalizing system that can also lend itself to totalitarianism, theory can do the same. And so, there is a wider point to be made here about the intersubjectivity of reading more generally – this reading does not *only* apply to thanatography. In modes of thought which reduce readers and writers to textual functions, the emotional affect of reading thanatography is dismissed as a mere effect of writing and naivety of reading. The transitivity of the word is proven – but the reader's and the writer's status as people (human beings, if I have to use the phrase, if I have to spell it out) is not. This, then, is an argument about the clash of abstraction and concretion – what I *think* and what I *feel*.

To put this another way, like most people, I know that one day I will die. To be alive and human is to be aware of the sense of an ending. Death is universal and ordinary. But whilst I know this abstractly, I generally live in the denial of that knowledge. And because I live in a world of relative material privilege, I am insulated from the confrontation with mortality that people who live in more dangerous and difficult places and times are forced to make daily. The process of dying in this place and time seems remote, rather than close, and feels as though it must be an unusual experience rather than a universal fact. In the western world, we live in a realm of health, and we have begun to think that death can be cheated, as previous generations were unable to believe. As early as the 1930s, in savagely ironic innocence of the trick history was about to play on Western Europe, Walter Benjamin put it like this:

> It has been observable for a number of centuries how in the general consciousness the thought of death has declined in omnipresence and vividness. ... in the course of the nineteenth century bourgeois society has, by means of hygienic and social, private and public institutions, realized a secondary effect ... to make it possible for people to avoid the sight of dying. Dying was once a public process in the life of the individual, and a most exemplary one; think of the medieval pictures in which the deathbed was turned into a throne toward which the people press through the wide-open doors of the death-house. In the course of modern times dying has been pushed further and further out of the perceptual world of the living. ... Today people live in rooms that have never been touched by death, dry dwellers in eternity, and when their end approaches they are stowed away in sanatoria or hospitals by their heirs. (Benjamin 1992, 93).

Death and dying have replaced sex as the great unmentionables, the major repressions of Western society. This fact has had a very peculiar effect on contemporary culture, for since the effects of the AIDS epidemic began to be felt in Europe and North America in the 1980s, and in a multiplicity of writings about cancer, the absolutely ordinary experience of dying has been transformed into the story of the shocking exception to the Western rule of a taken-for-granted longevity. At a very crude level, there is clearly a market for books about dying, fuelled by many motives: writers write for therapeutic purposes; they also write – let's not hedge around – for money; and readers read such narratives for some semblance of their own experience narrated back to them; and for therapy too; and – though they may not wish to admit it – in a spirit of partial prurience, to find out what dying is like. A plethora of AIDS narratives was published from the mid-1980s onwards; and, then, in the mid-1990s in Britain, at least, a number of cancer stories were also published, two of the most high-profile of which were John Diamond's *C: Because Cowards Get Cancer Too* and Ruth Picardie's *Before I Say Goodbye*, both of which originated in newspaper columns, and both of which, *in medias res*, charted the diurnality of dying, its ordinariness rather than its strangeness. Their focus was not on the meaning of life and death, but on the failure of meaning and on the failures of language itself to make meaning happen. The concretion of the dying experience evades the neatness of abstract thought – and it does this for both the dying subject and for the reader who scans these texts. These are narratives that force a confrontation with meaninglessness, with nihilism.

The will to construct meaning, the desire to find patterns of significance to attach to premature deaths, is perhaps the natural response of the literate subject, for in speech and writing, meaning is what we seek to fabricate. But at the same time, there are events that are beyond meaning, and which cannot be made meaningful. Susan Sontag, in *Against Interpretation*, long ago made the point that making significance is always a mode of fictionalization. In her two polemical pamphlets, *Illness as Metaphor* (1979, which considers the cultural 'meanings' of tuberculosis and cancer) and *AIDS and its Metaphors* (1989), she produces a cultural history and explanation of the discursive strategies that western societies have adopted to speak about diseases that are 'known' to be – without exception – fatal, and she investigates the metaphors that accrue to such diseases. One of her major insights is that once the pathology of a fatal disease is uncovered, and once its mystery has been dissipated and a cure found, as is the case with tuberculosis, its potency as a metaphor dissipates. From the Renaissance onwards, she suggests, tuberculosis was used both as a metaphor for 'disease' in the body politic, and as an index of the moral character of the sufferer. She notes the way in which TB became, ironically, a rather glamorous disease which made women thin, pale, sexy and beautiful and which seemed only to attach to very sensitive (even effeminate) men, especially those who exhibited artistic sensibility – painters, composers and poets. The misconception of the disease as one which conferred glamour to women and genius to male artists ignored the simple facts that tuberculosis was (and is) a disease of poverty, spread by squalid, cramped living conditions and gave alternative meanings to it, meanings that ignored the fact that, like most fatal illnesses, it is painful and often gruesome in its effects.

Cancer, Sontag suggests, has always had rather different meanings. Its aetiology (its operation and process) is mysterious, and because it cannot be explained in clear narratives of cause and effect, it is shrouded in obfuscation and greeted with fear. In 1979, when Sontag herself was diagnosed with breast cancer it was also 'known' always to be fatal. It proliferates metaphors of warfare, Sontag writes: cancer cells are an invading army, cancers are 'aggressive, cancer is a biological terrorist that kills the host body, and therefore patients must 'battle' against it. Often, too, it is associated with fault – with actions that the patient deliberately undertook, so that the disease is their own fault (for instance in relation to smoking-related cancers); more insidiously, it is associated with a particular kind of personality – the disappointed and the defeated get cancer in this discursive world, and if they were different sorts of people, if they didn't have these particular character traits, then they would be 'safe' and 'saved'. She notes the ways in which her fellow patients were often filled with disgust at their disease, which was also a sort of self-disgust – 'a kind of shame' (Sontag 1991, 97). And John Diamond, Gillian Rose and Ruth Picardie all pick up on the metaphors of warfare, on shame and on the accusation of personality disorders. Diamond disavowed the clichéd description of the cancer patient: 'I despise the set of warlike metaphors that so many apply to cancer. My antipathy has ... everything to do with a hatred for the sort of morality that says that only those who fight hard against their cancer survive it or deserve to survive it – the corollary being those who lose the fight deserved to do so' (Diamond 1999, 10). Picardie rails with fury against the euphemism that surrounds cancer – 'Cancer is all about fear, secrecy and euphemism – palliative care, advanced disease – all are euphemisms for dying. Oncology is the biggest euphemism in the world' (Picardie 1998, 13). Her objection is presumably precisely that periphrasis is a retreat from reality, but also that it implies that the patient should be ashamed, as if of an obscenity. Gillian Rose rejects 'the "cancer personality" described by the junk literature of cancer' because it 'covers everyone and no one. Characteristics: obesity, anorexia, depression, elation (manic depression), lack of confidence, no satisfying or challenging work, poor relationships' (Rose 1997, 78). The narratives of abject personalities, she argues, do not cover the individual cases at all.

The purpose of Sontag's pamphlet on *Illness as Metaphor*, she writes:

> was to calm the imagination, not to incite it. Not to confer meaning, which is the traditional purpose of literary endeavour, but to deprive something of meaning: to apply that quixotic, highly polemical strategy, 'against interpretation', to the real world this time. To the body. My purpose was, above all, practical. For it was my doleful observation ... that the metaphoric trappings that deform the experience of having cancer have very real consequences ... The metaphors and myths, I was convinced, kill ... [I hoped] to regard cancer as it were just a disease ... Not a curse, not a punishment, not an embarrassment. Without 'meaning'. And not necessarily a death sentence. (Sontag 1991, 100)

Giving cancer meaning is cruel, Sontag argues. Cancer does not mean: it simply is. Narrative and metaphor offer no comfort, therefore. And theories of its meaning involve a dangerous forgery.

Love's Work

Gillian Rose's *Love's Work* is a somewhat cerebral textual encounter.[1] Rose's professional status, as a philosopher, is present in her thanatography. *Love's Work* is a collage piece, drawing together very different narrative strands, which are juxtaposed though not exactly connected by causal links. The problem Rose raises in her text is the problem of representation itself; and Rose's view is that all explanations are to some extent explanatory fictions. The collage effect – a patchwork of disparate narrative fragments – is placed at the service of an argument that focuses attention on the reader's habit of insisting on interpretation (what is this story about?), and on what happens when we are deprived of the frame of causation that enables us to say with certainty what it is about.

It is also an unusual piece of life/death writing in that it displaces the reader's attention from the writing subject for much of its length. The principle of organization, if that is the right phrase, is to be found in the interplay of incongruous juxtaposition and Rose tells many other stories before she comes to her own, deferring her 'confession' of her terminal status until chapter 6 of a short (eight chapter, 135 page) book. Those 'other' stories demand to be read as the context for her meditation on the body that has betrayed her, and on the mind that sustains her. What they are resolutely not, however, are explanations – this is not an *apologia*, a confessional text with interpretative insight; rather the stories tell their readers about the proliferating mystery of the human condition, a condition that Rose defines as a kind of benign confusion.

The book opens with a first story that documents Gillian Rose's trip to New York sometime in the early 1990s. She travels to the US to visit her friend Jim, a gay man then dying of the late-twentieth-century's keynote disease, AIDS. She stays in the apartment of a nonagenarian woman named Edna, a woman slightly older than the century, who is, incidentally, suffering from cancer of the face, and who, in an image of utter comic grotesquerie, has a prosthetic nose which 'lacked any cosmetic alleviation. Smooth and artificially flesh-coloured, with thick spectacles perched on top, this proboscis could have come from a Christmas cracker' (Rose 1997, 4). Edna looks like a bad impersonation of Groucho Marx, and is thus associated with comedy; but the reason she looks so strange undermines the ease of laughter. There is a marked generic incongruity here, which destabilizes interpretation. But Edna's story also raises for Rose a massive rhetorical question. It later transpires that Edna has been a cancer patient on and off for eighty years, since 1913, when she was sixteen years old. Edna is a mystery: 'How can that be – that someone with cancer since she was sixteen exudes well-being at ninety-six?' (Rose 1997, 6). How can that be, when the 47-year old Jim is already dying? How do some people survive their bodily misfortunes and others succumb to them? The answer is that there is no answer.

This inability, refusal and unwillingness to impose an ordering on random contingencies is the point of the book. Before she gets to her own story, Rose documents other deaths and dyings – some of which are individual, local and personal (the death of her friend Yvette from breast cancer and of Jim from AIDS); some of which are historical and universally interpreted as significant ('my numbered but nameless dead in Poland,' the Holocaust deaths of Auschwitz [Rose 1997, 30]). She also elliptically describes being in love with a Catholic priest, a relationship fraught with specific contradictions which are also posited as being more generally true of all relationships: desire is both free and easy (as in the W. B. Yeats poem, 'Down by the Salley Gardens' where 'she bid me take love easy') and also hemmed in by biblical law and prohibition: 'Between the carefree song of Yeats and this wages of sin verse, my penance of love was solemnized. Does it not always proceed so?' (Rose 1997, 63). And in chapter 4, she produces the most nearly traditional autobiographical attempt to explain the woman Gillian Rose became through the excavation of her fragmented childhood. This story is at once highly individualized and idiosyncratic, the account of oddities of one particular family at particular moments of time, and also an emblematic of cultural history in that it is also the story of the inherited significance of Jewish identity, with its historical significance in the light of the events of the mid-twentieth century. Gillian Rose was the grand-daughter of Jewish migrants and refugees, families who disguised their origins by anglicizing their names – Stone 'substituted for the Polish-Jewish "Riddell" ... "Rose", English Rose, masked German-Jewish "Rosenthal", valley of roses' (36). Her own name, Rose, is further self-chosen because she adopted it from her stepfather, changing her name by deed poll on her sixteenth birthday. She offers an account of her resistance to her real father's outlook, a quasi-Freudian discussion of the necessity of rebellion for individuation. The resistance of the father is also a resistance of and a recuperation of the Jewish tradition more generally, for Rose became a philosopher with a particular interest in the German philosophical tradition which made her family refugees, shocking her family with her choice of subject matter. But autobiographical explanations, she implies, are at best, only partial, and at worst are deliberate falsifications. Who Gillian Rose became must also be explained in terms of the particular body that she inhabited – a function of biology as well as culture. Her preference for texts that are difficult to decipher, for example, is also explained by poor eyesight, a lazy eye in childhood that was eventually cured by an operation, but which rendered the girl Gillian dyslexic. Her experience of the confusions of the written word generally (and of the Word of God specifically) has made her stubborn. But confusion is also a state of mind, originally physical in origin, but also moral and cultural more generally.

As a child, the little Jewish girl, Gillian Rose, stole a hymnbook from a school friend because she 'adored' the Christian hymn, 'O Worship the King all Glorious Above'. The words of the hymn, she says, are seductive or enticing, and so she stole the book that contained it. The theft was discovered, the book returned to its rightful owner. But: the relief of being found out 'did not release me, because it was not completed by kind punishment or by any admonition whatsoever ... The outcome of such forbearance was not simple for me ... It left me at the mercy of a guilt that I could not begin to expiate myself' (Rose 1997, 47). The meaning of this tiny episode is suggested by reference to the Peter Weir film *Picnic at Hanging Rock*, based on Joan Lindsay's novel. The story is a simple one; on Valentine's Day 1900, during a school trip to a rock outcrop in Australia, three girls disappear, two of them for good. The one schoolgirl who has been excluded from the trip kills herself (in the novel, she is murdered); the headmistress, whose business has been destroyed by the various scandals, also kills herself by jumping off the titular rock. Neither novel or film offers an explanation of the central mystery at the heart of the story: what happens to the girls, why they disappear, is given consequences but no cause. The story, says Rose, 'offers us no solace of psychology or melancholy, which we yearn to find in it. It presents the pattern of a doom and a consummation' (Rose 1997, 49). The need for explanation, and for retribution, is the need for reassurance that the world is a just place, and that its workings are predictable and safe. It is childlike, and childish, to presume that the world might just be fair, that divine patterns of order exist, that poetic justice operates. In a life, Rose argues, against her childhood self, events sometimes just happen, and they have no meaning.

We exist, in other words, in the Lacanian realm of the 'Real' just as much as we exist in the Symbolic and Imaginary realms. For Lacan, the Real is the space of contingency, of non-interpretation, the realm 'that falls entirely and irretrievably outside the signifying dimension ... the Real is that which lies outside the symbolic process' (Bowie 1991, 94). And thus, Rose's preference for particularly difficult texts – Hegelian philosophy, the Ancient Hebrew of the Old Testament and the Kabbalah – is in part a recognition of the impossibility of interpretation; for no matter how hard one strives to find *the one meaning*, to decode the text, there is, in the end, no complete and total explanation.

These things are all a metaphor for cancer rather than representing cancer itself as a metaphor. Only in chapter 6 does the confession of cancer come into play. The aetiology of Rose's cancer (of the ovaries) is mysterious. It is an effect without a cause, or at least it has no cause that can be recuperated by narrative. Rose begins her confession with a hypothesis: what would her reader's response be if she now told them, at this late stage, that for the whole of the book so far she had been suffering from full-blown AIDS? Her answer is that she would 'lose you to knowledge, to fear and to metaphor. Such a revelation would result in the sacrifice of the alchemy of my art, of artistic "control" over the setting as well as the content of your imagination' (Rose 1997, 70). This loss of control would be the irretrievable result of, on the one hand, the unspeakable nature of death itself; and on the other, the fact that AIDS has a well-developed narrative structure – it has been 'overspoken', she says, by contemporary culture. By the same token, in her admission of terminal status from another cause, cancer, the very word also overdetermines the reader's response. She hypothesizes that her readers will imagine her tumours as discrete matter in the body, multiplying and attacking that body in the process; and she also knows that we are likely to see her diagnosis as 'a judgement, a species of ineluctable condemnation'. But she wants to posit an alternative position: 'To the bearer of this news, the term "cancer" means nothing: it has no meaning. It merges without remainder into the horizon within which the difficulties, the joys, the banalities, of each day elapse' (72). The problem with our intellectual knowledge is that it has nothing to do with experiential reality. Intellectual knowledge – theory, philosophy – works on the idea that narratives of various kinds will 'tell'; that we will uncover meaning by placing events in a certain order in retelling them, and that we will thereby deduce patterns of causes and consequences which reassure us of a minimal just order in things. But it isn't like that at all. After undergoing a failed operation to reverse a colostomy following the discovery that the original tumour has spread to the bowels, Rose narrates the failure of her two consultants to reconcile their two very different accounts of what they found inside her, and their two very different explanations of why they could not reverse the colostomy. Mr Wong 'informed me that there was considerable progression of the disease' (91); Mr Bates says in contrast: 'You look just the same as you did when we closed you up in April. No less cancer but no more either'(93). Both, clearly, cannot be right. Their conflicting interpretations of the bodily evidence dramatizes the fact that interpretations always conflict, whatever the context in which they take place.

For Rose, then, there is no comfort to be had from accounts that construct origins and significance for events that are essentially inexplicable and unmeaning. But she is also aware of the extent to which we demand a narrative that makes sense of things. In the context of her own colostomy bag, which produces a very different relationship with the waste products of her own body than that usually experienced in cancer-free existence, she discusses the kinds of resistance to meaninglessness that Holocaust historians have had to face. Not all the deaths at Birkenau and Auschwitz were *willed* Holocaust historian Robert Jan van Pelt has argued; not all the deaths were motivated by the enactment of Nazism's murderous fantasy. On the one hand we tell ourselves a story about the ruthless efficiency and appalling rationality that went into the planning of the death camps; on the other, we refuse to recognize that the camps were, in fact, 'designed with lack of foresight regarding the organization of sanitation, and this resulted in much *unplanned* death' (Rose 1997, 85, original emphasis). Van Pelt's argument is that people cannot cope with the idea that so much death was unwilled, or undesired, and especially resist that so much death came from the Nazis' inefficiency in managing shit. What is resisted, what cannot be borne, is the meaninglessness of it all, as if willed, planned, motivated and explicable deaths – Holocaust murders – are more bearable than deaths which were not quite murders, in which, as it were, no one cared enough to be the cause.

Gillian Rose ended her own story and chose the moment of her account's ending for herself. Her final chapter is taken up with what might be called the 'consolations of philosophy'. She argues that life is defined by the conditions of perplexity and melancholy; identity and subjectivity are defined by the personal (experiential) and philosophical (theoretical) responses one has to these conditions. Her chosen path is that of *euporia* – the recognition that the human condition is a comedy of benign confusion. 'Comedy', she writes, 'is homeopathic: it cures folly by folly'. The absurdity of the quest for meaning, which fixes things and totalizes them, is invoked and dismissed. Nonetheless, laughter does require 'a minimal just order. There are no collections of jokes associated with the Holocaust' (134). The minimum ethical requirement, presumably, has something to do with the admission of the other's humanity in a *face-to-face* encounter. The just order, though, requires constant renegotiation, in relation to concrete, material experience at least as much as to abstract theoretical principles. What Rose offers in the end is not a meaning for life, but a modus vivendi (and *moriendi*) – or rather a modus *laborandi*: living is love's *work*: her last words insist on a subjectivity that is made in relation to both mind and body, to the interplay between them, and to the individual in relation to the wider culture from which s/he is made. 'I will stay in the fray, in the revel of ideas and risk; learning, failing, wooing, grieving, trusting, working, reposing – in this sin of language and lips' (135).

There are, of course, theoretical models as well as literary critical approaches that could be applied to the thanatographical text, though the application might well be a kind of fakery. For example, Rose's text exemplifies that mode of being that Julia Kristeva has called abjection: that subject position which exists between subjectivity and the body as object in the world 'which draws me into the place where meaning collapses' (Kristeva 1982, 2). The proliferation of cancer cells in the body produces precisely the effects that Kristeva has described, and she even uses cancer as a metaphor for the process of abjection (Kristeva 1982, 11).[2] The effect of abjection is the effect of horror:

> A massive and sudden emergence of uncanniness, which, familiar as it might have been in an opaque and forgotten life, now harries me as radically separate, loathsome. Not me. Not that. But not nothing, either. A 'something' that I do not recognize as a thing. A weight of meaningless-ness, about which there is nothing insignificant, and which crushes me. (Kristeva 1982, 2)

But once I have identified an interpretative strategy – this is the Uncanny, the Abject, the Real – what else? What, in the end, is the adequacy of any theoretical account of my response? The risk of expla-nation is the risk of *explaining away*, erecting an explanatory fiction which consoles the reader merely by displacing emotion into an arcane vocabulary of distance and objectivity. The subjectivity I am most concerned with here, then, is my own. I want to find a way of reading narratives such as Gillian Rose's *Love's Work* – and other kinds of narra-tive as well – that connects the two halves of my own experience of Cartesian dualism: the theoretical academic reader with critical guns ablazing after all, inhabits the same body as the woman who cries at a sad story. To say that one response is more valid than the other is highly problematic. Each story calls into being a reader by its *face-to-face* appeal; and my sense is that we need to read both kinds of story, and we need to be both kinds of reader, otherwise various kinds of binarism remain appallingly intact. And it's something like the capacity to respond to the other as the other demands, or requests us to that I mean by strategic humanism.

Notes

1.   This is an ironic observation for me. When I read Ruth Picardie's *Before I Say Goodbye*, in the original form as columns in the *Observer* newspaper, I wept, despite the fact that I didn't know Ruth Picardie except as a 'textual sign'. However, if Picardie was just a name to me, Gillian Rose was some-one I actually knew, albeit briefly and fleetingly; and her text is resolutely not about provoking an emotional response in the reader – it asks us primarily to think. Nonetheless, the thoughts it provokes are profoundly disturbing, bringing together emotion and intellect in a highly uneasy cocktail.

2.   Kristeva describes the emotion of abjection thus: 'a language that gives up, a structure within the body, a non-assimilable alien, a monster, a tumour, a cancer that the listening devices of the unconscious do not hear, for its strayed subject is huddled outside the paths of desire'.

Glossary

Abjection: Term deriving from Kristeva's *Powers of Horror*. It refers to the discomfort (and horror) that is produced by the speaking subject's realization of him/herself as also an object (a body – that can be subjected to forces outside its own control).

Alterity: The condition of otherness which is often regarded as constitutive also of the subject: the subject is what the other is not, and therefore inhabits an ambiguous realm of difference, rather than the certainties of essence.

Binary Opposition: Any pair of terms which functions in opposition to each other to structure thought and knowledge – for example good and bad, black and white, night and day, man and woman. The contradiction at the heart of binarism is that whilst the pairing implies absolute difference between its two terms, in fact the two terms are mutually defining, and their meanings can therefore sometimes collapse into each other.

Dialogism: Deriving from the works of Mikhail Bakhtin, dialogism refers to the tendency of written words to inhabit more than one 'voice' in which no single voice assumes a position of authority and mastery.

Ego: The conscious component of the self in Freudian psychoanalysis, defined against the unconscious (chaotic and unstable) and the superego (the social forces that compel particular modes of action).

Epistemology: The philosophical question about the nature of knowledge: epistemology raises questions about how we know things – on what basis knowledge is generated. Depending on the philosophical model, the answers proposed may be broadly empirical (we know the world in relation to our bodily experience of it) or broadly metaphysical (we know the world only in relation to our subjective selfhood).

Humanism: The taking of the human subject, its will, desires and actions, as the central measure for all principles and the focus of aesthetic judgement. The term is usually used in distinction against theistic conceptions of the world (as made by God). Recently it has become a word very difficult to use with a positive gloss, for it has been strongly associated, especially in relation to the word 'liberal', with non-intellectual and commonsensical approaches to the world and knowledge of the world. Liberal humanism espouses values such as democracy, tolerance, rationality, a belief in human progress and individualism. It is also disapproved of for its failure to produce action in the face of totalitarian systems, and for its tendency to lapse away into idealism rather than practical action.

Identity: In the social sciences in particular, identity is the definition of the self in relation to larger social groupings – identity in relation to race and ethnicity, religion, politics, sexuality or nationality, for instance. Often it is used rather more loosely than this gloss implies, however.

Imaginary/Symbolic/Real: The three psychic realms in Lacanian thought. The imaginary refers to the state of illusion experienced by the newborn child from its birth to its initiation in the Symbolic order. The symbolic is associated with the prohibitions of the father, with rational language practices and with consciousness. The Real is the realm that is outside signification – beyond intepretation, in which what happens is purely random and contingent.

Materialism: The belief – often Marxist in inflection – that the material conditions in which the subject lives are determining of the kinds of thought the subject is able to think; a rejection of spirituality in the sense of religious belief in favour of the view that the measure of progress is actually the improved material conditions of the majority of the people.

Mirror Phase: Derived from Lacan's essay on the subject, the mirror phase describes the child's 'misrecognition' of its own image as itself. This mistake, however, institutes the child's subjectivity, for only at this point can it recognize itself as a separate and complete entity in the world.

Name/No of the Father (*le non du père*): Lacanian phrase to describe the subject's submission to the rules and prohibitions associated with patriarchal structures that infect every area of life – from language, to the family, from religion to social institutions.

Narrative: At its simplest, the recording of events, whether real or fictional. But narrative is more than mere story-telling. It also functions as an organizing principle, which structures events in such a way as to render them meaningful (or, aestheticizes them – renders them beautiful).

Oedipus Complex: The mechanism in Freudian psychoanalysis by which the child learns the necessity of repression for appropriate ego-formation. It consists of a fantasy in which the child experiences desire for its opposite sex parent, but learns that such desire must be repressed if the child is not to be punished. Its mechanical working is mysterious, but the child must learn to repress inappropriate wishes for one parent, and learn to identify him/herself with the other parent to achieve maturation and proper acculturation.

Ontology: Knowledge about the nature of 'being': but unlike epistemology, ontology focuses on the nature of 'real existence' as opposed to our knowledge of real existence.

Reverse Discourse: Term inaugurated by Michel Foucault in relation to the medico-moral discourses that surrounded the criminalization of homosexuality in the nineteenth century. Foucault argues in *The History of Sexuality* that the language practices which rendered homosexuality taboo were open to appropriation by precisely the people they also criminalized, who then used the language against its original intention.

Sign, signifier, signified, referent: Terms derived from the writings of Ferdinand de Saussure. The sign in Saussure's work is the combination of the signifier (the sound of a word, or its graphic or written equivalent) and the signified (the image produced in the mind of the person confronting the signifier). Saussure emphasized that signifier and signified occupy an arbitrary relationship, and also insisted that they had no connection to the referent – by which he designated the real object in the world to which sign wishes to refer.

Solipsism: Belief that only one's own experience is guaranteed – an absolute egotism.

Subject, speaking subject, subjectivity, subject-in-process: The subject is the self as conceived in language; a subject is therefore, always in some sense a speaking subject. Subjectivity relates to the processes by which selfhood attains subject status in language and in other social formations. The phrase subject-in-process (in French *sujet-en-procès*) is the term used by Julia Kristeva to describe the sense that subject, despite his/her illusion of autonomy is powerfully *subjected to* forces outside the self, and is therefore always a subject in the process of attaining its subject status, and always a subject on trial (tried by those external forces).

Supplement: Term deriving from the works of Jacques Derrida. The word literally means both an addition and a replacement. In its doubleness of signification it undermines the idea that the linguistic sign (written or spoken) can ever be fully present, can ever enact the fullness that it supposedly guarantees.

Uncanny: In Freud's essay on this subject, the word signals 'unhomeliness' (from the German *unheimlich*), and refers to the moments when that which seems familiar (or homely) is rendered strange and alien. Freud associates in particular with objects that appear to be human but are not (dolls, waxworks, dead bodies), and with subjects who are human, but appear not to be (e.g. clowns in full make-up). The confrontation with the uncanny produces a bodily response – a shudder, a turning away in horror.

Annotated Bibliography

Anderson, Linda. *Autobiography*. London: Routledge, 2001.

From the New Critical Idiom series, Anderson's *Autobiography* is the place to start one's investigations into written subjectivities. She offers a highly readable survey of the issues – theoretical, practical and material – at stake in the reading of subjectivity.

Burke, Seàn. *The Death and Return of the Author: Criticism and Subjectivity in Barthes, Foucault and Derrida*. 2nd edition. Edinburgh: Edinburgh University Press, 1998.

This is the only work of 'high' theory that I include in this annotated bibliography, but it is a model of its kind. Burke excavates the oft-stated view that the author is dead, first articulated by Roland Barthes, by a sustained and critical close-reading of the writings of the three most significant French thinkers in this area. He demonstrates the extent to which the author's death is a somewhat premature announcement and examines the ideological fissures in the project of reducing selfhood to mere textuality. It is a difficult book because the subject matter it confronts is complex. But it is also a highly rewarding and useful read.

Gagnier, Regenia. *Subjectivities: A History of Self-Representation in Britain, 1832–1920*. New York and Oxford: Oxford University Press, 1991.

An excellent corrective to the easy presumption that subjectivity is either a marker of an ahistorical human nature, or that the subjectivities of those outside the hegemonic classes can be measured by the models of the dominant groups. Gagnier's text discusses the material considerations that must go into the making of selfhood in a series of brilliant readings of under-read autobiographical writings, largely by British working-class writers of the nineteenth century. This book is essential reading for those wishing to pursue their interest in subject formation.

Hunt, Celia and Fiona Sampson, eds. *The Self on the Page: Theory and Practice of Creative Writing in Personal Development*. London: Jessica Kingsley Publishers Ltd, 1998.

A rather different book from most of those that appear here. This is a collection of essays by practitioners of various kinds – therapists, social workers, teachers and academics – that focuses on the purposes for subjectivity of self-writing. The essays are sociological in bent because they describe practice. But they also offer a theoretical model through that practice for thinking about the reasons why other autobiographers have committed themselves to paper. Given that many of the client groups for whom these people work are subjects in crises of various kinds, the practical element is a useful corrective to the more arcane reaches of theoretical thought.

Marcus, Laura. *Auto/Biographical Discourses: Theory, Criticism, Practice*. Manchester, Manchester University Press, 1994.

For those seeking a history of the ways in which autobiographical subjectivities have been described and discussed, this is without doubt, the best survey of the field. Marcus offers a wide-ranging discussion from the inception of the modern autobiography, and her comments are both judicious and readable. This is a highly lucid and yet also thoroughly theorized description of the subjectivities that can be submitted to 'literary' discourses.

Morraga, Cherríe and Gloria Anzaldúa, eds. *This Bridge Called My Back: Writings by Radical Women of Color*. New York: Kitchen Table, Women of Color Press, 1983.

I spend a great deal of professional career excising the personal voice from the writings of my students – an activity I am not always proud of. In this collection of critical writings, US women of colour write both autobiographically (using that first person voice) and theoretically to combat the racial stereotyping from which they suffer, and to celebrate their difference from the cultural models they are here attacking. This is a liberating experience to read, for it provides a useful model for all writers of how the 'I' need not be a disenfranchising, un-authoritative voice in mounting criticism: as well as its radical subject matter, its forms offer an opportunity to see how critique might be done differently.

Porter, Roy, ed. *Rewriting the Self: Histories from the Renaissance to the Present*. London: Routledge, 1997.

This very readable collection of essays, originally delivered as a series of lectures at the ICA in London, is, like Gagnier's text, a reminder that selfhood has a history: that the ways in which people have figured theirself to themselves have been a function of particular historical and material circumstances. It takes a series of snapshots of particular historical moments, and reveals the limitations of the model of human selfhood that appeals to human nature.

Smith, Sidonie and Julia Watson, *Women, Autobiography, Theory: A Reader*. Madison and London: University of Wisconsin Press, 1998.

The theorization of autobiography has been – in recent years at least – largely the preserve of feminist academics, who have been attracted to the personal voices of displaced and marginalized women usually excluded from literary canons of value. In one sense, I should be putting Sidonie Smith's monographs into this bibliography, for they have been extremely influential in this field (see Smith 1987 and 1993). For the purposes of the student reader, though, this anthology of recent interventions in the subject is an invaluable place to begin from. It offers extensive coverage in a single volume, and although there is always a caveat with anthologies, which always in some sense represent the particular interests of the editors, this text has comprehensiveness and useful scholarly apparatus to recommend it to the student reader.

Stanley, Liz. *The Auto/Biographical I: The Theory and Practice of Feminist Autobiography*. Manchester and New York: Manchester University Press, 1992.

Stanley is, as she announces in her book, a sociologist dissatisfied with some of the models that discourse offers for comprehending the social construction of selfhood. Her book is a series of case studies of famous and less famous women in which she argues that the bourgeois individualist self at stake in much representation of subjectivity is missing at least half the story of subject formation. Like Gagnier, though with a different set of materials, she argues for the importance of class and gender identities in subject formation and insists on the materialist basis of subjectivity. It is readable and interesting.

Williams, Raymond. *Keywords: A Vocabulary of Culture and Society*. London: Fontana, 1988.

I have recommended this book before, and I make no apology for doing so again. Williams' book is a dictionary of important cultural words. If, as this book has argued, subjectivity is primarily a linguistic process in its institution, the histories of the words we use to designate selfhood is an important part of our knowledge of selfhood. Williams repeatedly reminds us that the words we take for granted all have a history, and that history often erupts in unexpected ways as the ghosts of older meanings haunt the present. It is an important lesson, and not one to forget.

Bibliography

Abbs, Peter. *Autobiography in Education: An Introduction to the Subjective Discipline of Autobiography and its Central Place in the Education of Teachers*. London: Heinemann Educational, 1974.

Abbs, Peter. Introduction to *Father and Son*. Harmondsworth: Penguin, 1989: 9–31.

Ackroyd, Peter. *Dickens*. London: Minerva, 1991.

Adams, James Eli. *Dandies and Desert Saints: Styles of Victorian Masculinity*. Ithaca and London: Cornell University Press, 1995.

Allott, Miriam, ed. *Charlotte Brontë: Jane Eyre and Villette*. Casebook Series. London: Macmillan, 1973.

Anderson, Linda. *Autobiography*. London: Routledge, 2001.

Anzaldùa, Gloria. *Borderlands/La Frontera*. San Francisco: Aunt Lute Book Company, 1988.

Armstrong, Nancy. *Desire and Domestic Fiction: A Political History of the Novel*. Oxford: Oxford University Press, 1987.

Austen, Jane. *Northanger Abbey* [1818]. Ed. Anne H. Ehrenpreis. Harmondsworth: Penguin, 1972.

Bakhtin, Mikhail. *Speech Genres and Other Late Essays*. Trans. Vern W. McGee. Eds. Caryl Emerson and Michael Holquist. Austin: University of Texas Press, 1986.

Barnes, Julian. *Flaubert's Parrot*. London: Picador, 1985.

Barrett Browning, Elizabeth. *Her Novel in Verse, Aurora Leigh, and Other Poems*. Ed. Cora Kaplan. London: The Women's Press, 1981.

Barry, Peter. *Beginning Theory*. Manchester: Manchester University Press, 1995.

Barthes, Roland. *Image, Music, Text*. Trans. Stephen Heath. London: Fontana, 1977.

Belsey, Catherine. *Critical Practice*. London: Methuen, 1980.

Bennett, Alan. *Talking Heads*. London: BBC Worldwide Publishing, 1988.

Bennett, Alan. *Writing Home*. London: Faber and Faber, 1994.

Bennett, Alan. *Talking Heads 2*. London: BBC Worldwide Publishing, 1998.

Benjamin, Walter. *Illuminations*. Trans. Harry Zohn. London: Fontana, 1992.

Bernstein, Susan David. *Confessional Subjects: Revelations of Gender and Power in Victorian Literature and Culture*. Chapel Hill and London: University of Carolina Press, 1997.

Blake, Clare. 'A Strategy for Survival'. In Julia Swindells, ed. *The Uses of Autobiography*. London: Taylor and Francis, 1995: 56–63.

Bloom, Harold, ed. *James Joyce's A Portrait of the Artist as Young Man: Modern Critical Interpretations*. New York and Philadelphia: Chelsea House Publishers, 1998.

Bowie, Malcolm. *Lacan*. London: Fontana, 1991.

Brake, Laurel. *Subjugated Knowledges: Journalism, Gender and Literature in the Nineteenth Century*. London and Basingstoke: Macmillan, 1994.

Brodzki, Bella. 'Mothers, Displacement and Language'. In Sidonie Smith and Julia Watson, eds. *Women, Autobiography, Theory: A Reader*. Madison: University of Wisconsin Press, 1998: 156–9.

Brontë, Charlotte. *Villette* [1853]. Ed. Mark Lilly. Intro. Tony Tanner. Harmondsworth: Penguin, 1979.

Brontë, Charlotte. *Jane Eyre: An Autobiography* [1847]. Ed. and Intro. Michael Mason. Harmondsworth: Penguin, 1996.

Broughton, Trev Lynn. *Men of Letters, Writing Lives: Masculinity and Literary Auto/Biography in the Late Victorian Period*. London and New York: Routledge, 1999.

Burke, Peter. 'Representations of the Self from Petrarch to Descartes'. In Roy Porter, ed. *Rewriting the Self: Histories from the Renaissance to the Present*. London: Routledge, 1997: 17–28.

Burke, Seán. *The Death and Return of the Author: Criticism and Subjectivity in Barthes, Foucault and Derrida*. 2nd edition. Edinburgh: Edinburgh University Press, 1998.

Burnett, John. *Destiny Obscure: Autobiographies of Childhood, Education and Family from the 1820s to the 1920s*. Harmondsworth: Penguin, 1984.

Butler, Marilyn. *Romantics, Rebels and Reactionaries: English Literature and its Background, 1760–1830*. Oxford: Oxford University Press, 1981.

Byron, Glennis. *Dramatic Monologue*. London: Routledge, 2003.

Campbell, Jan and Janet Harbord, eds. *Temporalities: Autobiography and Everyday Life*. Manchester: Manchester University Press, 2002.

Carroll, Lewis. *The Annotated Alice: Alice's Adventures in Wonderland and Through the Looking Glass*. Ed. Martin Gardner. Harmondsworth: Penguin, 1970.

Chang, Jung. *Wild Swans: Three Daughters of China*. London: HarperCollins, 1993.

Charteris, Evan. *The Life and Letters of Sir Edmund Gosse*. London: William Heinemann, 1931.

Chin, Frank. 'The Most Popular Book in China'. In Sau-Ling Cynthia Wong, ed. *The Woman Warrior: A Casebook*. Oxford: Oxford University Press, 1999: 23–8.

Cobley, Paul. *Narrative*. London: Routledge, 2001.

Coleman, Patrick, Jayne Lewis and Jill Kowalik, eds. *Representations of the Self from the Renaissance to the Romantics*. Cambridge: Cambridge University Press, 2000.

Collins, Philip, ed. *Charles Dickens: The Critical Heritage*. London: Routledge and Kegan Paul, 1971.

Collins, Philip, ed. *Dickens: Interviews and Recollections*. 2 volumes. London: Macmillan, 1981.

Costanzo, Angelo. Extract from 'The Spiritual Autobiography and Slave Narrative of Ouladah Equiano'. In Werner Sollors, ed. *The Interesting Narrative of Ouladah Equiano, or Gustavus Vassa, the African, Written by Himself* [1789]. New York and London: W. W. Norton and Co., 2001: 348–50.

Cowley, Julian. ' "Snowed Up": A Structuralist Reading'. In Julian Wolfreys and William Baker, eds. *Literary Theories: A Case Study in Critical Performance*. Basingstoke: Macmillan, 1996: 41–56.

Culler, Jonathan. *On Deconstruction: Theory and Criticism after Structuralism*. London: Routledge, 1983.

Curran, Stuart, ed. *The Cambridge Companion to British Romanticism*. Cambridge: Cambridge University Press, 1993.

Day, Aidan. *Romanticism*. London and New York: Routledge, 1996.

Davies, Damian Walford. 'Thomas De Quincey, *Confessions of an English Opium-Eater*'. In Duncan Wu, ed. *A Companion to Romanticism*. Oxford: Blackwell Publishing, 1998: 269–76.

Davies, Tony. *Humanism*. London: Routledge, 1997.

De Man, Paul. *Allegories of Reading: Figural Language in Rousseau, Nietzsche, Rilke, and Proust*. New Haven and London: Yale University Press, 1979.

De Man, Paul. 'Autobiography as Defacement'. *The Rhetoric of Romanticism*. New York: Columbia University Press, 1984: 67–82.

De Quincey, Thomas. *Confessions of an English Opium Eater and Other Writings* [1822]. Ed. and Intro. Grevel Lindop. Oxford: Oxford University Press, 1985.

Derrida, Jacques. *Of Grammatology*. Trans. Gayatri Spivak. Baltimore: Johns Hopkins University Press, 1976.

Derrida, Jacques. *Dissemination*. Trans. Barbara Johnson. Chicago: University of Chicago Press, 1981.

Derrida, Jacques. 'The Law of Genre'. In Derek Attridge, ed. *Acts of Literature*. New York and London: Routledge, 1992.

Derrida, Jacques. ' "There is No *One* Narcissism": (Autobiophotographies)'. In Elizabeth Weber, ed. *Points … Interviews, 1974–1994*, Stanford University Press, 1995.

Derrida, Jacques. 'Emanuel Levinas'. *The Work of Mourning*. Eds, Pascale-Anne Brault and Michael Naas. Chicago and London: Chicago University Press, 2001.

Diamond, John. *C: Because Cowards Get Cancer Too. …* London: Random House, 1999.

Dickens, Charles. *The Personal History of David Copperfield*. Ed. and Intro. Trevor Blunt. Harmondsworth: Penguin, 1985.

Dickens, Charles. *Great Expectations*. Ed. and Intro. Angus Calder. Harmondsworth: Penguin, 1965.

Dickens, Charles. *David Coppefield: Authoritative Text; Backgrounds, Criticism*. Ed. Jerome H. Buckley. New York and London: W. W. Norton and Co., 1990.

Dollimore, Jonathan. *Sexual Dissidence: Augustine to Wilde, Freud to Foucault*. Oxford: OUP, 1991.

Dollimore, Jonathan. *Death, Desire and Loss in Western Culture*. London and New York: Routledge, 2001.

Doody, Margaret Anne. Introduction to Samuel Richardson, *Pamela*. Ed. Peter Sabor. Harmondsworth: Penguin, 1980.

Doody, Margaret Anne. 'Samuel Richardson: Fiction and Knowledge'. In John Richetti, ed. *The Cambridge Companion to the Eighteenth-Century Novel*. Cambridge: Cambridge University Press, 1996: 90–119.

Eaglestone, Robert. *Ethical Criticism: Reading After Levinas*. Edinburgh: Edinburgh University Press, 1997.

Eagleton, Terry. *Literary Theory: An Introduction*. 2nd Edition. Oxford: Blackwell Publishers, 1996.

Eagleton, Terry. *The Gatekeeper: A Memoir*. Harmondsworth: Penguin, 2001.

Elliott, Anthony. *Theories of Personality*. Cambridge: Polity Press, 2001.

Ellmann, Richard. *Oscar Wilde*. Harmondsworth: Penguin, 1987.

Equiano, Ouladah. *The Interesting Narrative of Ouladah Equiano, or Gustavus Vassa, the African, Written by Himself* [1789]. Ed. Werner Sollors. New York and London: W. W. Norton and Co., 2001.

Evans, Mary. *Missing Persons: The Impossibility of Auto/Biography*. London: Routledge, 1999.

Fleishman, Avrom. *Figures of Autobiography: The Language of Self-Writing.* Berkley: University of California Press, 1983.

Flint, Kate. 'The Middle Novels: *Chuzzlewit, Dombey,* and *Copperfield*'. In John O. Jordan, ed. *The Cambridge Companion to Charles Dickens.* Cambridge: Cambridge University Press, 2001: 34–48.

Flint, Kate. 'Women Writers, Women's Issues'. In Heather Glen, ed. *The Cambridge Companion to the Brontës.* Cambridge: Cambridge University Press, 2002: 170–191.

Foucault, Michel. *The History of Sexuality.* Volume I. *An Introduction.* Trans. Robert Hurley. Harmondsworth: Penguin, 1984.

Freud, Sigmund. *Art and Literature: The Penguin Freud Library, Volume 14.* Trans. James Strachey. Ed. Albert Dickson. Harmondsworth: Penguin, 1985.

Freud, Sigmund. *A Case of Hysteria; Three Essays on Sexuality; and Other Works.* The Standard Edition of the Complete Works of Sigmund Freud, Volume VII. Trans. James Strachey. London: The Hogarth Press, 1953.

Freud, Sigmund. *The Essentials of Psycho-Analysis.* Trans. James Strachey. Intro. Anna Freud. Harmondsworth: Penguin, 1986.

Gagnier, Regenia. *Idylls of the Marketplace: Oscar Wilde and the Victorian Public.* Aldershot: Scolar Press, 1987.

Gagnier, Regenia. *Subjectivities: A History of Self-Representation in Britain, 1832–1920.* Oxford and New York: Oxford University Press, 1991.

Gallop, Jane. *Feminism and Psychoanalysis: The Daughter's Seduction.* London: Macmillan, 1982.

Gates, Henry Louis, ed. *'Race', Writing and Difference.* Chicago and London: Chicago University Press, 1986.

Gates, Henry Louis. Excerpt from 'The Trope of the Talking Book'. In Werner Sollors, ed. *The Interesting Narrative of Ouladah Equiano, or Gustavus Vassa, the African, Written by Himself* [1789]. New York and London: W. W. Norton and Co., 2001: 361–67.

Gilbert, Sandra M. and Susan Gubar. *The Madwoman in the Attic: The Woman Writer and the Nineteenth-Century Imagination.* New Haven and London: 1979.

Glen, Heather, ed. *The Cambridge Companion to the Brontës.* Cambridge: Cambridge University Press, 2002.

Gordon, Lyndall. *Charlotte Brontë: A Passionate Life.* London: Vintage, 1995.

Gosse, Edmund. *Father and Son* [1907]. Harmondsworth: Penguin, 1989.

Greene, Gayle and Coppélia Kahn, eds. *Making a Difference: Feminist Literary Criticism.* London: Methuen, 1981.

Hara, Eiichi. 'Stories Present and Absent in *Great Expectations*'. In Roger D. Sell, ed. *New Casebooks: Great Expectations.* Basingstoke: Macmillan, 1994: 143–65.

Hartley, L. P. *The Go-Between.* Harmondsworth: Penguin, 1958.

Haslett, Moyra. *Marxist Literary and Cultural Theories.* Basingstoke: Macmillan, 2000.

Haslett, Moyra. *Pope to Burney, 1714–1779: Scriblerians to Bluestockings.* Basingstoke: Macmillan, 2003.

Hawkes, Terence. *Structuralism and Semiotics.* [1977] London: Routledge, 1988.

Henderson, Andrea K. *Romantic Identities: Varieties of Subjectivity, 1774–1830.* Cambridge: Cambridge University Press, 1996.

Henke, Suzette. *Shattered Subjects: Trauma and Testimony in Women's Life Writing.* Basingtoke: Macmillan, 1998.

Hoggart, Richard. *The Uses of Literacy* [1957]. Harmondsworth: Penguin, 1992.

Hong Kingston, Maxine. *The Woman Warrior* [1977]. London: Picador, 1981.

Hough, Graham. *The Last Romantics*. [1949]. London: Duckworth and Co., 1983.

Hunt, Celia and Fiona Sampson, eds. *The Self on the Page: Theory and Practice of Creative Writing in Personal Development*. London: Jessica Kingsley Publishers Ltd, 1998.

Jefferson, Ann and David Robey, eds. *Modern Literary Theory: A Comparative Introduction*. 2nd edition. London: B. T. Batsford, 1986.

James, William. *Principles of Psychology* [1890, 2 volumes]. New York: Dover Publications, 1950.

Jordan, John O., ed. *The Cambridge Companion to Charles Dickens*. Cambridge: Cambridge University Press, 2001.

Jouve, Nicole Ward. *White Woman Speaks With Forked Tongue: Criticism as Autobiography*. London and New York: Routledge, 1991.

Joyce, James. *A Portrait of the Artist as a Young Man* [1914–15]. Ed. and Intro. Seamus Deane. Harmondsworth: Penguin, 1992.

Keating, Peter, ed. *Unknown England: Selections from the Social Explorers, 1866–1913*. Manchester: Manchester University Press, 1976.

Keenan, Brian. *An Evil Cradling*. London: Vintage, 1992.

Kenner, Hugh. 'The *Portrait* in Perspective' [originally published as *Dublin's Joyce*, 1956]. Reprinted in Harold Bloom, ed. *James Joyce's A Portrait of the Artist as Young Man: Modern Critical Interpretations*. New York and Philadelphia: Chelsea House Publishers, 1998: 5–30.

King, Nicola. *Memory, Narrative, Identity: Remembering the Self*. Edinburgh: Edinburgh University Press, 2000.

Kitson, Peter J. 'Beyond the Enlightenment: The Philosophical, Scientific and Religious Inheritance'. In Duncan Wu, ed. *A Companion to Romanticism*. Oxford: Blackwell Publishing, 1998: 35–47.

Kohl, Norbert. *Oscar Wilde: Works of a Conformist Rebel*. Cambridge: Cambridge University Press, 1989.

Kristeva, Julia. *Powers of Horror: An Essay on Abjection* [1980]. Trans. Leon S. Roudiez. New York: Columbia University Press, 1982.

Kristeva, Julia. *Revolution in Poetic Language* [1974]. Trans. Margaret Waller. New York: Columbia University Press, 1984.

Kristeva, Julia. *The Kristeva Reader*. Ed. Toril Moi. Oxford: Blackwell, 1986.

Lacan, Jacques. *The Four Fundamental Concepts of Psycho-analysis*. Trans. Alan Sheridan. London: Hogarth Press, 1977.

Lacan, Jacques. *Écrits* [1966, trans. 1977]. Trans. Alan Sheridan. London: Routledge, 1988.

Lane, Harlan. *The Wild Boy of Aveyron*. London: George Allen and Unwin, 1977.

Langbaum, Robert. *The Poetry of Experience: The Dramatic Monologue in the Modern Literary Tradition*. Harmondsworth: Penguin, 1974.

Lawrence, D. H. *The Complete Poems*. Ed. Vivian de Sola Pinto and Intro. F. Warren Roberts. Harmondsworth: Penguin, 1972.

Lejeune, Philippe. *On Autobiography*. Ed. Paul John Eakin. Trans. Katherine Leary. Minneapolis: University of Minneapolis Press, 1989.

Levinas, Emmanuel. *Totality and Infinity: An Essay on Exteriority*. Trans. Alphonso Lingis. London: Kluwer Academic Publishers, 1991.

Lindop, Grevel. *The Opium Eater: A Life of Thomas De Quincey*. London: Dent, 1981.

MacLean, Charles. *The Wolf Children*. London: Allen Lane, 1977.

Malson, Lucien. *Wolf Children*. Printed as an Introduction to Jean Itard, *The Wild Boy of Aveyron*. Trans. Edmund Fawcett, Peter Ayrton and Joan White. London: NLB Books, 1972.

Marcus, Laura. *Auto/Biographical Discourses: Theory, Criticism, Practice*. Manchester: Manchester University Press, 1994.

McCarthy, John and Jill Morrell, *Some Other Rainbow*. London: Corgi, 1994.

McKeon, Michael. *The Origins of the English Novel, 1600–1740*. Baltimore and London: Johns Hopkins University Press, 1987.

Mill, John Stuart. *Utilitarianism; On Liberty; Considerations on Representative Government*. Ed. Geraint Williams. London: Everyman, 1993.

Miller, Jonathan. *The Body in Question*. London: Pimlico, 2000.

Moi, Toril. *Sexual/Textual Politics: Feminist Literary Theory*. London and New York: Methuen, 1985.

Montag, Warren. 'René Descartes (1596–1650) and Baruch Spinoza (1632–1677): Beginnings'. In Julian Wolfreys, ed. *The Edinburgh Encyclopaedia of Modern Criticism and Theory*. Edinburgh: Edinburgh University Press, 2002.

Moore, Oscar. *PWA: Looking AIDS in the Face*. London: Picador, 1996.

Morraga, Cherríe and Gloria Anzaldúa, eds. *This Bridge Called My Back: Writings by Radical Women of Color*. New York: Kitchen Table, Women of Color Press, 1983.

Morra, Joanne, Mark Robson and Marquard Smith, eds. *The Limits of Death: Between Philosophy and Psychoanalysis*. Manchester: Manchester University Press, 2000.

Morris, Pam. *Literature and Feminism: An Introduction*. Oxford: Blackwell, 1993.

Murphy, Geraldine. 'Ouladah Equiano: Accidental Tourist'. In Werner Sollors, ed. *The Interesting Narrative of Ouladah Equiano, or Gustavus Vassa, the African, Written by Himself* [1789]. New York and London: W. W. Norton and Co., 2001: 368–82.

Nash, Cristopher. *The Unravelling of the Postmodern Mind*. Edinburgh: Edinburgh University Press, 2001.

Nead, Lynda. *Myths of Sexuality: Representations of Women in Victorian Britain*. Oxford: Basil Blackwell, 1988.

Nestor, Pauline, ed. *Villette: Contemporary Critical Essays*. Basingstoke: Macmillan, 1992.

Newton, Michael. *Savage Girls and Wild Boys: A History of Feral Children*. London: Faber, 2002.

Nussbaum, Felicity A. *The Autobiographical Subject: Gender and Ideology in Eighteenth-Century England*. Baltimore: Johns Hopkins University Press, 1989.

Nussbaum, Felicity A. *The Limits of the Human: Fictions of Anomaly, Race, and Gender in the Long Eighteenth Century*. Cambridge: CUP, 2003.

Ong, Walter. *Orality and Literacy: The Technologizing of the Word*. London: Routledge, 1980.

Parke, Catherine N. *Biography: Writing Lives*. London and New York: Routledge, 2002.

Payne, Michael. *Reading Theory: An Introduction to Lacan, Derrida and Kristeva*. Oxford: Blackwell, 1993.

Peterson, Linda H. *Traditions of Victorian Women's Autobiography: The Poetics and Politics of Life Writing*. Charlottesville and London: University of Virginia Press, 1999.

Phelan, James. 'Reading for the Character and Reading for the Progression: John Wemmick and *Great Expectations*' [1989]. Reprinted in Roger D. Sell, ed. *New Casebooks: Great Expectations*. Basingstoke: Macmillan, 1994: 177–86.

Picardie, Ruth. *Before I say Goodbye*. Harmondsworth: Penguin, 1998.

Poovey, Mary. *Uneven Developments: The Ideological Work of Gender in Mid-Victorian England*. London: Virago, 1989.

Porter, Roy, ed. *Rewriting the Self: Histories from the Renaissance to the Present*. London: Routledge, 1997.

Pykett, Lyn. *Charles Dickens: Critical Issues*. London: Palgrave, 2002.

Rabaté, Jean-Michel. *Jacques Lacan*. Basingstoke: Macmillan, 2001.

Raby, Peter, ed. *The Cambridge Companion to Oscar Wilde*. Cambridge: Cambridge University Press, 1997.

Richardson, Samuel. *Pamela, or Virtue Rewarded* [1740]. Ed. Peter Sabor. Intro. Margaret Anne Doody. Harmondsworth: Penguin, 1980.

Richetti, John, ed. *The Cambridge Companion to the Eighteenth-Century Novel*. Cambridge: Cambridge University Press, 1996.

Richetti, John. *The English Novel in History, 1700–1800*. London: Routledge, 1999.

Riquelme, John Paul. 'The Preposterous Shape of Portraiture: *A Portrait of the Artist as Young Man*' [first published in Teller and Tale in Joyce's Fiction: Oscillating Perspectives, 1983]. Reprinted in Harold Bloom, ed. *James Joyce's A Portrait of the Artist as Young Man: Modern Critical Interpretations*. New York and Philadelphia: Chelsea House Publishers, 1998: 87–107

Robbins, Ruth. ' "And Judas always writes the biography": The Many Lives of Oscar Wilde' in Ruth Robbins and Julian Wolfreys, eds. *Victorian Identities: Social and Cultural Formations in Nineteenth-Century Literature*. Basingstoke: Macmillan, 1996: 97–118.

Robbins, Ruth. *Literary Feminisms*. Basingstoke: Palgrave Macmillan, 2000a.

Robbins, Ruth. 'The Genders of Socialism: Eleanor Marx and Oscar Wilde' in John Stokes, ed. *Eleanor Marx: Life, Work, Contacts*. Aldershot: Ashgate, 2000b: 99–112.

Roberts, Robert. *The Classic Slum: Salford Life in the First Quarter of the Century*. Harmondsworth: Pelican, 1971.

Roberts, Robert. *A Ragged Schooling*. London: Fontana, 1978.

Rose, Gillian. *Love's Work*. London: Vintage, 1997.

Roston, Murray. *The Search for Selfhood in Modern Literature*. Basingstoke: Palgrave, 2001.

Rousseau, Jean-Jacques. *The Confessions*. Trans. J. M. Cohen. Harmondsworth: Penguin, 1953.

Rylance, Rick. ' "Getting on": ideology, personality and the Brontë characters'. In Heather Glenn, ed. *The Cambridge Companion to the Brontës*. Cambridge: Cambridge University Press, 2002: 148–69.

Said, Edward W. *Orientalism: Western Conceptions of the Orient* [1978]. Harmondsworth: Penguin, 1991.

Said, Edward W. *Culture and Imperialism*. London: Vintage, 1993.

Schrag, Calvin O. *The Self After Postmodernity*. New Haven and London: Yale University Press, 1997.

Sedgwick, Peter. *Descartes to Derrida: An Introduction to European Philosophy*. Oxford: Blackwell Publishing, 2001.

Sedgwick, Eve Kosofsky. *Between Men: English Literature and Male Homosocial Desire*. New York: Columbia University Press, 1985.

Sell, Roger D., ed. *New Casebooks: Great Expectations*. Basingstoke: Macmillan, 1994.

Shaw, George Bernard. *The Portable Bernard Shaw*. Ed. and Intro. Stanley Weintraub. Harmondsworth: Penguin, 1977.

Smith, Sidonie. *A Poetics of Women's Autobiography: Marginality and the Fictions of Self-Representation*. Bloomington and Indianapolis: Indiana University Press, 1987.

Smith, Sidonie. *Subjectivity, Identity and the Body: Women's Autobiographical Practices in the Twentieth Century*. Bloomington: Indiana University Press, 1993.

Smith, Sidonie and Julia Watson, eds. *Women, Autobiography, Theory: A Reader*. London and Madison: University of Wisconsin Press, 1998.

Sontag, Susan. *Illness as Metaphor; AIDS and its Metaphors*. Harmondsworth: Penguin, 1991.

Spivak, Gayatri Chakravorty. 'Three Women's Texts and a Critique of Imperialism'. In Henry Louis Gates, Jr. *'Race', Writing and Difference*. Chicago and London: Chicago University Press, 1986: 262–80.

Spivak, Gayatri Chakravorty. 'Subaltern Studies: Deconstructing Historiography'. In *In Other Worlds*. London: Routledge, 1988: 196–211.

Stabler, Jane. *Burke to Byron, Barbauld to Baillie, 1790–1830*. Basingstoke: Palgrave Macmillan, 2002.

Stanley, Liz. *The Auto/biographical 'I': The Theory and Practice of Feminist Autobiography*. Manchester: Manchester University Press, 1992.

Steedman, Carolyn. *Landscape for a Good Woman*. London: Virago, 1986.

Steedman, Carolyn. *Past Tenses: Essays on Writing, Autobiography and History*. London: Rivers Oram Press, 1992.

Sterne, Laurence. *The Life and Opinions of Tristram Shandy, Gentleman*. [1759–67]. Ed. Graham Petrie. Intro. Christopher Ricks. Harmondsworth: Penguin, 1970.

Storr, Anthony. *Freud*. Oxford: Oxford University Press, 1989.

Sutherland, John. *Victorian Fiction: Writers, Publishers, Readers*. London: Macmillan, 1995.

Swindells, Julia, ed. *The Uses of Autobiography*. London: Taylor and Francis, 1995.

Taylor, Charles. *Human Agency and Language: Philosophical Papers*. Cambridge: Cambridge University Press, 1985.

Thompson, E. P. *The Making of the English Working Class* [1963]. Harmondsworth: Penguin, 1991.

Thwaite, Ann. *Edmund Gosse: A Literary Landscape, 1849–1928*. Chicago: University of Chicago Press, 1983.

Tolstoy, Leo. *Anna Karenin*. Trans. Rosemary Edmonds. Harmondsworth: Penguin, 1954.

Vicinus, Martha, ed. *A Widening Sphere: Changing Roles of Victorian Women*. London and Bloomington: Indiana University Press, 1977.

Vonnegut, Kurt. *Slaughterhouse 5* [1969]. London: Triad Grafton, 1979.

Waite, Terry. *Taken on Trust*. London: Coronet, 1994.

Warner, Marina. *Joan of Arc: The Image of Female Heroism*. Harmondsworth: Penguin, 1981.

Watt, Ian. *The Rise of the Novel* [1957]. London: Hogarth Press, 1987.

Wilde, Oscar. *The Complete Works of Oscar Wilde*. Ed. Merlin Holland. Glasgow: HarperCollins, 1994.

Wilde, Oscar. *Selected Letters of Oscar Wilde*. Ed. Rupert Hart-Davis. Oxford: Oxford University Press, 1979.

Williams, Raymond. *Marxism and Literature*. Oxford and New York: Oxford University Press, 1977.

Williams, Raymond. *The English Novel from Dickens to Lawrence*. London: The Hogarth Press, 1984.

Williams, Raymond. *Keywords: A Vocabulary of Culture and Society*. London: Fontana, 1988.

White, Hayden. *Metahistory: The Historical Imagination in Nineteenth-Century Europe*. Baltimore and London: Johns Hopkins University Press, 1975.

White, Hayden. *The Content of the Form: Narrative Discourse and Historical Representation*. Baltimore: Johns Hopkins University Press, 1987.

Wong, Sau Ling Cynthia. 'Autobiography as Chinatown Tour? Maxine Hong Kingston's *The Woman Warrior* and the Chinese American Autobiographical Controversy'. In Sau-Ling Cynthia Wong, ed. *The Woman Warrior: A Casebook*. Oxford: Oxford University Press, 1999: 29–53.

Woolf, Virginia. *Women and Writing*. Ed. Michèle Barrett. London: The Women's Press, 1979.

Woolf, Virginia. *To the Lighthouse* [1927]. Harmondsworth: Penguin, 1992a.

Woolf, Virginia. *Between the Acts* [1942]. Harmondsworth: Penguin, 1992b.

Wordsworth, Jonathan. 'William Wordsworth, *The Prelude*'. In Duncan Wu, ed. *A Companion to Romanticism*. Oxford: Blackwell Publishing, 1998: 179–90.

Wordsworth, Jonathan, M. H Abrams and Stephen Gill, eds. *The Prelude, 1799, 1805, 1850*. New York and London: W. W. Norton and Co., 1979.

Wordsworth, William. *The Major Works*. Ed. and Intro, Stephen Gill. Oxford: Oxford University Press, 2000.

Wright, Elizabeth. *Psychoanalytic Criticism: A Reappraisal*. Cambridge: Polity Press, 1998.

Wu, Duncan, ed. *Romanticism: An Anthology*. Second Edition. Oxford: Blackwell Publishing, 1994.

Wu, Duncan, ed. *A Companion to Romanticism*. Oxford: Blackwell Publishing, 1999.

Zhang, Ya-Jie. 'A Chinese Woman's Response to Maxine Hong Kingston's *The Woman Warrior*'. In Sau-Ling Cyntha Wong, ed. *The Woman Warrior: A Casebook*. Oxford: Oxford University Press, 1999: 17–22.

Index